Trends in Indo-African Relations

Trends in Indo-African Relations

Ajay Dubey

African Studies Association of India, New Delhi

In collaboration with

Manas Publications

New Delhi-110002 (INDIA)

MANAS PUBLICATIONS
(Publishers, Distributors, Importers & Exporters)
4402/5-A, Main Ansari Road
(Opp. HDFC Bank)
Darya Ganj, New Delhi-110 002 (INDIA)
Off. © 23260783, 23265523, Res. © 23842660
Fax: 011-23272766
E-mail: manaspublications@vsnl.com
www.manaspublications.in

African Studies Association of India,
351, School of International Studies,
Jawaharlal Nehru University, New Delhi-110067
Email: office@africanstudies.in
Website: www.africanstudies.in

ISBN 978-81-7049-359-4
Rs. 795

Typeset at
Manas Publications

Printed in India at
Jaico Printers, Delhi
and Published by Mrs Suman Lata for
Manas Publications, 4402/5-A, Main Ansari Road
(Opp. HDFC Bank),
Darya Ganj, New Delhi-110 002 (INDIA)

Contents

Foreword

This volume is the fruit of an academic conference held in New Delhi, with the theme of "Emerging Trends in Indo-African Relations". Involving participants from the Indian government, the diplomatic corps of African countries, commerce, independent research institutes, and academics from India, Africa and Europe, the conference was both pioneering, and—as subsequent events have shown—quite visionary.

Pioneering, inasmuch as this was the conference with which the African Studies Association of India (ASAI), which was formally constituted in October 2003, announced itself to the world. Since "Emerging Trends", ASAI has established itself as the hub for Africanists in South Asia, having held 9 major conferences, published a string of books and launched two journals, *African Review* and *Insight on Africa*.

A number of the speakers considered ways in which the dynamics of globalization, *inter alia* in the context of the rise of the Chinese and Indian economies, were undergoing significant modifications, which they suggested were making for new alignments, new options, new instabilities and conflicts, notably around energy access. Their focus and questions have anticipated subsequent developments which continue to highlight the problematic interface between good governance, respect for human rights and international investment and trade. This trade-off is manifested in ongoing divisions in the African Union around e.g. Sudan and Zimbabwe, and around issues of continental coordination, and is emphasized by US President Obama's call for responsible government as a requirement for aid to Africa during his visit to Ghana in July 2009. The precariousness of the current world economic order holds both threats and promise for Africa, with South Africa starkly illustrating both. Unemployment has risen significantly in recent months, but the G8 is set to expand to a G14, including India and South Africa, as well as Egypt, in an attempt to incorporate the Arab world, with its resources and resistance. Indian scholars' longstanding concern with both North and South Africa has indeed proved visionary.

This timely and insightful volume will be of interest and value to scholars, decision-makers and developers on both sides on the Indian Ocean.

Chris de Wet
Rhodes University, South Africa.

Acknowledgement

African Studies Association of India (ASA India) would like to thank Indian Council of World Affairs (ICWA) for its generous support in organizing the conference and Prof. Chris de Wet former Nelson Mandela Chair Professor at School of International Studies, Jawaharlal Nehru University for his support in academic coordination and preparing a very incisive Rapporteurs Report. We would also like to thank Ms. Jyoti Tyagi and Dr. Nivedita Ray for their support in the preparation of the manuscript.

Introduction

By the end of 20th century India and Africa witnessed new turn in their relations. These were many dimensions of old linkages that continue. Many drivers and rallying points of twentieth century like decolonization and racial discrimination disappeared. Many others like Afro-Asian resurgence, Non-Aligned Movement (NAM) and Collective Self Reliance (CSR) of South were subsumed by new forces and post cold war international architecture emerged. Two new developments at global level impacted Indo-African relations in significant ways. The first was the advent of globalization. It drastically affected the domestic scenarios in both India and Africa. It also threw the new direction, imperatives and parameters of international relations. Both India and Africa underwent Structural Adjustment Programme (SAP) and both shifted their priority from South-South linkage to global integration. States in both regions withdrew from economy. Market emerged as the prime instrument of economic cooperation. Unlike the past, private capital and private enterprise did not have same objectives as state policy instruments for international cooperation. The second factor was the rise of China and India as fast growing economies and rising global powers. Rapid growth of India changed Indian priorities, imperatives and needs. It looked for global engagement for technology, market, diplomatic support, raw materials and most importantly energy supply. In its search for market, Africa figure prominently. Stabilizing and steadily growing African economy (during 1990s and coup free African political system) made it an attractive market for cost competitive goods from India. Similarly the rising profile of India led it to demand for restructuring of institution of global governance like United Nations Security Council, World Bank and IMF. African support, because of their large number, remain crucial for Indian attempt to initiate restructuring of Security Council. India and Africa had trade relations in traditional items and balance of trade remained in favour of Africa. But during 70s and 80s Indian export of value added items in Africa wiped out the long lasting favourable balance of trade for Africa. As India started importing increasing amount of petroleum products from Africa trade balance started shifting again in favour of Africa. In twenty first century India emerged as an energy hungry country. Its energy requirement doubled every five years. India started securing energy supply from different parts of the world. African oil and petro-products became an important focus of Indian diplomacy in Africa. India made its largest public sector overseas investment in Sudan oil sector. It entered into supply contract with Nigeria. It bought stakes in oil blocks of several countries in Africa. It launched TEAM-9 initiative to establish closer relations with energy rich African countries.

Beside this India and African countries found common rallying points to work with concerted efforts to initiate several international trade negotiations. India, Brazil, South Africa and other countries of the region took strong positions in favour of developing countries stalling many decisions under WTO and other trade negotiation rounds which could have adversely affected developing economies. Indo-African cooperation extended to include other developing regions like Brazil, under India, Brazil, South Africa (IBSA) initiative. It is another new dimension of Indo-African framework of cooperation which included other developing regions like Latin America. This coalition of democratic South intends to develop these three countries as hubs for their respective region and to initiate inter regional cooperation.

The rising Indian economy and its international profile made India to proactively involve itself in peace keeping operations in Africa, though India was involved as early as 60s in peace keeping activities of Africa. Since 1960s, it increased its involvement over period of time. It also sent all women peace keeping units to Africa. Beside this, India increased its naval presence in Western Indian Ocean region. It increased its strength around the Gulf of Aden to protect its oil tankers and merchant ships from pirates in the region.

By mid 1990s India added another important factor in its global policies. It launched policy of engaging global Indian diasporas. Africa has around two million Indian diasporas spread in several countries of Africa–Anglophone, Francophone and Lusophone. In many countries their number is substantial and they form significant percentage of local population. In almost all countries they are affluent and well off compared to the native population. Most of them had gone as indentured worker. Some went as railway construction worker or trader. But almost all of them are fourth generation People of Indian Origin (PIO). They are settled since long time in Africa. They have been able to identify and establish themselves as African citizen. When India initiated its new diaspora policy many of its diaspora policy initiatives and instruments were used to establish contract with Indians in Africa. This served as an additional initiative and policy to accelerate closer Indo-African cooperation.

In other words Indo-African relations in 21st century shows new trends and intensity. The drivers and mutual interest are new though the foundation, understanding and goodwill are old. In order to mould this relation to contemporary expectations and demands an Indo-African Forum Summit was organized in April, 2008. The Forum Summit was represented by African leaders who were chosen by African Union and they represented and headed important regional organizations and AU bodies. The Summit intended to understand, negotiate and come out with plan of actions for putting Indo-African relation on a track where priorities, expectations and complementarities of both sides are taken into account to have a mutually beneficial and closer interaction.

The volume comprises of papers presented in an international seminar on "Emerging Trends in Indo-African Relations" organised by the African Studies Association of India. The papers shed valuable insights on various aspects of Indo-African relations. The issues covered relate to changing relations between India and Africa in the politico-diplomatic, economic, strategic and cultural context. Indo-African relations over the years witnessed various changes. It moved from a period of high political, diplomatic solidarity to a more material, concrete and pragmatic partnership. The article *'India-Africa Relations: Historical Connections and Recent Trends* provides a comprehensive and analytical account of the changing relations. It traces the trajectory of the relationship from historical to the current time and brings into focus how Indo-Africa relations over the years demonstrated change and continuity.The author examines the long historical ties between India and Africa and states that the relationship today is being shaped by the fundamental changes that are taking place in both territories. The focus has now shifted to economic emancipation and collective dreams of sustainable development in Africa. It argues that under globalization the economic relations with Africa are gainful for India, but as far as African perceptions are concerned the relations has to be qualitatively different from North-South relations. The author articulates that India should integrate priorities of Africa and be sensitive to their expectations and concerns. Currently resurgent Africa is exhibiting a sense of economic confidence but its future is beset with numerous challenges in terms of poverty, food insecurity, lack of democracy and good governance.

In regard to economic engagement the trade and investment partnership with Africa has increased considerably in the recent years. India launched a number of initiatives like Focus Africa Programme and TEAM-9 to increase trade with the continent. But is India doing enough to help Africa to achieve sustained economic growth is what the article *'Afro-India Economic Relations: Cup—Half Full?'* explores. The paper draws attention to the fact that promotion of merchandise trade as a pivot of the India-Africa relations has not paid enough dividends from the point of view of overall strategy of using economic diplomacy to prompt sustained economic growth in Africa.There is a need for commodity diversification. The author further points out that India has to complement Africa's attempts at sustained economic growth with additional initiatives on other areas of economic cooperation. These initiatives need to be in concert with the approaches of most of Africa's donors and the initiatives undertaken by many other developing countries of Asia and Latin America as part of South-South cooperation. The author points out that the IBSA initiative is a good initiative in this regard and on its part India needs to co-operate, rather than compete with other countries, in aid initiatives in Africa. It also emphasizes that while India needs to do more for Africa, initiative and impetus also have to come from the continent. Africa should do this by providing a conducive investment friendly environment, good governance and sound legal systems.

Trade and investments are increasing yet the existing levels of economic ties do not reflect the full potential. The paper *'India-Africa Economic Cooperation'* dwells on this aspect. It outlines the prospective areas of cooperation and the ways how both sides can benefit from each other. It articulates that there is a broad agenda of shared concerns which India and the countries of Africa can jointly address through mutual cooperation either at the bilateral or multilateral level. The author emphasizes that synergy that can emerge by enhancing mutual economic cooperation is immense but there are challenges which need to be addressed and those are not insurmountable. The article '*Indo-African Economic Relations: From 'Focus LAC' to 'Focus Africa'* examines the institutional mechanisms that have been sought to put the economic relations in sound footing. The author suggests India's 'Focus LAC' strategy has many lessons for the 'Focus Africa' strategy which has been adopted to strengthen the existing links with Africa. Under the Focus Africa programme India has been providing financial assistance to various trade promotion organisations, export promotion councils and apex chambers in the form of market development to facilitate economic engagement.

One of the major components of the current economic engagement between India and Africa is energy cooperation. The paper *'Energy Security Issues: Cooperation between India and African Countries'* deals on this subject. It highlights that the need to access energy can act as a catalyst for cooperation and conflict. It throws light on Africa's energy potential and India's rising energy needs as well as the challenges and risks that are involved for India in sourcing oil from Africa. It states that energy is currently a key driver of Indo-African relations.

India's engagement with Francophone Africa assumes significance in this context. The strategic implication of the Francophone African region, owing to its mineral and energy resources is immense for India. The paper *'India's Changing Engagement with Francophone Africa'* highlights the growing interactions of India's engagement with Francophone Africa. It outlines that the lack of clear cut Indian policy pre-90s kept the relationship at a low ebb but in the post-90s under globalization and liberalization India is proactively engaging the Francophone African countries by taking up initiatives like TEAM-9. The paper examines the initiatives that have been taken to foster cooperation in various sectors which includes trade and investment, energy, agricultural, human resource development; peacekeeping. It also draws attention to the challenges at the level of institutions and language that have proved to be impediments in promoting cooperation with the Francophone countries.

Apart from engaging the Francophone countries India has actively strived to promote cooperation with countries of other regions in Africa. With North African countries its relationship has intensified in the recent years. The paper '*Revitalising Indo-North African Relations*' throws light on India's relations with various North African countries including Algeria, Egypt, Morocco, Libya, Tunisia, and Sudan. It analyses the trade and economic ties as well as the widening technological collaboration.

For economic growth the African countries look towards Indian model as well as India's help and support. The article '*India-Africa Relations with Special Reference to Sudan*' emphasizes on this point. It states that Asian economies like India who have reached certain level of economic achievement can help the African countries through investment in large schemes of development, which are sure to build reliable infrastructure and by and by create a situation of healthy independent economy. In the similar lines the article on '*India- Ethiopia Relations*' dwells on the growing relations between both countries. It is stressed that for Ethiopia like any other countries in Africa, industrialization and modernization is the path ahead. It seeks India's cooperation in this regard for setting up joint ventures. For India, Ethiopia like many other countries in Africa is also turning out to be an attractive destination in terms of investments.

In Zambia India's cooperation in the areas of agriculture and science has restructured the relations. The paper '*Restructuring Developmental Identities in a Globalised World: Zambia-Indo Relations in Science and Agriculture*' presents an attempt to reconstruct the transition of the Zambia-Indo relations in the related fields of science and agriculture. It emphasises that India's overall ability to rise above most developing countries in the fields of science and technology and agriculture are cardinal experiences that ought to be engaged to see how other nations can traverse similar roadmaps and achieve similar scores. The author emphasizes that the Zambia-Indo relationship stands to gain greatly from such bilateral collaboration.

Similarly in the article '*Developing a Fruitful Partnership between India and D R Congo*' it is pointed out that there is a good potential for fruitful partnership between both sides. Since both sides have complementarities, especially now when India's energy demand has risen considerably, a fruitful partnership will be beneficial to both sides. The author emphasizes that creating an enabling environment for a fruitful partnership is also important.

In the context of India's relations with the countries of Horn of Africa the article '*India and Horn of Africa; Towards a Meaningful Relationship*' examines how the relationship between India and countries in the Horn of Africa is acquiring new meaning in the changing environment. It focuses on the growing desire in each side to enhance and promote partnership in various spheres. It highlights the strengths of each other where they can benefit from cooperation and the weaknesses where they can complement each other. The paper also discusses about the security challenges in the Horn of Africa region and India's role in promoting peace and stability through contributing troops for UN peacekeeping operations and cooperating with regional organizations like IGAD.

In promoting the relationship soft powers like, culture, education, literature and diaspora issues played an important role. The article titled '*Culture, Education, Literature and Diaspora as Issues and Factors in Indo-African Relations: Focus on Indo-South African Relations*' deals on this aspect with a focus on India and South Africa relations. It states that India and South Africa are amongst the foremost countries in the 'second world', they share common problems and they should adopt measures that will create solidarity. There is a need for exchanges in the fields of science, medicine and technology, as well as education. It furthers points out that as India and Africa are moving closer to each other. This relationship should be reflected in the Diaspora, where people of Indian and African origin begin to appreciate each others' concerns and needs.

Indian diaspora in Africa although have lived for a long period, are still conspicuous and not integrated to African majority. This issue of assimilation of Indian diaspora is brought into focus in the article '*African Indians: Settled Stereotypes and Limits*' in this volume. It is stated that both People of Indian Origin in East and South Africa have been the targets of racial animosity. But situation in South Africa is different where tensions between Indians and Blacks have grown after apartheid was abolished. It is argued that unless social, economic and political situation changes Indian insecurity will prevent them from integration.

Coming back to the issue of Indian culture it is largely seen that Bollywood films are very popular in African countries. It is perceived that somewhere there is a similarity in the culture which perhaps could be the key element for the popularity of Bollywood films. The article '*Hindu Dance Groups and Indophily in Senegal*' examines the interesting phenomenon of the love of Indian dance, music and films in Senegal—a country without an Indian expatriate community, and outside of the English sphere of influence. 'Indophily' relates to the massive success of Bollywood films and offers a way of being modern that is not Western. Bollywood make them think of their own culture.

The author talks of 'parallel modernities', i.e. imagining other cultures, not as homeland cultures, but as part of one's daily life. Bollywood offers a third space, between local Hausa or Fulani culture and Western culture, but people create their own Senegalese image of the orient, of India, in Bollywood and dance, filling in the gaps in their own imagination.

While culture, literature, language, education and diaspora played a critical role in bridging the gaps and bringing people closer, anxieties and dilemmas relating to political and socio-economic issues in Africa have created gaps. India is proactive for addressing the issues of democracy, governance and human rights in Africa. But today on the continental level a resurgent Africa is changing. Africa is increasingly embracing democracy and good governance. All member countries of AU have taken their promises of good governance seriously and signed up for the African Peer Review Mechanism (APRM), which is an offshoot of the New Partnership for Africa's Development (NEPAD) initiative launched by African countries in 2001.

The final article of this volume '*The New Partnership for Africa's Development: Making the African Peer Review Mechanism Work*' focuses on the concept of APRM. It provides an explanation of the concept of Peer Review and then describes the origin of Africa Peer Review Mechanism (APRM); its hierarchical structure, the types of reviews envisaged under APRM; justification of its existence highlights the contending views on it; and argues for a hybrid model to accommodate all contending views. The article throws a valuable and often repeated issues of African initiatives on good governance which is crucial even for long lasting and people centred Indo-African relations.

India-Africa Relations: Historical Connections and Recent Trends

Ajay K Dubey

India and Africa are two shore neighbours and it is this geographical proximity and navigable Indian Ocean that had made the peoples of the two regions known to each other. Beginning with early colonial days, the free and voluntary relations of the past had given way to colonial needs and preferences. The present relation, one between independent, self-respecting regions was formally established only after both sides got independence. However the contemporary relations based on equal regard and concerns for each other can be traced even before African countries became independent.

Historical Connections

Afro-Asian Resurgence: The idea of Afro-Asian emergence itself was a sign of emerging new relations between India and Africa. Jawaharlal Nehru, who was the architect of India's foreign policy, had a personal commitment to Afro-Asian resurgence In the Calcutta Session of Indian National Congress (1928), after returning from Brussels, he told about Africans that "listening to their harrowing tales of sufferings and their present unhappy conditions, one felt that obstacles in their way were far greater than any other countries' struggling peoples had to face and that full freedom would come to them only with the emancipation of all the peoples of the world."[1] After one month of Indian independence in September 1947, he said in a broadcast to the nation:

> *We believe that peace and freedom are indivisible and denial of freedom must endanger peace elsewhere and lead to conflict and war. We are particularly interested in emancipation of colonial and dependent countries and peoples and in recognition of the theory and practice of equal opportunity for all races.*[2]

The experience of discrimination of Mahatma Gandhi in South Africa had left an abiding influence in identification of the Indians with the freedom loving peoples of Africa. During his Prime Ministership Nehru's policy towards Africa demonstrated its support at two fronts; 1) to decolonisation of African states which India saw as a continuum of the process of Afro-Asian resurgence and 2) to struggles in South Africa to end the racial discrimination by White minority—a support which Indians extended even before its independence. For African countries still under colonial rule during this period, both were relevant to Africa's immediate concerns of decolonisation and Pan-African unity. The Bandung Meet (1955) and the Afro-Asian Peoples Solidarity Conference of Cairo (1958) demonstrated these Afro-Asian perceptions of each other.

However, by the end of 1950s, some problems arose in Indo-African relations. The divergence of views between Nkrumah and Nehru and passing of leadership of Afro-Asian movement from India to Egypt after Cairo Conference contributed to it. India's refusal to recognise the Nationalist Party of Algeria (CPRA) and its insistence of peaceful decolonisation along with its moderate stands on Congo Crisis displeased both conservative Brazzaville and militant Casablanca groups. Further its Anglo centric view resulting in not fixing the time limit for colonial withdrawal and the gulf caused between Indian settlers and Africans, by colonialist propaganda that India attempted to end White domination to replace it by Indians, brought differences in the open. Moreover, since Bandung onwards Chinese militancy and advocacy for armed struggle appealed more to Africans[3]. Indian isolation among African countries during Indo-Chinese War of 1962 was eye opener for it. Very few African countries supported India and many took openly unhelpful attitudes. The Cairo Conference of Non-aligned Countries (1964) further exposed India's isolation in a movement in whose birth it had played a significant role just three years earlier.

Chinese Factor : By mid-60s two developments are important for understanding these relations. India as a beacon of decolonisation in Africa, as one of the founders of Non-aligned Movement and a leader of Afro-Asian resurgence had been let down during Indo-Chinese War by those very peoples whose demands it had championed. The situation for India became more alarming when it observed that African countries belonging and professing to Non-aligned groups were ready to accept Chinese claims and versions which was a member of Communist Bloc. Therefore, it was time for India to do introspection of its relations with Africa who were not only non-aligned but numerically larger with a higher sense of a solidarity in Third World forums. Under these imperatives India went for a planned policy of long term objectives in Africa which was to be cultivated with consistency.

Second, it was by mid-60s that most of the African countries got independence and the Indo-African relations from that period onward was one between two independent and sovereign states. This period saw a complete metamorphosis in the state of Indo-African relations over a 20-year period. From a position of utter diplomatic failures, chaos and isolation India overcame its problems in diplomatic and political fields and established growing relations with African countries. Though one can also argue that by the end of the 50s, Indo-African relations were not in areas of priority in Indian foreign policy. Due to combination of various factors, India's global concerns seemed to extend beyond the limited horizon of Afro-Asian horizon. The business of cultivating close relations with Africa was left to the Indian diplomatic staff. India had taken a 'softer' approach on colonial issues in Africa. For India enlargement of area of peace amidst the super powers rivalry was the main concern. On the process of decolonisation in Africa, India gave diplomatic and moral support to Africans but it was a qualified support. For India, peaceful and constitutional path was the legitimate way. It believed that international balance of forces would force the colonial powers to wind up their empires in Africa. At the same time the leadership of Afro-Asian Movement had shifted to Africans by early 60s. The increasing numbers of independent African countries, with a feeling of African solidarity were becoming an important factor in Afro-Asian Movement. China, on the other hand, was providing a contrasting and radical posture as against India on many of the African issues.[4]

Chou-En-Lai had gone on an African safari, which enabled him to develop closer rapport with African leaders and to convince them of Chinese view points. Chinese stand on armed struggle as integral part of freedom struggle and assertion that no ruling power ever left its power voluntarily, along with Chinese material support, contrasted against the Indian qualified diplomatic support. Even India's limited support seemed to be hollow[5] and Indian image as staunch anti-colonial country was compromised. Nehru (1961) held the view that Goa's liberation was an exclusive Indian problem – similarly liberation of Mozambique and Angola were exclusive African problems.[6] At such a juncture, when China attacked India in 1962, there were not many friends in Africa to sympathise with Indian position. India got diplomatic support from four countries in Africa- Ethiopia, Libya, Nigeria, Congo (Leopoldville). Six others expressed sympathy and concern. Ghana, Tanzania and Guinea took an openly unhelpful stand towards India. This happened despite the fact India had consistently taken an anti-colonial and pro-liberation stand towards Africa in international forums like UNO. It had extended diplomatic and moral support to many of the liberation movements and maintained strict boycott of South Africa. African stands were unfavourable and embarrassing. India was isolated not only on the issue of Chinese attack but even in Afro-Asian and Third World meets. Indian diplomacy was in a state of disarray.

NAM Solidarity : In the second Conference of Non-aligned countries in October 1964 at Cairo, the moderates were largely in disarray. India without Nehru was reduced to insignificance. Krishna Menon had some very harsh things to say about Indian performance at Cairo. He said, "We became camp followers there...our personality did not make any impact on the conference or on the delegates."[7] Africans and Indians were at the two ends. In contrast to speech of Indian Prime Minister Lal Bahadur Shastri, who said: "First and foremost we believe in peace, in the settlement of all disputes with peaceful means," there was a speech by Kwame Nkrukah, who stated flatly, "as long as oppressed classes exist there can be no such thing as peaceful coexistence between opposing ideologies." In contrast to India's view that cold war was the root of all tensions, for Africans the root was not cold war but colonialism. Against Indian view of non-alignment as 'respect for peace and active coexistence among peoples and states,' Sekou Toure held that non-alignment 'perfectly expressed the wishes of states to free themselves from the domination of centuries.' "This conference represented 'combative' view of non-alignment and projected Sino-Soviet rivalry within the movement." Indian Prime Minister Shastri introduced a proposal to send a mission to China to try to persuade it to desist from developing nuclear weapons.[8]

Except Cyprus no other country gave any support to it and many thought it inappropriate even to introduce such a proposal.[9] India's isolation vis-à-vis China among African countries, inside NAM, was clear. In content it was a metamorphosis of Bandung (1955) sprit, if not of Belgrade (1961). But what was more important and in contrast to Bandung - it was Africa which took place of pride at Cairo Summit and it were African delegates who set the tone.[10] Further it was a success of Chinese approach as 'combatants' succeeded in pushing 'peaceful co-existence' from first to the fourth position in the list of items on Agenda. The Cairo Summit showed India beyond doubt the importance Africans had gained in NAM, the influence which China had over them, isolation which India faced among African countries and the sorry state which Indian diplomacy had come to.

It was in the above set of circumstances and imperatives that India's policy towards Africa had to be framed. It was not the simple failure of Indian diplomacy but these developments showed the lack of depth in Indian perceptions of various issues of African importance. The Heads of Missions in Africa and West Asia met in November 1963 at New Delhi. The task before India was to fix national diplomatic priorities with determined levels of urgency. These policy goals had to be adopted with suitable approach and style along with the importance that Africa enjoyed under the changed circumstances. Viewing from retrospect, the first priority of Indian policy goals in Africa was to isolate China and Pakistan which had signed "Boundary Agreement" with China ceding Indian territory of Pakistani occupied Kashmir. The second priority was to arrest and then enhance the falling influence of India amongst Africans who enjoyed greater numerical strength in NAM and other Third World forums. The strategy adopted was to be selective in approach to African countries and to make reliable friends there. Further each Chinese move was to be countered, like economic diplomacy, militant stands, visits by leaders, etc., and all other further leverage (Sino-Soviet rift, Indian settlers in Africa, an ex-colonial countries, etc.) which India had exclusively was to be exploited. These were some of the main considerations which guided India's Africa policy both for short and long term from mid-60s onwards.

South-South Engagement : Though priority of India's diplomacy till late 60s was to counter Chinese influence in Africa and make reliable friends there, at the same time India had started a determined move to develop strong economic relations with African countries. Though this helped India in meeting its political priorities in Africa policy, the economic consideration was also not less. The relatively higher level of Indian development and the umbrella of South-South cooperation under NAM gave India incentives in economic fields to fulfil its political end. Explaining the policy shift during early 70s the then External Affairs Minister said in Lok Sabha on 25 April 1972

> Proper training and orientation in economic work is given to all IFS (Indian Foreign Service) officers and the idea is to change them from being diplomatic agents to trade agents as far as possible. All our foreign service officers have been told very clearly that their promotion in future would depend on their performance in this field.[11]

On the economic front, by early 70s Africans started questioning the wisdom of dependent development. The increasing realisation for need of South - South cooperation both in India and Africa, for their own separate reasons, got articulated in various conferences. It was in Lusaka Summit of NAM in 1970 that both Africans and Indians underlined the need for its implementation. The resolutions on Nonalignment and Economic Progress were separated from fourteen other resolutions of the conference which for the first time dealt with a working programme and preliminary negotiations among non-aligned nations. The host, President Kenneth Kaunda in his opening address to the conference emphasised the need of economic unity.[12] Julius Nyerere of Tanzania pointed to the hope of developing countries in developing through the ideas of developed countries. Nyerere stressed that, "for in seeking to overcome our poverty we each inevitably run the risk of being sucked into the orbit of one or other of the Great Powers", and "it is through these questions of trade and aid that our action in world affairs can be influenced, if not be controlled." He, therefore, asked the Lusaka Conference to consider "the question of how we can strengthen Nonalignment by economic cooperation." Indian Prime Minister Mrs. Indira Gandhi elaborated in details, at the same conference, the potential areas and logic behind South-South cooperation. She assured the conference that "if we decide and, I hope we shall, India will be glad to play her modest part."[13]

By the first half of 70s there were many outstanding achievements by India at domestic front which injected self confidence in it. In 1971 India won Bangladesh War despite the combined threat of Pakistan, China and USA. Indian diplomacy scored a point at this stage when it obtained the support of one Super Power against the other by Indo-Soviet Friendship Treaty of 1971, keeping intact Indian status as a non-aligned country. Indian explosion of nuclear device in 1974 showed Indian progress in scientific and technological areas. Overnight it placed India in the restricted categories of countries which had mastered nuclear technology. The achievement of self-sufficiency in foodgrain production projected Indian economic and managerial capacity. The launching of its geostationary satellite again placed India among the few advance countries.

The two major implications of these developments were that, firstly, India succeeded in arresting the reverses at diplomatic front which it was suffering since Indo-Chinese War of 1962. Now onwards Indian policy and diplomacy became positive, including towards African countries, compared to 60s when its major concern was to contain China and Pakistan. Secondly for Africa, India again became a power to turn to, for help and assistance. Indian diplomacy during this period changed its priority. India's major concern in Africa was to foster economic cooperation under the umbrella of South-South cooperation. India utilised all its diplomatic strength under all international forums like UNO, NAM, 'Group of 77', etc., to develop South-South cooperation. Policy to make friends in Africa and to gain their diplomatic support on various issues, shifted to creation and cultivation of gainful economic links. In any Third World cooperation India was not only going to gain like other partners but because of its relative advancement in economy and technology it had chances of gaining more than others.

The China factor which had been obsessing India by early 70s was also over by mid 70s. Mrs. Gandhi took personal interest in Africa since her China Safari of 1963-64. During Lusaka and Algiers Non-aligned Summits Mrs. Gandhi took personal interest in meeting and interacting with African leaders. An active and aggressive role in world forums and effecting South-South Cooperation was the main thrust of her policy towards Africa. During the period of Janta Party Government and Rajiv Gandhi's

Government there has not been any qualitative policy departure or addition. Over the years Indian stand on issue of Namibian independence and abolition of apartheid in South Africa became more supportive. It is a different issue that though economic diplomacy came to have greater thrust, the result had not been very encouraging.

India again became important in NAM. Since Lusaka (1970) to New Delhi meet of 1983, the main running issues in all these summits were: (1) the changing concepts of NAM; (2) support to national liberation struggles and (3) the case of South-South cooperation. The question related to the definition and purpose of NAM had always surfaced in one way or other. We discussed that during Cairo Summit the difference between India and Africa was on NAM's priority—peaceful co-existence or national liberation. To India NAM as a movement, equidistant from super power's rivalry, 'was the main source of its power.'[14] However, as Heismath and Man Singh had observed "the power derived from Non-alignment existed only in relation to those states, whose peculiar interests were attacked when that posture was assumed by another state."[15] This explains the Indian adherence to its earlier philosophy for NAM. In operation it accepted and encouraged economic dimension also but it hardly changed from position which was very close to provide the peculiar gain which India was having by that position. In Cairo (1964) when the tone was of militancy, 'combative' view was the predominant style, India did not change its stand on that count. In Lusaka Summit (1970) most of the militant leaders were absent, notably Nkrumah from Sub-Sahara, Ben Bella from Algeria and, Nasser of Egypt, etc., who had vigorously championed the case of militant struggles. Lusaka Manifesto on Southern African had already toned down the appeal for armed struggle. This manifesto emphasised peaceful and non-violent change as a method to liberate the oppressed black majority. However, the issue was not left untouched. African concern for liberation struggle did have its impact in the Final Declaration. Though stating that there was no need to redefine NAM there were nuances of these leaders perceptions in the final charter. It no longer defined non-alignment as an 'irreplaceable instrument for solution of contemporary world and establishment of international relations based upon principles of active and peaceful co-existence' but rather as 'an integral part of the changes in the present structure of international community in its entirety, and production of anti-colonialist revolution.'[16] At Algiers Summit (1973), again Cuba floated the opinion that as NAM is anti-colonial and anti-imperialist, Soviet Union is its natural ally. This time change in definition of NAM was based on different elements. Despite India's reservation, in Economic Declaration it was observed that *detente* was no longer sought by non-aligned nations, "did not have any beneficial effect on developing countries and international cooperation". At Colombo Summit (1976) the Cuban thesis of 'natural ally' was not accepted. It was at Havana Summit (1979) that controversy over the concept of natural ally became very sharp. Senegalese Foreign Minister M. Moustapha accused Castro of exploiting his position as a host "to favour his interest and his political opinions."[17] It was Nyerere of Tanzania who restored the balance. Expressing his doubt whether the movement and permanent enemies and permanent friends, let alone natural ones he warned that natural alliance between non-alignment and Soviet Bloc would cause the movement to "cease to be an influence on the world and fall apart." In growing divergent position on the nature of NAM, India helped along with Nigeria the host delegation in preparing the final draft, which was a compromise but it underlined the primacy of the unity of the movement. It was in New Delhi Summit and Harare Summit that this controversy was completely side-tracked. The main thrust and focus of non-alignment shifted to and for the cause of economic cooperation. In the changed circumstances of 80s NAM's earlier relevance for India had given way to more tangible concept of South-South cooperation in economic matters. In Delhi this issue was the first item of Agenda as well as in Final Declaration. In the earlier successive summits India had yielded here and there to make a dent on more relevant and useful concept of South-South economic cooperation.

Liberation Struggles : On the issues of liberation struggles in Africa India gave continued support at bilateral and multilateral levels. It had vigorous campaigned against Apartheid and occupation of Namibia. With rapid increase in the number of Afro-Asian members within UNO, India adopted a quieter role, as the African group itself took the role to represent the African problems. In 1970 the General Assembly adopted the resolution on the right of people of South Africa to end colonialism by "all means at their disposal" including armed struggle. This resolution was backed by India and it was a clear departure from its earlier insistence on peaceful decolonisation. In 1977, the UN Security Council adopted a resolution on a mandatory armed embargo against South Africa. India worked hard with Afro-Asian countries to get these resolutions passed.

On 5 October 1976 the UN Committee Against Apartheid was specially convened in New York to pay tribute to India for its crusade against Apartheid. It was for the first time during twelve years of this Committee's existence that it honoured a member state. Delegates from all over the world showered praise on India for its principled stand against apartheid during the last thirty years. Ambassador Leslie O. Harriman of Nigeria, the chairman of the Special Committee said on the occasion:

> We, in this Special Committee, owe particular appreciation to India for its consistent cooperation. When this Committee began its work on 2nd April 1963, the very first document before it was a letter from India offering full cooperation. When this Committee appealed in 1964 for assistance to political prisoners, the very first contribution came from India. We found a response from India for every request we made in the cause of South Africa[18].

Rajiv Gandhi and successive Indian Prime Ministers continued this Indian policy. Nelson Mandela visited India after his release from jail. Prime Minister V.P. Singh offered him a cheque of US$ 5 million and he was conferred the highest Indian award Bharat Ratna. When Mandela was sworn in as President of South Africa and apartheid came to an end, India participated with one of the biggest delegations to rejoice the success for which it had worked so long and so hard.

On the issue of Namibian liberation struggle India worked consistently and aggressively in the United Nations. When the International Court of Justice deferred in 1971 its decision on terminating South Africa's illegal occupation of Namibia, Indian Minister of External Affairs asserted that, "it is a political question, which has to be dealt with by the conscience of mankind. It is incumbent on international community to close this ugly chapter in the history of international relations". In 1982 India proposed a global meet on Namibia to force South Africa to free it and it was adopted by 130-0 votes in UN. India accorded full diplomatic status to SWAPO in Delhi in 1985 while commemorating the 25th anniversary of SWAPO at an extraordinary meeting of NAM. The meeting also pledged all possible diplomatic, military and material support stressing the need for greater political as well as more tangible 'material assistance' to SWAPO. Rajiv Gandhi committed that "India would make further contribution to the Non-aligned Solidarity Fund for the Liberation of Namibia." The diplomatic recognition of SWAPO was in sharp contrast to earlier legalistic approach of India on issue of Algerian crisis, Mau Mau rebellion etc. Both the Indian Prime Minister V.P. Singh and opposition leader Rajiv Gandhi attended the independence celebration in 1990 at Windhoek.

Rhodesia was another country which was fighting for its independence during this period. Earlier in 1965 when Unilateral Declaration of Independence (UDI) was made, India was again the first country in the world to break off diplomatic relations with the Rhodesian regime and it was the first to impose total trade embargo. However unlike in South Africa or Namibia where despite the presence of multiple parties fighting for freedom, one party had overwhelming support and it was easy for India to provide its diplomatic and material support to the dominant party, in Rhodesia India made a false start by extending its support to party led by Joshua Nkomo and not to party led by Robert Mugabe which came to power after independence in 1980. India took corrective action as soon as Mugabe came to power at the conclusion of Lancaster House conference. But nevertheless it was a failure of Indian diplomacy to correctly assess the Rhodesian situation.

Besides providing diplomatic support for liberation struggles in fora like UNO, Commonwealth, NAM etc., India had started backing its diplomatic support with finance and material support. It was an addition to earlier policies of India when it used to give mainly diplomatic support. Its own economic limitation did not enable India to provide meaningful material or financial support to liberation struggles. However these material and financial supports were largely provided through multilateral channels like bodies of OAU. In 1969 Indias had spent around Rs. 1.2 million to assist African Liberation movement. By 1977 this amount went up to Rs. 5 million. The enormous increase in this amount during this period shows that India's commitment to African liberation was based on solid grounds-no matter which party was in power in India-not on the rhetoric or personal commitment of any particular leader. During 1977-78 it further allotted Rs. 31 million to add strength to its diplomatic moves. India provided ANC and SWAPO with facilities to man their respective missions in New Delhi. Material and technical assistance were given to South African and Namibian liberation struggles. India also made contribution to UN Fund for Namibia, UN Institute for Namibia, UN Educational and Training Programme for South Africa. Indian External Affairs Minister Atal Behari Vajpayee had pledged at the Foreign Ministers' Conference of Commonwealth that India would definitely consider any request for arms made by guerrillas fighting against White minority regime of South Africa. At Harare NAM Summit (1986), Rajiv Gandhi was chiefly responsible for the establishment of Action for Resisting Invasion, Colonialism and Apartheid (AFRICA) Fund which is better known as AFRICA Fund. He was made its chairman. The plan of action was finalised in close consultation with Southern African Development Coordination Council (SADCC). The nine member group chaired by Rajiv Gandhi launched the Fund with an initial capital of US$ 70 million with an Indian contribution of US$ 40 million. The purpose of the Fund was to enable NAM to help all the victims of apartheid in South Africa, Namibia and in the frontline states.

Indian Diaspora in Africa : Along with economic interaction and support to liberation struggles in Africa, the third issue of continued interactions between India and African states was the presence of Indian settlers in Africa. In comparison to Nehru period Indian policy shifted on this count. Making amends to earlier dependence on diplomats, Mrs. Indira Gandhi went with a high power delegation for an African Safari in 1963-64. The main task of this safari was to (1) assess China's influence in Africa; (2) explaining the factors behind India's reverse in the border war; (3) assessing the future of 420,000 people of Indian origin settled in Africa, and (4) effecting technical and economic collaboration with African Countries.[19] For the first time large numbers of PIOs in Africa were also taken into policy considerations. Indian move was to include them in larger Africa policy of India. In 1963 African Safari, apart from her other engagements, including calling on Heads of State, Mrs. Gandhi never missed an opportunity to meet the Indian leaders and members of Indian community, though their number in certain small locations was not exceeding even fifty. The constant refrain in her speeches was that Indians settled in Africa must identify themselves completely with African peoples and make their fullest contribution to the society in which they lived. This was the continuation of Nehru's stand but its importance has changed under the changed circumstances. Nehru was somewhat impatient with Indian settlers in Africa. He refused to accept the thesis that they were entitled by virtue of their Indian origin to Indian protection. But, Mrs. Gandhi described them as "Ambassadors of India", a subtle contrast from Nehru's view which sounded outright dissociation of Indian migrants from policy considerations of India. Not only this exhortation to Indian settlers by an Indian politician pleased African leaders but gave a chance to Indian leaders to establish a close *rapport* with leaders of Indian settlers in Africa.

The report of the Congress delegation presented to Indian government emphasised two points that–Africa's new leaders were not pro-Chinese and that there was abundant goodwill for India which ought to be made use of. Later throughout her Prime Ministership, Mrs. Gandhi continued to take interest in African Affairs and there were streams of African dignitaries who visited New Delhi just to see her and seek her counsels.[20] The inclusion of 'PIOs' in Africa in policy frame of India was more apparent in Kenya where India initiated with the Government of Kenya the plan for the formation for Africa-India Development Association (African-do) with a long term objective to seek the integration of Indian community in the economic life of Kenya. Though ultimately it could not materialise due to reasons other than disinterest of India, it did show the inclusion of settlers in Indian policy and the contrast which it provided along with other economic initiatives in Kenya to the pro-Chinese Tanzania which also had PIOs.[21]

By end of 70s she had unsuccessfully tried to intervene in Kenyanisation. It earned the wrath of Kenyan government. The local government and people of Kenya saw Indians as those who only made exorbitant profits in Africa but did not identify themselves with the majority community or the country. The litmus test of India's policy towards Asian settlers in Africa and that of

Indian settlers expectation from Indian government came during expulsion of Asians from Uganda in 1972. Idi Amin like Kenyatta wanted to put Ugandan economy in hands of Ugandans of African origin. He said that 80,000 Asians in Uganda were sabotaging the economy and encouraging corruption and therefore there was no room for them in Uganda. Asians had not taken the citizenship of Uganda. All Asians who were Kenyan citizens, British or Indian passport holders had to leave Uganda in 90 days before 8 November, 1972. Amin called the expulsion of Asians "as part of war of liberation". The Indian President while in Lusaka denounced the expulsion and stated, "The happenings in Uganda leave a heavy cloud of doubt and uncertainty over the minds of many people of Indian origin in several countries of Africa. The pernicious doctrine of racialism may permeate even free Africa." Other African countries like Mauritius, Tanzania and Zambia also condemned the expulsion but no African country volunteered to accept even a single Asian family from Uganda.

Indian Deputy Minister of External Affairs said in Parliament, "We are in touch with the Ugandan authorities and I can assure the house that we shall do everything we can to protect the interest of Indians there". India made it clear that it was going to support any international move that would persuade Amin for extending the expulsion deadline. India did not take toughter line because (i) a purely racial issue would have been interpreted as Indian interference and design in Africa, (ii) the Afro-Asian solidarity would have been damaged and (iii) there was "nothing to be gained by using strong words if they cannot be backed by meaningful action in Uganda as any show of strong sentiment may trigger off an anti-Asian wave."[22] India refused to take back Asians who held passport other than Indian. This forced Britain to accept responsibility for British passport holders and allow them to come back to UK. Once Britain accepted its responsibilities and opened its door for them India too permitted Asian settlers to come to India with their money and accept Indian citizenship. They did not opt to come to India which they wanted to intervene very strongly in Uganda. Both Indian government and Asian settlers realised the limits of their expectation from each other. However the restrained approach of India succeeded in getting Amin agree to pay compensation for business and properties of Indian passport holders which was not given to Indians or other nationalities.

In many African states Asian settlers had to bear the wrath of its government and people. Zambia, in whose freedom struggle India contributed a great deal, its leader Kenneth Kaunda got his political training in India, Asian settlers were subjected to harsh treatment by government. In February 1988 para-military troops pushed into clothing shops of businessmen of Indian descent in Lusaka in early morning to enforce a law that parliament had passed just a night before. This law provided for seizure of business thought to be trading in black market. The owner of such business had no legal recourse. Kaunda said, "We have been forced to do this to deal with the selfish minority of businessman because we must protect the silent majority." The Asian bashing in Africa had brought home another point to India. The consistent support to African freedom struggles and Afro-Asian solidarity must not make India expect that African government would reciprocate by taking care of 'suspected' Asian settlers.

In South Africa as well, India exhorted Asian settlers to join black against apartheid and made no special gestures towards Asians. Because of its experience in East Africa it is not surprising that in the aggressive diplomatic and economic initiatives towards free South Africa the issue of Indian settlers in South Africa hardly finds any important place. However the real test of this policy would come when Indian settlers have to share the burden of economic and social restructuring programmes undergoing in South Africa. Perhaps due to long isolation of South Africa from India during apartheid period, they will not have unlike East African Indians a 'dependency attitude' towards India, making Indian diplomatic task easier. But it does not mean Asian settlers have no place in Indo-African relations. For Asian settlers India still remains a source of cultural strength and inspiration. Cultural tourism is one potential area where Asian settlers would remain a priority both for business and religio-cultural organisations.

Proactive Diplomacy: Besides these major components of Indo-African relations, we find that Indian diplomacy was alert and aggressive on occasional crisis and issues of African states. In April 1986 when US bombers attacked Libya, India condemned the attack. Foreign Ministers of Non-aligned countries met in an emergency meeting chaired by India and unanimously condemned the US administration for "dastardly, blatant and unprovoked aggression" and deputed a six member ministerial team headed by Indian Foreign Minister to Tripoli as a special gesture of solidarity with Libya.

The 'award diplomacy' was initiated. All important leaders of African countries were given one after another Jawaharlal Nehru Award For International Understanding—J. Nyerere (1973), K. Kaunda (1974), Nelson Mandela (1979), L. Senghor (1982) and others. Nelson Mandela was further given Bharat Ratna the highest Indian award when he visited India first time. Large number of the lesser dignitaries were awarded doctorate (Honoris causa). This award diplomacy was further enforced by sharp increase in visits of Indian leaders to Africa. Nehru visited only one sub-Saharan Africa country but Indira Gandhi, Rajiv Gandhi and successive prime ministers made frequent visits to African countries. If one scans the Annual Reports of Ministry of External Affairs, Government of India, over the years, one finds that there is massive increase in visits of head of state and government from both India and Africa. The visits by joint commissions, specialised commissions, ministry delegates, public sector delegates etc., increased tremendously. Indian diplomacy was backed by financial and mutual support, joint ventures, production cooperation and trade agreements.

Another new feature of India's Africa diplomacy during 1990s was its emphasis on South Africa since its liberation from internal colonization. The annual income of South Africa equalled to half the gross income of the entire sub-Saharan Africa. It has concentration of world's biggest trading, mining and manufacturing corporations. The euphoria of India on the end of apartheid was just not because Indian settlers and blacks have become free from racialism but to a great extent because India wanted to convert its goodwill for South Africa, that time, not for Indian settlers, but into economic gains by having a preferential access to its large and strong economy.

In fact the award diplomacy, rapidly increasing visits and interactions of government and non-government people was to provide a newer thrust to economic cooperation. However by the end of fifty years of Indian independence Indo-African relations faced challenges. What were the major challenges that India faced on the eve of 21st Century? The most important challenges were that the new umbrella of South-South cooperation was already showing its problems as Indo-African relations has not been able to emerge qualitatively different from North-South relations and looked like a new pecking order. The relevance of NAM was lost and apartheid and decolonisation of Namibia were over from Indo-African agenda. Indian diplomacy had to find agenda which had to be equally relevant for Africans and provided equally effective rallying points for Indians and Africans. The regional cooperation through Indian Ocean Rim framework or inter-regional cooperation like through SADC provided India with newer opportunities and challenges.[23] India's Africa policy indicated a slight change as also some consistency. Thrust was changing towards promoting economic cooperation, preserving peace and assisting the African defence forces.

Peacekeeping Operations : India extended its participation in UN peace keeping mission even since UN involved itself in conflict management situation in Africa. India participated in more than forty UN peace-keeping operations in Africa. The first Indian participation was dating back to 1960 in Congo. It has contributed nearly 100,000[24] troops who are well experienced in low intensity conflict. India's support in peacekeeping operations in Africa demonstrates its commitment at bringing peace and development to the continent.[25]

Indian troops were present in Ethiopia-Eritrea border operation (UNMEE), Democratic Republic of Congo, Liberia and Sudan (2007). India also responded to the call by the UN Secretary General for female personnel in field Missions by sending its first full 'Female Formed Police Unit' for peace-keeping mission in Liberia. This Unit also reached out to women and children, in addition to performing its normal peace-keeping functions[26]. The professionalism and the social/community sensitivity of the Indian troops in African countries is well known.

India provides military training to officers of the African defense forces. It is an another important component of India's Africa policy. Africa does not have enough military training institutions. They send their military officers abroad for training. Since 1960s, India provided military training to Africans primarily from the Anglophone African region. The training covers security and strategic studies, defence management, artillery, electronics, mechanical, marine and aeronautical engineering, logistics management services.[27] During the last decade and a half around more than 1000 senior level officers from African countries have been provided training by the Indian army.

Interactions in the 21st Century : The Indo-Africa relations over the years have demonstrated both change and continuity. In the 21st century there are discernible changes that are visible in India- Africa relations and there are new imperatives that are shaping this relationship. It is being shaped by the fundamental changes that took place in both the regions. India's rise as an economic power, its vibrant democracy and its greater integration into the world economy and on African side democratic, economic growth and its continental and regional integrations are major factors that are shaping this relationship. The ability to complement each other is far greater today than it was in the past. There is a desire to work on their complementarities and build partnership based on mutual benefit. The focus has now shifted to economic development and the interactions are now moving beyond government to embrace track II interactions. India is cooperating with the African countries within the limits of its capacities and capabilities, in their efforts to achieve democratic vibrancy and economic development.[28]

At the Pan-African level India stepped up its relations with African Union which was formalised by the recently held India-Africa Summit in April 2008 [29]. In a way the Summit institutionalised the decade-old partnership between India and Africa. The Summit was attended by African leaders selected by the African Union. India views the African Union as embodying the spirit of resurgent Africa. India has been fully supportive of AU programs and objectives. India now is not just an observer but is a dialogue partner in the African Union.

At the regional level India is engaged in forming partnership with regional organizations. India made good progress in developing cooperation with the regional organizations like COMEASA, EAC, SADC, ECOWAS and is trying to do similar progress with others. The regional cooperation programs include several areas like feasibility studies, consultancies, joint projects in expansion of railway networks. It also includes food and health security, pilot projects on the establishment of micro, small and medium enterprises and ICT for development. India has strength both in medium and small industries as well as in IT areas. India extended large credit lines to the East Africa Development Bank, the PTA Bank for the COMESA region, West African Development Bank (BOAD) and most recently a line of credit of $250million to the Economic Community of West African States (ECOWAS) Development Bank in West African region. The last one is to help finance sub-regional projects[30].

Indian partnership at various levels aimed at strengthening the South-South cooperation. There are enormous possibilities for further Indo-African cooperation, both in economic and political areas especially in the context of multi-polar and globalised world. Both sides agree that institutions of international governance have become anachronistic and need to be democratised and reformed. Both sides had been broadly working together for UN reforms and are want to make the UN more representative and democratic. They stand together in global negotiation on critical issues as in multilateral trade negotiations, climate change, fight against terrorism and in international financial institutions.[31]

India-Africa Trade : Owing to economic liberalisation in both India and Africa, trade and investment partnership with Africa has increased considerably in the recent years. In the last decade, India has launched a number of initiatives for a closer co-operation with Africa, which includes the Focus Africa programme to increase trade with the continent and the TEAM-9 initiative in 2003 to enhance co-operation with West and Central African countries. India's bilateral (non-oil) trade with Africa has grown exponentially. Figure speaks volumes. From $ 4812.27 million almost in 1998 it has grown to $ 34379.91 billion in 2008. During this 10 year period while imports have risen from $2915.53 million to 20475.67 billion, exports have gone up form a mere $394 million to $5.4 billion (Graph 1). What is significant to note is that the balance of trade has been in favour of Africa and Africa's share in India's global trade has increased from 5.8% in 2002-2003 to 8% in 2006-2007 (Graph 1). A region wise analyses of India- Africa trade shows India's trade with Western African region has become higher (due to increased imports of petroleum products) followed by Southern Africa, Northern Africa and Eastern Africa (see Graph 2).

Graph - 1

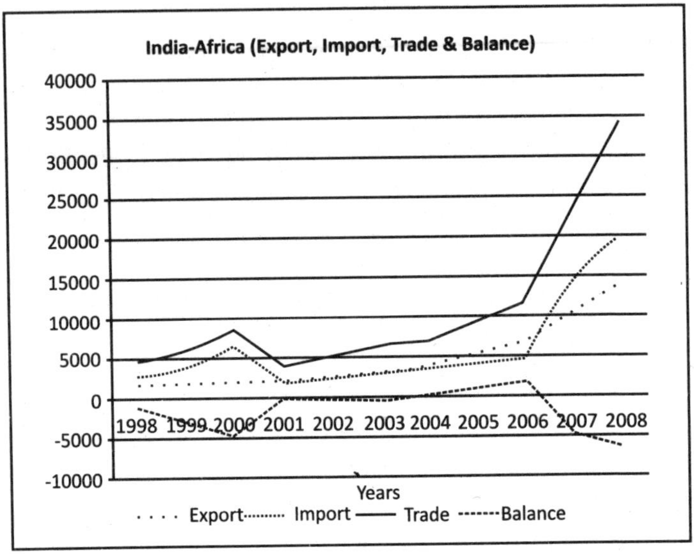

Source: Ministry of Commerce, Government of India

Graph - 2

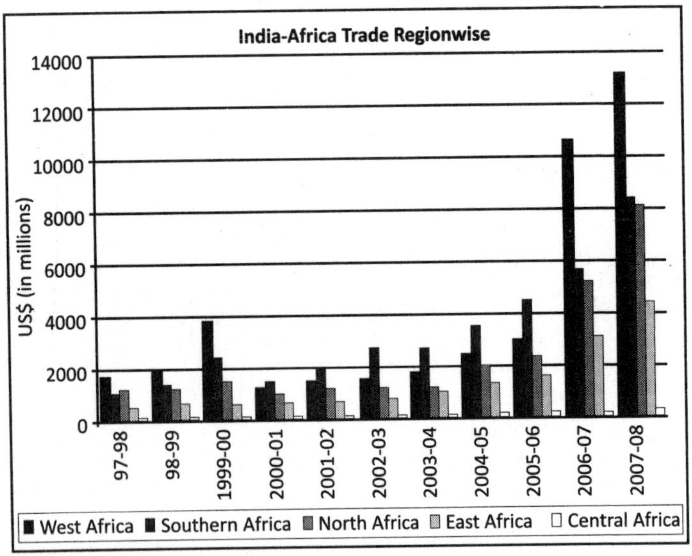

Source: Ministry of Commerce, Government of India

India is however mindful about the need of providing greater market access to imports from Africa. In accordance with its commitment at WTO it has decided to extend a duty free preferential tariff scheme for 34 least developed countries in Africa.[32] The government of India is also working with the Indian private sector in forging project partnerships. The India-Africa project partnership conclaves held in 2004, 2005 and 2006 reflect the growing investment and trade ties. Indian government is impressing upon the Indian industry, Indian entrepreneurs, and agriculture and service personnel to have non-exploitative engagement and build new cooperative partnerships in Africa. Indian industry is realising the importance of Africa especially in commercials terms. But there are challenges as to whether the Indian multinationals operating in Africa behave differently from those of the Western multinational and can they be equal partners in Africa's development process. As far as Indian government is concerned, to facilitate the economic engagement, it has been providing financial assistance to various trade promotion organisations, export promotion councils and apex chambers in the form of Market Development Assistance under the "Focus: Africa" programme and even increasing lines of credit for executing projects in African countries.

Human Resource Development and Capacity Building : One of the strong focuses of the current India's initiatives towards Africa is empowerment of people through capacity building and human resource development.[33] India recognises Africa's need for human resources development on overcoming the gap for development in indigenous capacities. By adopting a people centric development approach in Africa, India differentiates itself from other players in Africa. Such approach combines the use of lines of credits with deployment of Indian expertise to create assets in Africa and to establish people centric projects. Local skill development is part of the projects. India has augmented its development packages to Africa. It has doubled financial package for development of the continent to $5.4 billion over the next five years. It pledged another half a billion dollars in projects related to capacity building and human resource development. It increased scholarships and number of training slots for African students. Under ITEC programme it has been involved in training Africans, deputation of Indian experts and implementation of African projects. Africa is the largest recipient of India's ITEC programmes. The Pan-Africa E- network costing over $100 million is a project that illustrates India's commitment at sharing its progress in information technology sector and bridging the gap of digital divide. The project aims to promote tele-education and tele-medicine in all 53 members of African Union. Senegal has been designated by African Union as the hub for the entire project.[34]

NEPAD Initiative : India has supported the vision of New Partnership for Africa's Development (NEPAD) initiative since its inception in 2001. It is another step indicative of its move to assist Africa in achieving its development goals. India committed $ 200 million to the NEPAD to increase economic interaction with Africa.[35] The aim was to forge closer economic co-operation in the fields of mining, agro-processed products, motor vehicles and components, and Information and Communication Technology (ICT). NEPAD offers large opportunity and an appropriate framework for India- Africa partnership.

Energy Cooperation : Energy cooperation emerged as prominent area of partnership between India and Africa. It is one of the prime drivers of the current partnership. At preset India is the sixth largest energy consumer in the world and projected to emerge as the fourth largest consumer after the United States, China and Japan, by 2010.[36] India requires to expand its energy supply to sustain its growth levels required to attain the developmental goals and especially to eradicate poverty. It is seeking to diversify its energy sources, for which it is investing in energy assets outside. In this context Africa's energy potential is very significant for India. About 24% of India's crude oil imports are sourced from Africa (including the North African countries).[37] The Oil and Natural Gas Corporation Videsh Limited (OVL) has largest overseas investment lower 2 billion $US invested in Sudan. It has also acquired stakes in Senegal other countries like Ivory Coast, Libya, Egypt, and Nigeria and Gabon. For its energy requirements India is willing to share with Africa its expertise in exploration, distribution, refining, storage and transportation. Indian investment in this sector should directly assist in the building up of a trained and skilled local workforce capable of efficiently running the assets. India is keen for energy resource supply from Africa. But major issue is as how India is going to reciprocate by policy and acts which is qualitatively different from traditional buyers in Africa. India has proposed to support food security, human resource development market access and anything that their 'collective' leadership suggest and which India can provide.

Maritime Cooperation : Maritime cooperation is another component of India's current engagement with Africa. The growing concern in the Indian Ocean owing to piracy, smuggling, drug and arms trafficking, terrorism etc. threatens the security of the sea lane of communication. Frequent acts of piracy in the Somalian waters has made that country's waters the most dangerous for merchant shipping in the world. Indian ships are not immune. At the regional level the IGAD sub-region has significant importance for India for maritime security in the Indian Ocean. India's involvement and contribution, particularly in peace consolidation and post-conflict reconstruction in both Somalia and South Sudan would ensure security both for the region and India.

At the national level over the past few years, India deepened security and diplomatic co-operation with various African countries such as South Africa, Seychelles, Mauritius, South Africa, Madagascar and Mozambique. South Africa is in the strategic neighbourhood of India and its coastline being strategically important, India entered into an agreement[38] with South Africa, (March 2006), to improve cooperation in merchant shipping and related activities. The agreement provides for facilitating Indian companies to establish joint ventures in the field of sea based transportation and ship building/repairs. Furthermore, the pact also facilitates the exchange of information for accelerating the flow of commercial goods through and at port and promotes the strengthening of cooperation between merchant fleets.[39]

The Indian Navy has been doing naval exercise in the Indian Ocean. It provides maritime security cover to most of the Western Indian Ocean African islands. It has been patrolling the Exclusive Economic Zone of Mauritius since 2003. It has entered into similar agreements with Seychelles in 2003 to patrol its territorial waters. The Indian Navy is planning further joint exercises with the Seychelles. India has set up in Madagascar its first listening post on a foreign soil in July 2007.[40] It has set up a radar surveillance station with high-tech digital systems to observe shipping movements. It is seeking a long-term lease of the Agalega islands in Mauritius. But the established lobby is opposing this. In strategic terms, it could serve as a small base between India and the important shipping lane of the Mozambique. African East coast being the strategic maritime neighbourhood of India, efforts are underway for greater maritime presence and stronger ties with the African countries to secure the sea lanes of communication (SLOCs).

In the 21st century India and Africa are confronted with new challenges at the domestic and international level and there is a need to be partner for mutual benefit. The historical connections provide the goodwill to foster the present interactions. The Delhi Declaration adopted by India and Africa in the India-Africa Summit Declaration calls for South-South solidarity and provides a blueprint for further cooperation in 21st century.

Conclusion

India–Africa relation over the years has witnessed various changes. It has moved from a period of high political, emotional and moral solidarity to a more material, concrete and pragmatic approach. Indo-African diplomatic relations by mid 60s had gone to a very low ebb. Indian policy was unrealistic in perceiving both, the role Africa was going to play due to its numerical strength and sense of solidarity and secondly in importance and priority which Africans attached to issues like decolonisation and racial equality. India had failed to realise that any such issues like peaceful co-existence, highly relevant and important though they were for India, had to be integrated with African impatience for decolonisation. India stuck to its priority of peaceful co-existence but it paid the price in the group of Afro-Asian countries. Once India started integrating the priorities of African countries it was able to convince to a certain extent the importance and relevance of its own stand and views on different issues. International situations and India's achievements at home played an important role in India's move to befriend African countries but it was the planned, systematic and persistent attempt of its policy pursuits that took the problems in its stride and exploited the favourable circumstances that came its way.

Second, India provided increasing support to African liberation movements, both for decolonisation and end of racialism. During early period India's support was not strong in material terms. Even its qualified diplomatic support was not pursued with tact and care. The result was that it was branded as the one having 'softer' feelings on issues like colonialism. Though during seventies and eighties, material assistance was added to Indian diplomatic efforts, they remained meagre due to India's own limitation to give more in those terms. However, the diplomatic alertness and initiatives were so vigorously pursued that they bridged the gaps of less material assistance and projected India as a champion and uncompromising fighter against colonialism and racialism. Third, as was discussed, Indian diplomacy did succeed in filling the gaps in Indian desires and its effective role in African liberation struggles but how far did it succeed in providing a coherence to India's economic relations within emerging South-South concept? India had added economic dimension to its diplomacy and policy toward Third World for meeting its political imperatives in mid 60s. Through its ITEC and other programmes it started to counter the growing Chinese economic diplomacy in Third World. Selective and aggressive initiatives for friendship through economic diplomacy did help India. Over the years the political urgency passed away, but this 'means' itself was gainful and worth pursuing. Under the umbrella of NAM this became the main policy goal and other diplomatic endeavours became supportive and adjunct to it in Africa. The Economic relation which emerged in the context of Indian initiatives in the umbrella of South-South was not very encouraging. Indo-African growing trends in economic areas demand that in the light of India's past experiences, it should be sensitive to African concerns and expectation. The present interactions calls for partnership and south-south solidarity and focuses on economic empowerment and sustainable development in Africa. But the challenge is whether the horizontal relations would be different from the vertical relations. If the growing trends in Indo-African economic relations do not distinguish itself qualitatively from North-South relations, then it creates problems for Indian moves in Africa. The economic relations of India with Africa under globalisation are gainful for India but it has to be qualitatively different from North-South relations as far as African perceptions are concerned. Can India translate its historical and cultural goodwill along with its credential of a fast developing ex-colonial country as a competitive edge to push its new economic agenda formulated under India-Africa-Forum summit 2008?

Endnotes

1 "Calcutta Session of AICC 1928," *AICC Background to India's Foreign Policy* (New Delhi, 1950), Appendix.

2 "Selection Speeches of Jawaharlal Nehru, September 1946-April 1961," *India's Foreign Policy* (Publications Division, New Delhi, 1961), p. 2.

3 Foreign Minister Oscar Kambona of Tanzania said in the early 60s that he and others were willing to agree that India's leadership of Asia was decadent and China was an emergent force. Quoted in D. Kimche, *The Afro-Asian Movement: Ideology and Foreign Policy of the Third World.* (Jerusalem, 1973), p. 246.

4 Anirudha Gupta, "India and Africa South of the Sahara", in Bimla Prasad, (Ed.) *India's Foreign Policy* (New Delhi, 1979).

5 The limitation of India's moral and diplomatic support to African cause was apparent when Whitehall succeeded in getting Apa Saheb Pant, the first Indian High Commissioner in East Africa, recalled from Kenya. His home in Kenya was haven to political leadership of Southern Rhodesia, Uganda, North Rhodesia, Nyasaland, and Burundi. All these leaders had got a message in early years of Indian independence that New Delhi could be fully depended on for its support to the African cause despite the pressures of colonial masters on India. Therefore recall of Pant from Kenya, exposed the limitation of India for their cause.

6 Anirudha Gupta, *op. cit,* p. 269.

7 M. Brecher, *India and World Politics—Krishna Menon's View of the World* (London, 1968), p. 226.

8 C.H. Heimsath and Man Singh, *A Diplomatic History of Modern India* (New York 1971), p. 173.

9 Similarly when Jakarta preparatory meet for Algiers-Bandung type conference was being held, Egypt put the proposal that no dispute like the Sino-Indian should be considered as pre-condition for such a meet.

10 African countries constituted 60% of total participants in Cairo (28 Africans out of total of 47) *Africa Research Bulletin* (London) Vol. 1, No, 1-31 October 1964.

11 *Foreign Affairs Record,* MEA (Govt. of India) April 1973, pp. 161--162.

12 Kaunda said: "We must move non-alignment with what critics consider mere political and idle rhetoric. We must work out and agree on common action to give substance to the movement not only in political field but in the economic and technical field which will add to our unity and strength. See *Africa Research Bulletin* (London), 1-31 November 1970, p. 1879.

13 *Selected Speeches of Indira Gandhi 1969-72,* Publications Division, Government of India, New Delhi, pp. 629-97.

14 C.H. Heimsath, *op. cit,* p. 61.

15 *Ibid.* p. 61.

16 Sadiq Ali *op. cit,* p. 61.

17 *Ibid.* p. 17.

18 See, "Solidarity with the Struggles for freedom in South Africa: Tribute to India" *United Nations: Apartheid Special Committee* (New York, 1976).

19 Anirudha Gupta, *op. cit,* p. 270.

20 Ajit S. Gopal, *op. cit,* p. 12.

21 The reason for failure of Africendo was the exodus of Asians which began after passing of British Immigration Bill of 1968 and hesitation of Indian settlers to contribute money due to lack of political security. The other economic initiatives in Kenya were the government encouragement to Indian industrialists in investing to build twenty two industrial units in Nairobi.

22 *Times of India* (Delhi) 6th October, 1972.

23 Ajay Dubey, India Africa State Relations, *Africa Quarterly,*

24 Ministry of External Affairs (UNP) Division, 'United Nations Peacekeeping and India's Contribution" http://www.indianembassy.at/content/multilateral/documents/UNPKandIndiascontribCorrectedVersion, Accessed on January 2004.

25 Some of the UN missions in Africa in which India participated by sending its troops are as follows in Mozambique (ONUMOZ, 1992), Somalia (UNOSOM, 1993-95, UNOSOMII), Rwanda (UNAMIR, 1994), Angola (1995, UNAVERM, MONUA,) and Sierra Leone (UNAMSIL, 1999-2000,), *ibid.*

26 Inderjit Rao, Minister of State, External Affairs 2006, India, Africa Ready to Embrace Global Destiny http://meaindia.nic.in/interview/2006/01/25in01.htm, 15 January.

27 *Government of India, Annual Report, 1999-2000,* Ministry of External Affairs; New Delhi, pp. 97-98

28 Dr. Manmohan Singh, 2008, Opening Remarks, Plenary Session, India-Africa Summit in New Delhi, 8 April

29 Pranab Mukherjee, 2008,Address by External Affairs Minister, India- Africa Business Luncheon, New Delhi, 9 April

30 "Exim Bank Extends Credit Line of US$ 5 mn. to PTA Bank to Boost Exports to Africa," *www.eximbankindia.com/old/press011112.html*

31 Delhi Declaration, April 2008, India-Africa Summit

32 No. 25

33 India-Africa Framework of Cooperation, India–Africa Summit, 9 April 2008

34 No. 24

35 *Ibid.*

36 HIS. energy

37 Middle East Economic Survey, 2006,Vol.XLIX,No.15,1 May

38 The bilateral Maritime Shipping Agreement aims at increasing cooperation between India and South Africa in the field of shipping and to promote development of contacts between shipping organisations of the two countries. A Maritime Liaison Committee would be set up under the agreement for promoting merchant shipping and other maritime-transport related matters between India and South Africa.

39 'India, South Africa Sign Maritime Pact', *Business Line,* March 24, 2006.

40 'India activates listening post on foreign soil: Radars in Madagascar' http://www.defence.pk/forums/indian-defence-military/6345-india-activates-listening-post-foreign-soil-radars-madagascar.htmlascar, Accessed on July 2007

Afro-India Economic Relations: Cup – Half Full?

Parvathi Vasudevan

Economic relations between countries or between a country and a group of countries has to be viewed in terms of not merely merchandise trade but also a number of other aspects of international economic cooperation. Economic relations to be fruitful has necessarily to be dynamic, capable of responding to economic and political circumstances of the countries concerned as well as to the evolving global international framework. Inevitably, the context in which the relations have to be viewed needs to be first understood before we analyze the new opportunities and challenges.

This paper is organised into five sections. In Section I, the context is explained in brief. Section II deals with the trade policy initiative taken by the Government of India through issuance of the 'Focus Africa' document. Section III provides a view of the Indian initiatives from the early 1990s to date in respect of other areas of economic cooperation and economic contact. This section also gives an idea of the actual operations of other select countries vis-à-vis Africa. Inevitably, the account in the section being selective could be viewed as not representative but the important point is that it highlights the thrust of the arguments in favor of the main contention of this paper. In Section IV, the international initiatives for Africa and the new opportunities they offer are discussed keeping in view India's participation in it. Here too our effort has been to limit ourselves to the major initiatives. The final section gives perspectives from our analysis and provides some policy implications.

I

It is by now well recognized that in the last few years, especially since about the middle of the 1990s, a significant number of African economies have exuded a quiet but definite sense of economic confidence that was not seen before. This is particularly relevant since several observers have suggested that the twenty-first century could well be 'Africa's century'[1]. Evidence to this optimism is traced to the fact that a large number of African countries have accepted that Africa's problems of poverty and social deprivation can be overcome only with high economic growth on a sustained basis. This implied that notwithstanding some reservations, African economies have generally recognized the imperatives of adjustment—stabilization and structural[2]. Those that have undertaken adjustment processes could turn the 'lost decade of the 80s' and the trying decade of the 90s to be the springboards for improved performance in the present century. This is no mean achievement: in fact, it is a positive development and an important step forward giving credence to the hope that spillover of growth and improved economic performance to the rest of the continent could occur sooner than expected. All this is good news, but the much spoken about renaissance of the African economy is nowhere on the horizon.

The reasons for not being overly optimistic are not far to seek. Even as Africa moves forward, Africa is aware that the future is filled with numerous challenges, one of which is to resolve the problems of the past and at the same time grapple with the overarching reality of the contemporary mores of globalization. The latter, viz., globalization, with its relentless move for integration of the world economy into a seamless entity has fuelled the fear that Africa would be increasingly marginalized[3]. The African leadership is aware that Africa is already lagging behind the rest of the world in so far as meeting minimum human needs—potable water, decent sanitation facilities, affordable health care, and meaningful education—are concerned. Equally disconcerting is the negative image that the rest of the world has of Africa, of pandemics, interminable conflicts, as also the inability to break out of the vicious spiral of stunted growth and arrested economic development. Several Africa observers believe that today most countries of sub-Saharan Africa (SSA) are in a state of greater poverty than they were when they achieved independence[4]. Per capita GDP in SSA as of June 2004 is estimated to be nearly US $ 200 lower than what it was in 1974—a decline of approximately 11 per cent in a period of three decades. This is in contrast to the rest of the world that experienced much higher growth rates on a sustained basis. The East Asian countries for example had posted high per capita incomes that give considerable hope that they would converge rapidly with the levels recorded by developed countries. If Africa is not to be by-passed in the development profile of countries, it has to take more bold economic decisions towards adjustment and reforms and align with the global economy. The point at issue is: can Africa do this all on its own steam?

Most experts believe that Africa needs friends who would assist the continent leap-frog stages of development—friends who could help invest in people and enhance human development, improve Africa's competitiveness and deepen the economies by substantially expanding trade and investment[5]. This would imply that Africa has to continue with the difficult reform process further by deepening and widening it. Equally important for Africa is to ensure that its trade-related infrastructure—ports, railways and roads—is functioning essentially because 30 per cent of African countries are land locked. Telecommunications and energy sectors too need to be reformed in order to make them both cost effective and efficient. Africa's ability to enhance international trade is directly proportional to the quality and volume of trade related inputs such as the quality of human capital, the quantum of finance, insurance, the use of modern technology, the size of the market, the quality of market related institutions, and above all, the quality of the governments. While the reform processes have attempted to address some of these shortcomings, it is important that Africa gains in competitiveness through technological innovation, and in terms of higher growth potential by attracting additional investments in new and modern industries and services through flows of direct foreign capital. So far the record of foreign direct flows to SSA has been very dismal. In 1991-96, as the UNCTAD publication, The World Investment Report 2003 shows, SSA received mere US $ 2 billion. Thereafter, foreign direct investment to SSA was in the range of US $ 6-8 billion a year, with the exception of 2001 when foreign direct investment touched an unusually high figure of US $ 14 billion. The major recipients of foreign direct investment were Angola, Nigeria, Chad, Sudan, Mozambique, and Equatorial Guinea because they have hydro carbon reserves; Uganda, Tanzania and Namibia because of relative macroeconomic stability; Congo and Zambia owing to copper resources; and South Africa since it is regarded as Africa's growth engine. Although foreign direct investment flows have so far been limited, the fact is that such flows would help improve trading possibilities of Africa with the developed countries, as also the advanced developing nations of Asia and Latin America. Intra-African trade could also improve but given the high tariffs and other non-tariff barriers including the convoluted transit systems, inadequate physical infrastructure, and inadequate commodity diversification for trade, the scope for enhancing intra-regional trade is likely to be modest[6].

These facts call for a proactive approach to be followed as much by African governments as by Africa's friends. Relationships among the African public, the friendly trading partners and the policy makers in Africa and at the international (multilateral) levels have to be forged upon into sound partnerships for helping African development. Inevitably, assistance for development would take numerous forms and would be on much larger scale than is presently made available.

Fortunately for Africa, the international environment for growth is conducive. The paradigmatic shift in world affairs, with the collapse of the Soviet Union resulting in the United States emerging as the lone superpower, the international financial institutions placing emphasis on large conditional lending, and the massive movement of capital across the world literally at the touch of a button, have contributed to the emergence of a vibrant civil society across the world demanding for 'adjustment with a human face' and calling for alternative development strategies. These developments have resulted in change in the perceptions of the international community including multilateral institutions about the need to be sharply focused in assisting Africa. This explains the various initiatives that have come about in recent years at the international level. The NEPAD is an excellent case in point[7]. These initiatives build upon the earlier initiative of the International Monetary Fund and World Bank to provide assistance through what is called the HIPC initiative[8]. There are also individual developed country initiatives to help African countries to help themselves.

II

Against the background outlined in Section I, we shall discuss how far India could prove to be a time-tested and reliable friend willing to help Africa. India's Ministry of External Affairs (MEA) has placed emphasis on the economic content of foreign policy towards Africa—economic diplomacy, as the Ministry would refer to. This explains the sharper focus, inter alia, on improvement of trade, removal of economic barriers, promotion of investment, support for regional economic groupings, free trade agreements, technical cooperation, and working in unison with like-minded economies on critical issues at the World Trade Organization (WTO) as part of economic diplomacy. However, trade rather than other areas gains in importance in the policy matrix of the Government of India.

The Focus Africa Program is the document that provides a glimpse of India's economic diplomacy towards Africa. Brought out by the Ministry of Commerce and Industry first in 2002 and later expanded in 2003, it represents a statement of intent. To the extent it does not give forward looking profiles of trade diplomacy, it is not a vision document either. But it is the latest available reference point for discussion on India's contribution to and cooperation with Africa. It is, therefore, important to deal with the document in some detail.

The Focus Africa document highlights the assistance that the Government of India would extend to Indian exporters and the members of the Export Promotion Councils should they visit African countries as part of the Marketing Development Assistance Scheme. It also gives details about the responses of exporters, and the need for interactions through Joint Business Councils and Joint Trade Committees. It lists out the various trade delegations to India from African countries in the calendar year 2003. It gives prominence to the role played by the ECGC and EXIM Bank of India and calls for a proactive role to be played by the Export Promotion Councils, the apex Chambers of Commerce and Industry and the Indian Missions located in Africa. The document also gives a brief idea of the major indicators about 24 select countries of Africa and spells out as to what constitutes India's imports from and exports to the select countries.

While the document is considered to be useful by the corporate officials of the organized export and apex chambers, the medium and small exporters who form a significant proportion of the market players do not seem to share this view. Markets, according to the medium and small exporters, provide enough signals about the problems and prospects of trading with African countries[9]. Strangely enough, the present Minister of Commerce, Mr. Kamal Nath, appears to have made no reference to the relevance or otherwise of the Focus Africa program nor did he propose his policy viewpoint towards trading relations with Africa on the occasion of the announcement of India's Foreign Trade Policy for the period 2004-09 made on August 31, 2004. The fact that the EXIM Bank of India had opened new lines of credit to Africa on the same day, however, leaves the impression that the general thrust of the Focus Africa program would continue.

In terms of facts relating to the trade diplomacy with Africa, it is clear from the Focus Africa document that trade between India and Africa had gone up noticeably in the period 2000 and 2003. This could be partly due to the incentives provided to Indian exporters by the Government of India and partly due to improved economic performance of African countries in recent years. In value terms, imports by India (exports by 24 African countries) were higher than exports by India (imports by 24 African countries) in the latest year, i.e., 2003 (See table 1 at the end of the paper for quick reference). There was thus an overall trade deficit. But this was mainly due to large trade deficits incurred with five of the 24 select countries, namely Cote D'Ivoire (formerly Ivory Coast), Morocco, Senegal, South Africa and Tunisia. With the rest of the countries, India enjoyed trade surplus. The large trade deficits with the 5 African countries were on account of substantial imports by India of cashew nuts (from Cote d'Ivoire), inorganic chemicals (from Morocco as well as Senegal and Tunisia) and gold (from South Africa).

It is not that the trade deficit with the select 24 countries was very critical. In fact the deficit was worth US $ 1 billion. If gold imports that amounted to more than US $ 1 billion were not reckoned in our calculations, there was trade surplus! Since gold is used for consumption purposes, imports for purposes of production did not give rise to trade deficit. Interestingly enough, the dollar value of imports from Africa in any one commodity group exceeded double-digit mark only in the case of Egypt, Cote d'Ivoire, Morocco, Mozambique, Nigeria, Senegal, South Africa, Tanzania, Tunisia and Zambia. The main imports from these countries commodity group wise are as follows: from Egypt, raw cotton, from Cote d'Ivoire, cashew nuts and wood products, from

Morocco, inorganic chemicals and fertilizer crude, from Mozambique, cashew nuts and raw cotton, from Nigeria, wood products, metalifer ores and metal scrap, and cashew nuts, from Senegal, inorganic chemicals, and fertilizer crude, from South Africa, gold, coal and coke, and inorganic chemicals, from Tanzania, cashew nuts, pearls and stones and pulses, from Tunisia, inorganic chemicals, from Zambia, pearls and stones. The major exports from India to the select African countries were: transport equipment, metals and metal manufactures, plastics and linoleum, drugs and pharmaceuticals, cotton yarn, paints, manmade yarn, iron and steel, machinery, rice (often not basmati), oil meals, and readymade cotton garments. Barring Botswana, Libya, Madagascar, Mozambique, Namibia, Seychelles, Zambia and Zimbabwe, the maximum dollar value of imports of any commodity group in respect of 16 select African countries from India hardly exceeded the double-digit mark.

Both imports from and exports to Africa were largely low value based for any commodity group. This is reflected in our classification of the trade values in millions of US dollars in different size classes. This is provided in table below:

Size class	Number of Commodity Groups	
Millions of US $	Imports from India	Exports to India
Less than 1	56 (21.3%)	102 (49.8%)
1-5	95 (36.1%)	59 (28.8%)
5-10	55 (20.9%)	20 (9.8%)
10-20	32 (12.2%)	8 (3.9%)
Over 20	25 (9.5%)	16 (7.8%)
Total	263 (100)	205 (100)

From the above table, one could find that about 78 per cent of imports from India were less than US $ 10 million for any one individual commodity group. Africa's exports to India too showed similar trend: 88 per cent of such exports were less than US $ 10 million for any one individual group.

In the over US $ 20 million class, African countries' imports were mainly by three countries: Egypt (largely due to the group, 'cotton yarn, fabrics, made-ups etc), Nigeria (largely due to groups, 'drugs and pharmaceuticals and fine chemicals', 'machinery and instruments', 'manufactures of metals', 'transport equipment', 'rice other than basmati', and 'cotton yarn, fabrics, made ups etc), and South Africa (largely due to groups, 'rice other than basmati', 'ready made garments of cotton including accessories, 'cotton yarn, fabrics, made ups etc, and 'drugs, pharmaceuticals and fine chemicals'). On the other hand, in the US $ 20 million class, African countries' exports to India were mainly due to Cote d'Ivoire, Morocco and South Africa.

For trade to grow there is a need for commodity diversification as well as further focus on how to improve the size at least in terms of values. A recent survey conducted by a business group in India shows that Africa is 'virgin territory, they need everything'[10]. The report points out that India Inc could expect higher returns in conducting business with Africa since inflation in most countries of Africa is within manageable level. In 2002, only 11 out of the 54 African countries had double-digit inflation. The report observes that while India's traditional trading partners have been Ghana, Mauritius, Kenya, Uganda, Tanzania, Egypt, Nigeria and South Africa, some countries in the continent are turning out to be 'emerging markets' with potential of becoming India's trading partners. These include Libya, Algeria, Senegal, Sudan, Mozambique, Morocco, and Tunisia. These economies are rich in commodity wealth and seek Indian expertise in agricultural and food processing technology, engineering goods and pharmaceuticals. Some of these economies as also other African economies need infrastructure—power, road and railways.

The potential to export goods and services to Africa is widely acknowledged in the official and business circles in India. But the potential imports from Africa hardly receive any mention! There is a presumption that once the African economies stabilize and post high growth rates, they would be able to diversify their export base as well. In the meantime, there would be a trade gap that would be filled, so goes the assumption, by aid at rates that are sustainable. While this approach has considerable merit, there are certain limitations to improving the size and composition of trade that need to be urgently attended to. Top on the list of such limitations is the lack of a sufficient large base of middle class. As a result, Africa's imports cannot grow very rapidly. Besides, there are maze of unstable and excessive regulations on trade in a number of African countries. Moreover, exporters to African countries have to often contend with large official fees in handling transactions and with the recovery of even legitimate receipts owing to unreliable banking systems and practices[11]. These limitations, however, should wane as adjustment processes take root and governance improves.

III

Promotion of merchandise trade as a pivot of the Indo-African relations has not paid enough dividends from the point of view of the overall strategy of using economic diplomacy to prompt sustained economic growth in Africa. While rapid growth alone would not be sufficient to bring about reduction of poverty, it still is a necessary condition. The time has therefore come for India to complement Africa's attempts at sustained adjustment with initiatives on a number of other areas of economic cooperation. These initiatives need to be in concert with the approaches of most of Africa's donors and the initiatives undertaken by many other developing countries of Asia and Latin America as part of what has come to be known as South-South Cooperation (SSC). The launching of IBSA-the special regional economic grouping in early 2004 by India, Brazil and South Africa is hopefully a good initiative in this regard. Should IBSA reach its full potential it could well emerge as the vital bridge linking the three continents and the vast areas bordering the Indian Ocean Rim[12]. These areas with limitless resource endowments if thoughtfully harnessed could render the developing South to be a powerhouse able to talk to rather than be talked down by the developed North.

It is in this context that one has to understand South-South partnerships. Traditionally, SSC, which is a few decades old as a concept and as one that is put into practice has been viewed as a sharing and caring exercise among the developing countries, with the more advanced of them assisting the others in the group to help jumpstart growth and speed up development. The SSC has, therefore, placed its emphasis mainly on technical assistance and economic cooperation in its broad sense covering the areas of finance, investment, trade and technology flows. Over time, SSC has been extended to include the non-traditional areas such as human rights, electoral assistance and peace and security. The extended coverage is based on the argument that for the core areas to be effective, democracy and the absence of strife are imperatives for all nations—developing and developed. In its implementation,

SSC involves the provision of experts in various fields of activity for a period of two to three years to work with the community in the agreed areas of cooperation. This could be in the rural or urban areas. The number of experts needed for the purpose is determined on a case-by-case basis but must be sufficient to provide a critical mass as also to ensure that all the regions of the countries are covered. Experts ensure planning, implementation and monitoring of the activities in question. The approach of the SSC is thus to opt for policies that facilitate the access of the poor to human, physical and financial assets to improve the earning capacities of the ordinary Africans too.

The core area of focus of cooperation among the developing countries has been agriculture, particularly in the context of food security. Viewed thus, the centrality of agriculture for Africa is never contested. But to ensure that African agriculture survives and provides a basis for diversification of economic activities, the international trading environment has to be conducive. This is where Africa is faced with severe challenges in recent years. To appreciate this point, it is necessary to note that for long, Africa's exports of cash crops topped the continent's export chart. But in the last two decades, Africa faced enormous difficulties in facing the challenge posed by large subsidies provided by the developed countries to their own farmers. To elaborate this point, Japan subsided its farmers to the extent of 60 per cent of incomes, the OECD gave 31 per cent and the US farmers got about 20 per cent of their incomes in the form of government support. Cotton, meat, rice, sugar, tobacco and wheat in fact enjoyed over 40 per cent subsidy in the US, with the subsidy to cotton alone amounting to US $ 3.9 billion in 2001-02[13]. This translated into significant losses in the export earnings of African cotton exports from Mali, Benin, Cote d'Ivoire, Burkina Faso, Cameroon, Chad and Togo. The loss was estimated at about US $ 334 million for the period 1999-2001[14]. Similarly, domestic production support and export subsidies enabled the EU tomato farmers to capture approximately 80 per cent of the tomato market in West Africa by setting a price cheaper than the ones of locally produced tomatoes. This resulted in shift away from tomato cultivation as also in the closure of tomato processing plants (into powder, paste) in Burkina Faso, Senegal, Ghana, Gambia and Mali. This story is repeated in several other areas: Kenya's generation of fresh milk owing to large imports of milk powder, Benin's domestic production of chicken and meat, and Mozambique's sugar. The development caused by subsidies and government support by developed countries for their own farm producers led to not only loss of revenue but also loss of jobs in Africa. Besides, the continued domination of large multinational firms in world trade in coffee, cocoa, cotton, vegetables, oil seeds, tobacco, jute, fruits, to cite a few instances, have acted as a dampener to Africa's efforts at improving value addition to these products in which its trade had been significant. Africa's abilities to participate in the global agricultural markets have thus been substantially eroded.

India's help in the uplift of agriculture in Africa has largely been in the form of technical assistance. As part of the Indian Technical and Economic Cooperation (ITEC) program that was started in 1964, India has trained several thousand Africans in the field of hydrology. In fact 60 per cent of training slots were reserved for Africans under the ITEC program. In more recent years, India has provided technical assistance in the food security project in Eritrea, entered into an agreement with Uganda in agriculture research. India provided agricultural goods and implements as gifts to some of the African nations—tractors to Senegal, water pumps and corn grinding mills to Togo and cooking oil and milk powder to Namibia. India is also supporting projects in rice and cotton in Senegal[15]. Nevertheless, India's participation in the African efforts at renewal in agriculture is dwarfed by the efforts of China and the other nations of Asia and Latin America.

Although China is geographically distant, it has not allowed this as a barrier to come to Africa's rescue. Since China shares many of the environmental and climatic challenges that Africa faces, it has lent its helping hand in the FAO's program of the Special Program for Food Security (SPFS) by sending its experts to northern Nigeria. 20 Chinese experts accompanied by over 500 field technicians with varied and specific expertise have been posted to Africa for 3 years to live amidst the Nigerian farmers in 109 locations. Initially, there was some skepticism about the language barrier but the field experience has indicated the ability of the Chinese to pick up the local language as also being sensitive to the cultural needs of the local people. Such an interactive/participative approach has helped China to be gender sensitive too, in that farming women in Africa could learn about poultry and livestock raising, improve food processing, grain storage, raising small ruminants as part of managing water resources. The principal areas of focus related to improving food security at the household levels by ensuring farm irrigation, dam construction, increased soil fertility, pest control services, marketing of agricultural commodities and management of food stocks. Apart from being involved with Nigeria, China has attempted such confidence building measures in Ethiopia, Mauritania, Mali, Ghana and South Africa. Such assistance has enabled these economies to improve their productivity besides a sense of food security. The success of the collaborative approach among China, Africa and FAO owed a great deal to the attitude of the principal actor in listening, teaching, learning, planning, and monitoring, and to the responsibilities that were shared by the stake holders, policy makers and external donors. In Tanzania, the China State Farm and Agri-Business Cooperation has helped in the rehabilitation of sisal farms that helped boost the incomes of local farmers and sisal processing units in a substantial manner[16].

Vietnam, a small Asian economy, had also similarly signed tripartite agreements by the mid-1990s with Benin, Senegal, and Madagascar, and by 2000 with the Republic of Congo. The SPFS program has also helped Morocco assist Niger, Burkina Faso and Central African Republic; Egypt assist Tanzania and Cameroon; Bangladesh assist Gambia even as Bangladesh is itself being assisted by China; Cuba assist Cape Verde and Guinea Bissau even as Cuba is itself being assisted by Venezuela; Myanmar assist Malawi; and Pakistan assist Swaziland. As of now, Vietnam provides over 2000 agricultural specialists in addition to hundreds of other technical experts at Angola and Algeria.

By September 2004 fifteen similar agreements have been entered into whereby nearly 20 advanced developing economies with a workforce of over 2800 experts and technicians will help realize the objectives of the SPFS in an all comprehensive manner almost on the lines of China's commitment to Nigeria [17].

The SSC as it has evolved between Latin America and Africa indicates the strength of the relationship, the primary attempt being to lower Africa's poverty concerns.

Latin American assistance to Africa's agricultural development is worth noting for the reason that it has focused to a large extent on providing an enduring push to agricultural productivity. The International Centre for Tropical Agriculture (CIAT) with its focus on improving the crop germ plasm of the ordinary bean has enabled timely dispersal of the results of its experiments by strengthening sound management practices in collaboration with national programs through regional networks. The latter include ECABREN – the Eastern and Central Africa Bean Research Network – the SABRN – the Southern African Bean Research Network – that liaise with their counterparts in Latin America, viz., PROFRIZA – the Regional Bean Project for the Andean Zone and the PROFRITOL – the Cooperative Regional Bean Program for Central America, Mexico and the Caribbean. These efforts helped ensure new and increased bean germ plasm for the small farmers in Africa and Latin America and reduced the hazards posed by the use of pesticides. While incomes have gone up, it is important to note, that with the improvement of the quality of the bean, protein intake has also gone up with positive effects on the dietary patterns of the ordinary African.

Similar success has been achieved by research in the areas of improving the quality of roots and tubers that occupy a central place in the food menu of African countries. The International Potato Centre has ensured the creation of several national and regional research networks that helps the scientists from the Caribbean, Latin America and Africa harmonize research, share information and multiply the benefits. As a result, the quality and the quantity of potatoes and sweet potatoes have increased. Latin America has helped set up a root crop research network in Southern Africa with emphasis on potato and sweet potato programs.

At the bilateral level, some instances of cooperation between Latin American countries and Africa are worth noting. Uruguay has been assisting Angola while Brazil has been assisting Mozambique, Angola, Sao Tome and Principe, Namibia and Guinea Bissau through cooperation agreements that aim at strengthening local agricultural research institutes, supporting rural areas with emphasis on subsistence farming or transfer of technologies in special areas of farm production such as cocoa, tropical fruits and legumes as well as on the irrigation of rice. Yet another initiative involves Cuba that sent its experts in agriculture and fishing to Cape Verde with the support of the FAO. The UNDP has also contributed to agricultural research in West Africa by supporting the discovery of NERICA – the New Rice for Africa program and the establishment of WARDA – the West African Rice Development Association. These efforts ensured new varieties of rice that were created by crossing the best species of both the African and Asian varieties. The result was higher yields which also matured 30 to 50 days earlier, are high in protein content, more disease, drought as also insects-pest resistant and out compete weeds. With appropriate technical assistance, the West African farmers have played a key role in developing 'super crops' whilst ensuring that these new varieties were user friendly even by those who could not afford fertilizers or herbicides i.e. basically the small farmer, possibly the farm hand. The net result has been a boost for food security all over Africa.

In the field of education and technological advancement, India's relations with African countries were largely in the nature of providing educational facilities in India often along with scholarships and fellowships. At any point of time, there are, and this has been so especially since the early 1990s, over 12,000 African students in Indian universities and colleges attending courses that will get them a Bachelor's or Master's degree in the faculties of humanities, sciences, law, medicine, and computer science and in other professional courses. A few of these students stay on to do doctorate studies. These programs involve some amount of subsidy that the Indian exchequer bears as part of India's commitment to raise the levels of education of the people of Africa. This is besides the training programs under the ITEC under which several thousand Africans get training in fields as diverse as small and medium industries, agriculture, financial management, diplomacy and information, communication and telecommunications. ITEC has also initiated programs such as entrepreneurship and employment planning in Africa itself. Most recent and more important has been the offer by the former Indian President. Speaking in South Africa Mr. Kalam categorically assured the Africans that India would willingly assist Africa to bridge the digital divide. The Government of India, he said, had decided 'to provide seamless and integrated satellite, fibre optics and wireless networks connecting 53 African countries for education, tele-education, tele-medicine and e-services. This will connect 53 leading centers, 10 super-speciality hospitals and 53 end locations in rural areas at an estimated cost of $56 million and was to be completed in three years.'[18]

India has also been supporting projects in Africa relating to solar energy, transportation, telecommunications, oil exploration and production, in particular upgradation of refineries, and ventures in the field of chemicals. As of 2002, Indian enterprises had invested US $ 330 million in a variety of projects in Egypt. Indian enterprises are active in chemicals ventures in Morocco and Tanzania, copper mining in Zambia, oil in Mauritius and Madagascar, and telecommunications and textiles in Malawi. In Uganda, India is now the third largest source of foreign direct investment (after UK and Kenya). In 2003, Oil and Natural Gas Commission (ONGC) invested in Sudanese oil exploration and production and won contracts to build a 720 kilometre oil pipeline and upgrade an oil refinery. Total investments by ONGC in Sudan that year touched US $ 1.6 billion. This is a very large sum considering the fact that total foreign investments for the entire continent reached only US $ 11 billion the year before. India has also been lending help in the specialized area of pharmaceuticals especially in the context of the outbreak of HIV/AIDS.

In contrast to India's participation in social sector development, the Latin American initiatives seem to be far more effective. Early on itself Latin America entered into cooperation agreements in the health sector, mainly to combat the HIV/AIDS pandemic based on comprehensive strategies. At the bilateral level, cooperation has involved the capacity building support and technical assistance: Brazil to Angola, Botswana, Burundi, Guinea-Bissau and Sao Tome and Principe is a prime example. Brazil donated massive quantities of antiretroviral drugs. On the basis of a pilot project, Brazil attends to 115,000 patients at their homes and also organizes prevention campaigns in collaboration with civil society. The objective is to encourage recipient governments to take charge of the project, once the treatment routine is in place. In November 2003, Brazil entered into an agreement with Mozambique that will facilitate Brazilian technicians to transfer technology and provide technical assistance for setting up a factory that can manufacture the generic version of antiretroviral drugs locally so as to make them affordable. At the request of the governments of Angola, and Namibia, Brazil has agreed at the cost of US $ 30 million in the first phase to render similar help by setting up pharmaceutical units that will focus on HIV/AIDS and also manufacture condoms.

Mexico and Cuba have also lent support to SSA countries to combat HIV/AIDS. Cuba has sent 4000 medical personnel to Africa, set up medical department in the region that will provide comprehensive help on a war footing in areas where needed and has also made available free antiretroviral drugs for 30,000 patients on a yearly basis. Cuba, more than any other nation, has its trained medical teams working in tandem with the respective public health systems. This often involves being located in remotest areas in several countries of Africa where the population is afflicted by severe poverty and/or affected by major natural catastrophes. Cuba also imparts training to thousands of men and women from over 40 developing countries including those in the continent, pursuing a medical career free of charge in the International Medical School located in Havana.

In the area of human resource development too, Mexico, Cuba and Brazil have signed numerous agreements with the specific purpose of raising the levels of literacy where it matters most—at the level of the primary schools. Brazil in particular deepened its relations with the Portuguese speaking countries in Africa—Mozambique, Sao Tome and Principe and Cape Verde, by providing financial incentives to families that keep their children in schools. Besides primary education, Brazil has offered scholarships to students from Africa to complete their graduate and postgraduate studies in Brazil. Mexico has extended similar facilities to enable students from 35 African countries to receive education in Mexican institutions of higher learning. Mexico has also initiated programs to enable their top experts to collaborate in the areas of science and technology with emphasis on applied research programs. As for Cuba, it offers opportunities for African students keen on higher education. In more recent times, it has sent teaching personnel to train African students in vocational education. But it is Cuba's initiative in medical education that is outstanding: it has set up schools of medicine staffed by Cuban medical professors in Equatorial Guinea, Gambia, Eritrea, Guinea Bissau and Ghana.

Latin American countries in concert with the United Nations have been helping the African countries to combat drought and desertification too. Venezuela for example has pledged one million US dollars apart from lending financial assistance to select non-Government Organizations (NGOs) working on sustainable development projects. Benin, Burkina Faso, Cameroon, Cape Verde,

Mali, Mozambique, Niger, Senegal and Togo are the beneficiaries with special emphasis being placed on women and youth. The projects encompass both rural and urban areas. The core concern is protection of environment using information gathered by the Latin American counterpart.

In more recent times, Latin America's civil society has involved itself in areas such as human rights, and economic and corporate governance in Africa [19].

IV

India's contribution to the international initiatives to help Africa cannot be measured but as a member of various international organizations and intergovernmental groups, it has played an important part to see that Africa obtains both economic and political benefits. Historically, India's role at the Bandung Conference in Indonesia in 1955 to promote Afro-Asian solidarity was well known and well received too. But less well known is India willingly agreeing to forego its claim to a financial facility exclusively available for the world's poorer countries in 1985 in favor of African nations[20]. This was known as the Structural Adjustment Facility (SAF) that was later enhanced in 1987 to become ESAF. India also gave unreserved support to the HIPC (Highly Indebted Poor Countries) initiative that was introduced in September 1996 jointly by the IMF and the World Bank with a view to reducing or writing down the external debt burdens of all eligible countries to a sustainable level in a relatively short period of time. The HIPC problem has a major African slant: 33 of the 41 eligible countries are in sub-Saharan Africa. India also supported the Enhanced HIPC initiative in 1999 that provided a link between debt relief, poverty reduction and social policies[21]. In the same year, the ESAF was replaced by a newly labeled Poverty Reduction and Growth Facility (PRGF). PRGF aimed at making poverty reduction efforts the centerpiece of a new growth-oriented economic strategy of countries that avail of the facility. In May and June 2003, India contributed to IMF as a lender given its strong balance of payments position and large accumulation of foreign exchange reserves. India contributed GBP 180 million to a reserve fund meant to be used to bail out countries in distress. India also wrote off GBP 12.5 million that seven countries – Mozambique, Tanzania, Gambia, Zambia, Guyana, Nicaragua, Ghana and Uganda owed India[22].

South Africa initiated at the turn of the present century the New Partnership for Africa's Development (NEPAD) and India welcomed the initiative[23]. NEPAD has recognized the need for Africa's adjustment for growth as well as for integration with the international economy and focused on projects and programs relating to infrastructure and agriculture. Around the time the NEPAD was launched (July 2001) the G-8 leadership (consisting of 8 major developed countries) had indicated its willingness to engage itself in a variety of ways to help Africa. NEPAD was seen as facilitating North-South engagement in a manner that strengthens South-South cooperation in a more meaningful fashion.

India set up in early 2003 India-Africa Fund worth US $ 200 million to be used in the forms of loans to projects that enhance African economic integration within the NEPAD framework.

V

India's relations with Africa have been very cordial and cooperative. India is also aware of the poverty and the challenges of development that Africa is faced with, being herself one of those coping with the tasks set out by the UN supported Millennium Development Goals (MDGs) under which targets are set to improve social development across Africa. The focus of the MDGs is on primary education, gender equality, empowerment of women, reduction of infant and child mortality rates, reduction of maternal mortality ratios, halting and reversing the spread of HIV/AIDS, malaria and other diseases, implementing strategies for sustainable development so as to reverse the loss of environmental resources, developing global partnerships for development, and making available access to safe drinking water and basic sanitation latest by 2015[24]. India has helped to improve trade and foster non-trade relations without being substantial and qualitatively high in effectiveness. As a result, the visibility of India as a major partner in Africa's development is conspicuously low, notwithstanding the fact that it has historical ties with Africa partly owing to a large Indian population and partly owing to geographical proximity.

It is probably the presence of a large Indian population in some of the African countries that could have contributed to the absence of innovative initiatives by New Delhi and Indian business houses which if done could have triggered new businesses and collaborative ventures between India and Africa. Traditionally, the Indian settlers in Africa were mostly traders who like all traders were only motivated by profit maximization. As traders, they were in contact with the local population, but they were unwilling to absorb the local population in their businesses even in administrative positions. They generally fraternized amongst themselves and did not show any inclination or evidence of giving back something tangible to Africa that they called home. As a result, they alienated themselves from the sensitivities of the needs and the aspirations of the local population. The large exodus of Indian traders from Africa right from the 1960s to India and to the West resulted mainly because the local political regimes took advantage of the Indian alienation from the local African communities and made life difficult for them. The Indian Government on its part had no choice but to be passive. It had to do a balancing act of being sympathetic to the Indian population and at the same time show solidarity with the African aspirations for the sake of promoting the Third World interests. In the result, the continent suffered for want of adequate Indian investments. The domestic saving rate and the foreign investment inflows being low, the African continent had to contend with raising enough resources from out of its meager incomes to undertake new businesses. The Indian Government's view of cooperation has been to extend some financial and material support, subject to its budget constraints and to promote foreign trade between the Indian exporters and African importers.

All this, is in contrast to what some of the other countries of Asia have done since the 1990s for Africa. For instance, the Malaysian Business Centre was set up in Uganda to explore mutual trade and investment opportunities. China has set up almost a dozen such centers throughout Africa Further, with strong support from the governments of Singapore and Malaysia, and UNDP, Malaysia has promoted Asia-Africa economic linkages. One outcome of this initiative is the Asia-Africa Business Forum set up in 1999 supported through a triangular management with the Japan Human Resources Fund. Another initiative is the Asia-Africa Small and Medium Enterprises Network with a hub operated by a Singapore based regional business organization. UNDP also facilitates the Credit Analysis and Development Finance in Africa – a project that brings African financial executives to the

Development and Infrastructure Bank of Malaysia for intensive training programs. Malaysia also offers technical training to Africans under the Malaysian Technical Cooperation Program initiated as early as 1981. Under this program, it offers nearly 90 courses each year in Malaysian institutions. By mid 2003, more than 2000 participants from 46 African countries have benefited. These courses focus on transferring technical knowledge, improving management and planning skills. Malaysia has also been actively involved in strengthening local micro credit schemes in South Africa with particular emphasis on empowering women and the economically disadvantaged section of the South African black community.

Malaysia's State owned oil company, Petronas, has oil production or oil exploration ventures in more than a dozen countries with a principal focus on Chad where Petronas has 35 per cent in a consortium and has built a 1000 kilometre pipeline through Cameroon. Also Petronas operates approximately 1600 petrol stations in South Africa and Botswana. Similarly Malaysian companies are involved in the telecommunication sectors in Ghana, Malawi and South Africa, palm oil production in Gabon, banking in Mozambique and tourism in Seychelles. Under the AGOA scheme, Malaysia in 2001 set up also a textile and garment manufacturing unit in Namibia. By 2002, it exported textiles to the US markets that is expected to touch US $ 185 million. More importantly this has created several thousand jobs at the local levels.

Yet another Asian nation that recognized the need to support programs and projects in Africa on a sustained basis is Japan—the world's second largest economy. In 1993 Japan authored TICAD—the Tokyo International Conference on African Development. TICAD is more than a conference. It is a major global framework for Africa intended to promote development in a comprehensive manner in partnership with likeminded players. Japan thus funneled most of her developmental assistance under the aegis of UNCTAD, UNIDO, the Asia-Africa Investment &Technology Promotion Centre, the UN Office for Project Services, United Nations Volunteers and the WARDA. Japan also incorporated NEPAD and the Africa Union to help her get her priorities right in Africa. This is particularly evident when one examines the contextual relevance of each TICAD round. TICAD

I held in 1993 centered on the political and economic reforms, private sector development, regional co-operation as also sharing the Asian experiences in development and international cooperation. TICAD II held in 1998 called for poverty reduction through accelerated economic growth and sustainable development as also for an effective integration into the global economy. TICAD III held in 2003 talked in terms of enhancing Africa's attempts at consolidation of peace, governance, agriculture development, infrastructure, HRD (education, health and gender issues) HIV/AIDS and other infectious diseases; water, ICT and the involvement of the private sector given the vastness of the development agenda. .TICAD III also emphasized the need for deepening the SSC. On Japan's part, it's aid to Africa between 1993 and 2003 was to the tune of $12 bn., had accepted more than 10,000 trainees from Africa and had sent over 7,000 Japanese experts to Africa to provide technical training and lend project support. Clearly, the basic premise of TICAD is that there can be no be pockets of prosperity in a vast sea of poverty[25].

These examples from China, Japan, Malaysia, Cuba, Brazil, and Mexico provide many perspectives. The efforts of these countries are seen in a number of countries and in a number of activities. Besides, they attempted to improve the human skills within those countries through training and educational programs with their own country experts sent to African countries specifically for the purpose. These programs are specific to the activities and local conditions. On the other hand, the Indian contribution to development of African skills was largely in terms of providing scholarships and fellowships to Africans in Indian educational institutions but this hardly ensured that the skills acquired were actually deployed for African development.

Very few major Indian companies have taken initiatives to move into Africa with direct investment plans in recent years. Also, there are very few instances of Indian experts being sent to African countries for purposes of training or undertaking specialized teaching. Nor are there very many cases of sharing research outcomes in agriculture and health care. There are not too many examples either of India partnering with other emerging economies or international organizations in providing assistance in a manner that would have an enduring and a positive impact on Africa's development.

It is time that India takes a proactive stance in building economic relations with Africa for the sake of economic convergence. This is the right time for taking such a stance since NEPAD is in place. For this purpose, India has to zero in on the special areas where India's strength is known to be not insignificant. Such a move would help raise the level, though not overnight, of the cup of economic diplomacy. For instance, India could involve itself more intensely with Africa's human resource development with special focus on affordable health care and value-based education. Such an involvement would enhance income opportunities for the ordinary Africans and would be in line with one of the explicit aims of NEPAD, which is to ensure technical and financial support from the rest of the world for Africa so as to eradicate poverty and reverse the marginalisation of the continent. In regard to imparting of value-based education, it should be centered on information, communication and technology, the area in which India's strength lies. India can assist Africa in adapting technology to suit the local needs. Although the levels of investment required for entry are low and knowledge required for entry is in the public domain, adaptations to local situations require a certain skill that Indian information technology experts possess[26]. What most African economies require is not a cutting edge technology, but help to create, diffuse and use new ideas that could be applied to the traditional/'brick-and-mortar' sectors. For instance, this would be helpful for upgrading or innovating processes and products in the areas of textiles and machinery, help set up small and medium enterprises, and most importantly in the area of food security. The possibility of the green revolution in Africa could be based on similar successful revolutions that occurred elsewhere. What is important is to create, disseminate and use knowledge with the express intent of bridging the gap between the farmers, the general public in various government bodies and international institutions. In the case of agriculture, India could consider accessing the information that is made available by the Consultative Group for International Agricultural Research (CIGAR) that exclusively focuses on agriculture. The question is not whether India can, but whether India will take the initiative to liaise with CIGAR. This will be in addition to India's own experience in the agricultural arena that can help give insights about bridging the gap between the local potential of agriculture and the requirements of the African economies. That all this is within India's ability is not a matter of doubt—what India needs is the will.

Indian scientists and bio-technologists can, taking advantage of the massive research efforts in their areas of specialization help Africa achieve better harvests. For better harvests African farmers would need, nutrients for the soil—both mineral and organic fertilizers, small-scale irrigation and technologies for collecting rain water, sturdier higher yielding seeds; and a team of master farmers, trained in up-to-date agricultural techniques who would be posted in African villages for a substantial period of time. These farmers would serve as extension workers providing comprehensive advise and in keeping with the local variations. By providing such assistance, India can help triple food production in Africa by 2015. This would mean that finally African farmers can step up the crop yields from the present average of 1500 pounds of cereals per acre to 2,300 pounds as in India and may even touch the 4,900 pounds as in China. Indian extension workers can also help Africa reclaim land for increased agricultural use through appropriate fertilization and through more environmentally sensitive techniques such as nitrogen based agro-forestry and also the cultivation of pest tolerant plant crops which would reduce the need for insecticide and pesticides. Such an aggressive and pro-farmer assistance by India would help Africa usher in the next green revolution[27]. Once soil and water requirements are taken care of biotechnology can step in and fortify African food crops so that the nutritional content of the continent's staple foods are enhanced.

A rise in crop yields would *ipso facto* ensure food security. This would enable Africa's women who constitute approximately 80 per cent of farm labor and who work mostly without tool or modern technologies to work off thê farm; would enable more girls to stay in school and facilitate children to have more and better food to eat. Women's empowerment would lead to lower population growth, to greater advances in children's health and education. Yet another offshoot of these improvements could be additional demands for locally grown foods helping Africa to strengthen its agriculture profile. What would the total costs be to achieve all these results? A back of the envelope exercise indicates it would be approximately $50 per person in the first year and then decline[28]. While India cannot afford it all on her, she can enter into a triangular, or quadrangular partnership with the developed economies—the US., Japan, Canada, Australia along with the FAO.

The information about the manner in which women movements in India have managed to combat the stresses and strains of every day life and the various entrepreneurial skills that have empowered women in different areas—fuel use, micro-credit and environment—would also be of help in resolving some of the ecology related issues and governance initiatives at the local level in Africa.

The use of digital telecommunications for development is well recognized[29] but its use in Africa has been very low. The tele-density remains below one line per 100 people, and service costs are high. Cross border linkages within the continent and across the continent are negligible. Besides, the availability of trained ICT professionals remains small as also the absence of software that is locally applicable based on an awareness of Africa's special needs add to the impediments that Africa has to contend with. This is where the Indian President's offer is very apt and timely. But, the offer needs to made operational which means that India's public and private sector IT professionals co-ordinate with the UN Task Force, the G-8 Dot Force and other bilateral donors help Africa by connecting schools and youth centers in Africa and setting up a network of training and research institutions to building high levels of manpower. India could also help Africa focus on the areas of higher education that would include engineering, medicine, legal studies, marketing management, finance, audit and accounts to name a few. This can also be by way of a triangular partnership -between India, UNESCO and/ or UNDP and an African country. An African component is a must so that the efforts and commitments would be of a sustainable nature.

In the area of healthcare too, India could lend its helping hand to address the widespread prevalence of communicable diseases such as HIV/AIDS, tuberculosis and malaria. Africa compares very poorly in the health profile when compared with the rest of the world. In 2001, the infant mortality rate for SSA was 105 per 1000 live births, the corresponding figures for China being 31, India, 67, East Asia, 34. Life expectancy at birth in 2001 was 46 years for SSA, 70 years for China, 63 years for India and 69 years for East Asia. Less than 20 doctors are available per 100,000 inhabitants in Africa. This situation is worsened by the absolute poverty levels that are reflected in very low nutritional position. The average daily intake of calories in Africa is poor restricting the population's capacity to address their livelihood strategies.

India could enter into a public-private partnership and with the help of WHO, and local NGOs in Africa, take a lead in making Africa conscious of health literacy, health infrastructure and health management, besides providing affordable drugs. The Indian pharmaceutical companies could set up manufacturing units in Africa wherever the investment environment is conducive. Also India's skills in alternative health care therapies could be provided. Maybe India could send para-medical and auxiliary health personnel too and popularize the concept of bare-foot doctors particularly in Africa's rural areas as this would make medi-care available not only where and when needed but also affordable[30]. Clearly, the emergence of a healthy Africa is the bed-rock on which all else—education, employment, poverty elimination and prosperity—can be factored in.

To conclude, while India could certainly help enhance the quality of the social sectors of Africa, help her also to enjoy higher levels of food security and consequently help reduce the absolute number of people below the poverty line, the initiative and impetus has to come from within Africa. The continent can and should do this by providing a conducive investment environment, property rights and sound legal systems. When there is convergence of interests in favor of socio-political and economic reforms and adjustment, India as an emerging economy could contribute to Africa's human security. In the words of Amartya Sen, this could enable Africa to enjoy the 'freedom to do what it wants to do and what it wants to be'. It is now or never for India's economic diplomacy to bear the fruits of perseverance.

Table 1: India-Select African Nations' Merchandise Trade in 2002-2003

(US $ millions)

No.	Country	Exports to India	Exports by India	Trade Balance of India
1.	Algeria	2.17	54.58	+52.41
2.	Angola	7.13	29.62	+22.49
3.	Botswana	0.01	3.34	+ 3.33
4.	Egypt	223.32	237.56	+14.24
5.	Ethiopia	10.45	49.32	+38.87
6.	Ghana	18.46	104.60	+86.14
7.	Cote d'Ivoire	84.97	39.38	-45.59
8.	Kenya	32.03	164.23	+132.20
9.	Libya	2.91	17.49	+14.58
10.	Madagascar	3.91	11.96	+ 8.05
11.	Mauritius	15.99	163.32	+147.33
12.	Morocco	197.83	75.62	-122.21
13.	Mozambique	27.49	46.27	+18.78
14.	Namibia	3.24	4.09	+ 0.85
15.	Nigeria	71.82	361.56	+289.74
16.	Senegal	168.88	50.89	-117.99
17.	Seychelles	0.05	4.96	+ 4.91
18.	South Africa	2050.92	377.60	-1673.32
19.	Sudan	24.23	103.98	+79.75
20.	Tanzania	90.31	94.44	+ 4.13
21.	Tunisia	92.66	47.97	+44.69
22.	Uganda	1.95	65.38	+63.43
23.	Zambia	14.27	30.72	+16.45
24.	Zimbabwe	13.89	15.76	+ 1.87
Total	3158.89	2154.64	-1004.25	

Source: Government of India, Focus Africa, New Delhi 2003

Endnotes

1 *The World Bank.* 2000. 'Can Africa Claim the 21st Century?' Washington DC: The World Bank

2 For reservation, see *UNECA*. 1989. 'Africa's Alternative to Structural Adjustment Programmes for Socio-Economic Recovery and Transformation'. Addis Ababa: UNECA; for imperatives of adjustment, see Vasudevan, Parvathi. 2001. *The Political Economy of Africa's Adjustment.* Mumbai: Himalaya Publishing House.

3 Cheru, Fantu. 2002. *African Renaissance: Road Maps to the Challenge of Globalisation.* London: Zed Books Ltd.

4 Arbadi, Ela and Xavier Sala-I-Martin. 2004. 'The Economic Tragedy of the Twentieth Century: Growth in Africa' in *The World Economic Forum. Africa Competitiveness Report,* Released at the African Economic Summit in Mozambique.

5 Amoebae, K.Y. 2000. Executive Secretary of the UNECA at OAU Meeting in Lome in July 2000. *Hindu Business Line,* August 2.

6 *Global Coalition for Africa,* 2004. *2003/2004, Annual Report.* Washington DC.

7 Waal, Alex De . 2002. 'What's New in the New Partnership for Africa's Development?', *International Affairs,* vol. 78, no. 3, July.

8 *The Economist.* 2004. 'How to Make Africa Smile: A Survey of Sub-Saharan Africa', January.

9 At the Workshop on 'Doing Business with Africa', Centre for African Studies, University of Mumbai, India, March 2003.

10 *Indian Express,* 2004. Sunday edition, September 05, p. 11.

11 *The Economist.* 2004. 'The Risks and Rewards of Doing Business in Africa', January 17.; also *The World Bank.* 2004. 'Doing Business in 2005—Removing Obstacles to Growth'. Oxford University Press.

12 For the full potential of Indian Ocean Rim, see Gwyn Campbell (ed). 2003. *The Indian Ocean Rim: Southern Africa and Regional Cooperation.* London: Routledge Curzon.

13 *Global Coalition for Africa, op. cit.*

14 *Ibid.*

15 See *Africa Recovery,* vol. 12, no. 2, 1998; also see Embassy of India, Washington DC, 'India's Foreign Relations', 1998-99.

16 *Africa Recovery,* 'Africa and Asia for Strategic Alliance' 2004. vol. 18, no.1.

17 For details of the Special Programme for Food Security (SPFS), see FAO website: <http://www.fao.org/SPFS>

18 *The Hindu,* 2004. 'Satellite Network to link African Union' 17 September.

19 *United Nations.* 2004. 'South-South Cooperation in Support of the New Partnership for Africa's Development—Experiences

of Africa-Latin America and the Caribbean'. New York: Office of the Special Adviser on Africa.

20 Both India and China agreed to forego the use of the facility in favor of low income countries in 1985. See James Boughton. 2001. *Silent Revolution—The International Monetary Fund, 1979-1989,* Washington DC: International Monetary Fund, pp.646-47.

21 Vasudevan, Parvathi, *op. cit.,* pp.159-162. Also see, *International Monetary Fund.* 1999. 'Debt Relief for Low-income Countries, The Enhanced HIPC Initiative'. Washington DC: International Monetary Fund.

22 Tripathi, Salil . 2003. 'Who has Written off African Country Debts and Now Lends to IMF?' *New Statesman,* July 21.

23 *NEPAD.* 2002. 'Background to South Africa Department of Foreign Affairs' website:<www.dfa.gov.za/docs/nepad 2 htm>.

24 *The World Bank.* 2003. 'The World Development Report, 2004.' Washington DC: The World Bank, Box 1, p.2.

25 'Patterns of Africa-Asia Trade and Investment, Potential for Ownership and Partnership' website: <http://www.ticad.net/ > accessed on November, 2004.

26 Chandrashekar, C P. 2003. 'The Diffusion of Information Technology—the Indian Experience', *Social Scientist,* vol. 31, no. 7 & 8, July-August.

27 Sanchez, Pedro. 2004. 'The Next Green Revolution'. *New York Times,* October 6.

28 *Ibid.,* Also see Scott, Andrew & Margaret Foster. 2002. 'Gender, Technology and Livelihoods', in Desai, V and R B Potter eds., *The Companion to Development Studies.* London: Arnold Publishers.

29 The World Bank. 1999. *The World Development Report, 1998/99, Knowledge for Development,* Delhi: Oxford University Press.

30 This suggestion made by the author was well received by the South African President and the South African Minister for Health in their meeting with the Indian Captains of Trade and Industry, sponsored by the Confederation of Indian Industry, New Delhi at Mumbai, on October, 18, 2003.

Indo-African Economic Cooperation

B.P Dhaka

Introduction

Most of the developing world is characterised by slow economic growth, growing unemployment, high debt-servicing burden, balance of payments problem, diminishing net inflow of funds from developed countries, falling share in world trade and adverse terms of trade, widening energy gap and severe infrastructural bottlenecks.

In the last two decades, though the developing world as a whole has witnessed a higher average annual rate of economic growth than the developed world, it has been a highly skewed growth and limited to a few countries. The average annual rate of world economic growth was 3.3 percent in the period 1980-1990 and 2.7 percent in the period 1990-2002. The comparable average annual rates of economic growth in the two periods were 3.3 percent and 2.5 percent for developed countries, 3.2 percent and 3.4 percent for developing countries, and 1.6 percent and 2.6 percent for Sub-Saharan African countries. Consequently, the disparities between the developed world and the top few rapidly growing economies of the developing world and the rest of the developing world have continued to widen. This widening of gap with the developed world is especially true for most countries of Africa.

The significant dependence on foreign capital and assistance to fuel economic growth in several developing countries, especially the least developed countries, and the diminishing net inflow of funds from developed countries to most of the developing countries have intensified the need for greater South-South co-operation. Driven by this approach, developing countries are increasingly looking towards each other to provide themselves with an engine of growth through enhanced economic and technical co-operation amongst themselves.

The changes in industrial capacities and capabilities of some developing countries like India and China have led to the emergence of a new dynamic force in the promotion of South-South trade and economic co-operation. These countries can now offer intermediate capital goods, machinery and technology in most fields that are more suited to the requirements of labour-surplus and capital-deficient developing countries than the high-cost capital-intensive technologies offered by the developed world.

The developing world, taken as a whole, possesses almost all the necessary inputs required for economic growth and development. It possesses enormous natural resources, including minerals and oil, and large reservoirs of skilled, semi-skilled and unskilled manpower available at comparatively lesser cost. It has a strong agricultural base and is rich in a wide variety of agro-produce. It has the capability to manufacture a diversified range of goods, both industrial and consumer, and possesses the technical know-how to produce virtually everything. Therefore, there exists a huge potential for South-South co-operation and it must be realised that the common problems of trade and development, aid and technology cannot be possibly overcome without a concerted and renewed effort towards promoting increased economic and technical co-operation among developing countries themselves.

From the East-West Cold War rivalry, there is now an economic confrontation between the North and the South at the global level. Individually, developing countries have not been able to effectively take action on the world economic arena, but collectively they can make their voices heard.

Though the World Trade Organisation (WTO) has been emphasising the creation of multilaterism in trade, regional trading and economic blocs have been gaining importance the world over. In the changing international scenario of globalisation and liberalisation, coupled with the emergence of several trade blocs, promotion of intra-regional trade, investment and co-operation amongst developing countries for mutual benefit has become essential and necessary to exploit the vast economic potential of their region to the fullest.

In the last two decades, especially in the 1990s, many governments of Africa undertook wide-ranging market-oriented economic reforms. These included giving due prominence to the private sector and recognising its dynamic role in economic growth and development, economic deregulation and liberalisation, financial and monetary stabilisation, ambitious privatisation programmes, liberalisation of foreign exchange regulations and currency depreciation, relaxing controls on foreign direct investment (FDI) and free repatriation of investment proceeds and profits, etc. Though structural rigidities have hampered the process and results have been at best modest, these steps have slowly but surely led to a changing perception about Africa as a lucrative investment destination.

It is being increasingly realised that Africa is the continent of the future, offering the maximum amount of opportunities. The advantages offered by Africa are fertile soil, low cost of land, low population levels, abundant availability of natural resources, well-educated populace in the cities and high aspiration levels.

The share of Sub-Saharan Africa in world merchandise exports declined from 1.98 percent in 1990 to 1.41 percent in 2002. Similarly, the share of Sub-Saharan Africa in world merchandise imports declined from 1.63 percent in 1990 to 1.29 percent in 2002. There has been an increase in the importance of industrial goods and services as opposed to traditional commodities in the export basket of Africa. Though FDI inflows into Sub-Saharan Africa have been growing, the growth has been less than that witnessed in some other developing regions of the world, in spite of the widespread liberalisation of restrictions on inflow of FDI. The share of Sub-Saharan Africa in total global FDI inflows has risen from 0.48 percent in 1990 to 1.24 percent in 2002. The leading sectors attracting FDI in Africa are telecommunications, food and beverages, tourism, textile and clothing and mining and quarrying. The African countries perceived to be the most attractive to foreign investors are South Africa, Nigeria, Botswana, Ivory Coast and Tunisia.

Indo-African Economic Cooperation : Some Obstacles and Suggestions

There is a broad agenda of shared concerns which India and the countries of Africa can jointly address through mutual co-operation either at the bilateral or multilateral level. Developing countries have to look towards themselves to find effective solutions to their common problems. Transplanting economic models from the developed world in developing economies will not effectively address their unique problems. For example, the experience of India in ushering a green revolution through cost-effective and innovative techniques is more suited to the requirements of African countries, rather than a capital-intensive model of the developed world.

Despite the huge potential that exists for trade between Africa and India, Africa accounted for only 6.01 percent of India's exports (US $ 3,825 million out of US $ 63,623 million) and 4.15 percent of India's imports (US $ 3,206 million out of US $ 77,237 million) in 2003-04. Whereas in the year 2007-08 Africa acounted for 7.09 percent of India's export and 7 percent of India's import. However the export and import basket has remained very limited and narrow over time, restricted to only a few items.

While major items of Indian exports to Africa include drugs and pharmaceuticals, cotton textiles and garments, engineering goods, machinery and instruments, chemicals and allied products, manufactures of metals, transport equipment, food and agro products, etc., major items of Indian imports from Africa include gold, precious and semi-precious stones, petroleum, coal, raw cotton, non-ferrous metals, inorganic chemicals, metaliferrous ores and metal scrap, crude fertilisers, etc. In spite of the growing confidence of the Indian industry to invest abroad, less than 10% of Indian joint ventures abroad are in Africa.

India and countries of Africa share common historical experiences of colonisation and are now being called upon to jointly confront the challenges of the post-colonial and post-cold war era. While removal of under-development and illiteracy and upliftment of living standards of their people are the foremost goals, the emerging new world economic order also requires immediate attention and concerted action.

Africa, for Indian business, is still a largely uncharted territory. The existing level of business ties between India and Africa does not reflect the full potential. The consolidation of Indo-African economic co-operation, bilateral and multilateral, can usher in a new era of South-South co-operation in the new millennium.

Economies of India and many African countries are complementary to each other and stand to gain tremendously from increased trade and economic co-operation. To promote the development of economic, commercial and technical relations between India and Africa, efforts should be channelised towards identifying and building upon the complementarities between the economies of India and that of the African countries.

Commercial information about several African countries is not readily available and this information gap needs to be bridged. Lack of knowledge of specific projects, business opportunities and commercial information is an obstacle in greater Indian business interest in Africa. Similarly, there is lack of awareness in most African countries about India's diversified industrial base and capabilities. It must also be mentioned that in most African countries strong economic linkages with the erstwhile colonial powers (European) continue making it difficult for other countries to make significant inroads.

Wrong perceptions exist in Africa about the poor quality of Indian products and in India about payments problems from Africa. Indian products are a lot cheaper than and almost as good quality-wise as European and American products. Similarly, the payments problem though in existence vis-à-vis most African countries is not as endemic as perceived by Indian businessmen. Dealing with only genuine parties on both sides is essential to avoid problems and the help of chambers of commerce and diplomatic missions can be taken to verify the credentials.

Since it is always advisable to have local partners, a mechanism for identifying reliable partners should be put in place in African countries. There is also a need for the buyers and the sellers to directly negotiate with each other to avoid middlemen and price mark-ups. Many Indian products are routed through Europe to Africa after being re-branded and with a high mark-up.

EXIM Bank of India is also providing several lines of credit to many African countries and this information should be publicised amongst Indian industry. Lack of long term supplier's credit on competitive terms and the foreign exchange problems faced by many African countries have also hindered bilateral trade.

Another problem area faced by Indian companies is that there is no direct freight or shipping services to most of the African countries and this result in high transportation costs making exports/imports uncompetitive. Similarly, the distribution networks need to be strengthened in African countries and warehousing facilities created.

Africa possesses immense mineral wealth and bulk of world reserves of several minerals. India and African countries can undertake joint exploration and mining of minerals, petroleum and petroleum products and precious stones, gems and jewellery and this can be utilised for value-addition.

Infrastructural constraints have impeded the economic growth of many African countries and there exists substantial scope for setting up of joint ventures in the fields of construction of roads and bridges, railways, power, telecommunications, construction materials based industry and low-cost housing complexes. India can especially target development projects under multilateral funding. The Indian construction industry would be willing to develop infrastructure projects in Africa on build-operate-transfer (BOT) basis provided information on specific opportunities, loans offered by international financial and aid institutions, identification of reliable local partners with some equity participation, government regulations on land allotment, housing finance companies which would lend to prospective customers, etc. was made available.

India has developed a huge reservoir of technical manpower through its wide network of technical training institutes and can help Africa immensely by sharing its expertise in setting up the infrastructure geared towards the needs of developing economies. India has emerged as a leader in the field of information technology and in this area it can help Africa by sharing its expertise and training personnel.

There exists immense potential for export of engineering goods from India to several African countries like agricultural implements and machinery, machinery for construction of roads and bridges, irrigation equipment and water pumps, diesel sets, mining machinery, etc.

Other potential items of exports from India to Africa include textiles and garments, drugs and pharmaceuticals, electronic goods, household appliances, bicycles and parts, automobiles and auto components, gems and jewellery, foodstuffs, leather goods, rice, tobacco, machine tools, processed fruits and vegetables and their products, computer hardware and software, scientific instruments, etc. India could carve out a niche for itself by exporting the wide variety of intermediate technology that India possesses and is required immensely by many African countries. Similarly, India can offer consultancy services on a much wider scale to African countries in many areas.

Potential items of imports from Africa to India include wood pulp and wood products, crude minerals and mineral products, plastic materials and artificial resins, chemicals, asbestos, newsprint, rough diamonds and other precious stones, various types of agro-produce, etc.

The African continent as a whole, with subsistence farming and generally no land ceilings provides substantial opportunities for Indian companies in the fields of agriculture and agro-processing.

Tourism is the one area in which both India and Africa have tremendous potential and there is a lot that can be learnt from each other in this field. African countries can develop tourism packages and market them in India as Indians are increasingly becoming international tourists.

India has developed sufficient expertise in setting up of small and medium units and this is one area in which India can play a major role in Africa's development. Some potential areas for setting up of joint ventures and technology transfers between India and Africa and where India has acquired requisite expertise are textiles, cement, paper pulp, sugar, jute, pharmaceuticals, drugs and chemicals / petrochemicals, tea processing, rubber, light engineering industries, electronics, machinery, oil processing, food and agro processing, tourism and tourism related industries, etc.

India is poised to give the African countries appropriate technology, right-sized industrial enterprises, marketing and management know-how as also capital investments since Indian industry is increasingly looking outwards for growth and investments and is now more confident of expanding its horizons and stepping into the international arena;

Most countries of Africa offer manufacturers and exporters preferential access / quota-free access to various countries and economic blocs and also enjoy GSP (Generalised System of

Preferences) status. There are also many economic groupings in Africa that allow goods manufactured in one member country free or preferential access to the markets of all other member countries. Indian manufacturers can base their operations in these countries and enjoy preferential access to the markets of Africa, the European Union and the United States. There is also a need to bring about a uniform trade policy and harmonisation of tariffs amongst these groupings.

Some of the economic groupings in Africa are as follows:

- The Economic and Monetary Community of Central Africa (CEMAC)–Cameroon, Central African Republic, Chad, Republic of Congo, Equatorial Guinea, Gabon and Sao Tome and Principe;
- The Economic Community of the Countries of Great Lakes (CEPGL)–Burundi, Democratic Republic of Congo and Rwanda;
- The Common Market for Eastern and Southern Africa (COMESA) – Angola, Burundi, Comoros, Democratic Republic of Congo, Djibouti, Egypt, Eritrea, Ethiopia, Kenya, Madagascar, Malawi, Mauritius, Namibia, Rwanda, Seychelles, Sudan, Swaziland, Uganda, Zambia and Zimbabwe;
- The East African Community (EAC)–Kenya, Tanzania and Uganda;
- The Cross Border Initiative–Burundi, Comoros, Kenya, Madagascar, Malawi, Mauritius, Namibia, Rwanda, Seychelles, Swaziland, Tanzania, Uganda, Zambia and Zimbabwe;
- The Economic Community of Central African States (ECCAS)–Angola, Burundi, Cameroon, Central African Republic, Chad, Democratic Republic of Congo, Republic of Congo, Equatorial Guinea, Gabon, Rwanda and Sao Tome & Principe;
- The Economic Community of West African States (ECOWAS)–Benin, Burkina Faso, Cape Verde, Cote d'Ivore (Ivory Coast), Gambia, Ghana, Guinea, Guinea Bissau, Liberia, Mali, Mauritania, Niger, Nigeria, Senegal, Sierra Leone and Togo;

- The Indian Ocean Commission-Comoros, Madagascar, Mauritius, Reunion and Seychelles;
- The Mano River Union (MRU)-Guinea, Liberia and Sierra Leone;
- The Southern African Development Community (SADC)-Angola, Botswana, Democratic Republic of Congo, Lesotho, Malawi, Mauritius, Mozambique, Namibia, Seychelles, South Africa, Swaziland, Tanzania, Zambia and Zimbabwe;
- The South African Customs Union (SACU)-Botswana, Lesotho, Namibia, South Africa and Swaziland;
- The Central African Customs and Economic Union (UDEAC)-Cameroon, Central African Republic, Chad, Republic of Congo, Equatorial Guinea and Gabon;
- The West African Economic and Monetary Union (UEMOA)-Benin, Burkina Faso, Cote d'Ivore (Ivory Coast), Guinea Bissau, Mali, Niger, Senegal and Togo; and
- The Arab Maghreb Union (UMA)-Algeria, Libya, Mauritania, Morocco and Tunisia.

Investment authorities / agencies in the respective African countries should be more proactive and have all the basic parameters in place to attract foreign investment. Feasibility studies/ project reports / market surveys should be prepared by the authorities and then offered to international investors in specially organised 'investmarts'. If the authorities do not have in-house staff to undertake these studies, then international consultants could be entrusted this task. International aid agencies would be willing to give grants for these activities.

Some steps, which should be undertaken to enhance co-operation between India and African countries, are as follows:

- Identify products which can be sourced from each other based on comparative cost advantage on account of resource endowments and technological capabilities;
- Encourage counter trade by tying imports with exports and vice-versa. Historically, payments have obstructed greater co-operation;

- Identify and draw more on each others' experience, technology, expertise and resources;
- Undertake joint marketing and promotional strategies for common products in which distinct comparative advantage exists so that the effort to undercut each other are stalled;
- Engage in joint harnessing of natural resources by pooling resources and technical know-how;
- Identify specific projects and areas for setting up of joint ventures and collaborations, especially at the small and medium enterprise (SME) level, between Indian and African partners in Africa which can be used for third country exports or under buy-back arrangements;
- Create joint research and development institutions to develop appropriate technologies and the mechanisms for technology transfers and absorption;
- Encourage people-to-people and institution-to-institution contact by exchanging business and other delegations and by organisation of trade fairs and exhibitions;
- Ensure manpower training and human resources development by setting up collaborative institutions imparting training on skill and technology upgradation and entrepreneurial development; and
- Create institutions with pooled resources for developing data banks and institutionalise mechanisms for exchange of commercial intelligence and information on business opportunities and available technologies to bridge the existing information gap.

To conclude, it can be said that the synergy that can emerge by enhancing mutual economic co-operation is immense.

India's Major Export Sources

Countries	US $Million					%Change					% Share				
	2002-03	2003-04	2005-06	2006-07	2007-08	2002-03	2003-04	2005-06	2006-07	2007-08	2002-03	2003-04	2005-06	2006-07	2007-08
World	52856	63623	103091	126,262.67	162,983.90	20.19	20.37	23.41	22.48	29.08	100	100	100	100	100
Africa	3139.9	3825.3	5441.7	8404.97	11554.3	8.38	21.83	42.25	54.45	37.46	5.94	6.01	6.11	6.6567	7.0943
Egypt	299	366.4	672.43	760.41	1396.91	-35.6	22.54	51.20	13.08	83.71	0.57	0.58	0.5324	0.6022	0.8571
Kenya	204.1	226.2	576.54	1,314.47	1597.51	30.39	10.84	35.14	127.99	20.16	0.39	0.36	0.5593	1.0411	0.9691
Mauritius	164.8	203.2	199.43	735.95	1086.57	0.81	23.34	-22.76	269.02	47.64	0.31	0.32	0.1935	0.5829	0.667
Nigeria	450.2	566.2	874.03	902.78	1083.87	-20.32	25.75	33.58	3.29	20.06	0.85	0.89	0.8478	0.715	0.665
South Africa	485.2	535.8	1526.9	2244.74	2658.67	37.01	10.43	55.16	47.02	18.44	0.92	0.84	1.4811	1.7778	1.6312
Americas	12990	13434	21368	24225.64	27645.58	28.01	3.42	64.11	51.1	42.89	24.58	21.12	20.7275	18.4667	16.964
Asia(Excluding Middle East)	15428	19593	6552.2	7953.28	11031.75	34.41	26.99	37.27	64.75	43.53	29.19	30.79	6.3557	6.299	6.7686
Europe	13578	16444	23228.84	26,784.99	34,507.04	15.43	21.11	27.29	15.31	28.83	25.69	25.89	22.5325	21.2137	21.172

India's Major Import Sources

Countries	US $Million					% Change				% Share				
	2002-03	2003-04	2005-06	2006-07	2007-08	2003-04	2005-06	2006-07	2007-08	2002-03	2003-04	2005-06	2006-07	2007-08
World	61571.6	77236.7	149,165.73	185604.1	251562.26	100	33.76	25.43	100	100	100	100	100	100
Africa	3446.5	3205.6	5441.7	8404.97	11546.3	25.34	22.11	51.10	32.21	5.6	4.15	5.27	6.65	7.08
Egypt	227.2	98.5	220.44	1741.65	1983.74	-6.99	44.42	13.08	13.9	0.37	0.13	0.14	0.93	0.78
Kenya	33.6	42	48.52	56.44	86.55	-56.65	3.84	16.32	53.37	0.05	0.05	0.03	0.03	0.034
Mauritius	16.2	7.6	7.33	14.5	10.08	25	2.02	97.79	-30.49	0.03	0.01	0.05	0.01	0.004
Nigeria	78.3	75.8	72.46	7021.44	7619.82	-53.25	49.72	95.58	8.52	0.13	0.1	0.5	3.78	3.02
South Africa	2098.9	1897	2,471.80	2469.73	3614.86	-3.18	12.47	-0.08	46.37	3.41	2.46	1.65	1.33	1.43
Americas	6074.6	6666	21368.11	24225.64	27648.58	-9.62	64.08	51.1	42.89	9.87	8.63	20.72	19.18	16.96
Asia(Excluding Middle east)	13564.3	19549.4	6552	7953.28	110311.75	9.73	37.27	64.75	43.53	22.03	25.31	6.35	6.29	6.76
Europe		16183.3	19785.3	26784.99	34507.04	44.12	27.29	15.31	28.83	26.28	25.62	22.53	21.21	21.17

Source: Directorate General of Commercial Intelligence and Statistics (DGCI&S) and Ministry of Commerce and Industry

Indo-African Economic Relations: From Focus LAC to Focus Africa

R. L. Chawla

Introduction

Over the years, the world community has been deeply concerned about the persistent critical economic situation in Africa in general, and Sub-Saharan Africa, in particular. As a sample of World Bank studies on Africa, its report titled 'Sub-Saharan Africa: From Crisis to Sustainable Growth' (1989) provides an analysis of the broader development perspective of these countries, emerging out of the protracted crisis of several years. Its another Policy Research Report 'Adjustment in Africa: Reforms, Results and the Road Ahead' (1994) examines the extent of policy reforms and their impact on growth and poverty in 29 countries of Africa that were undergoing adjustment in the second half of 1980s. 'Can Africa Claim the 21st Century,' is one more revealing study of World Bank at the turn of the new millennium, again highlighting the deplorable plight and tasks ahead in this continent. This is just to provide an illustration list rather than to attempt an exhaustive compendium on World Bank's studies on Africa.

Notwithstanding the many revealing aspects of these studies and a variety of policy measures, the continent has, still, been bedeviled by a heavy debt burden, low level of savings and investment, depressed commodity prices, declining levels of ODA, and insufficient FDI inflows. The continent suffers from acute poverty with detrimental impact on the political stability of most countries and regions. Close to 350 million people live below poverty line i.e., below $1 a day or less in the whole continent. An indication of the marginalisation of the continent in the world economy is the very low absolute value of its exports and its consistently declining share in world trade. Deriving mostly its GDP from mineral and agricultural sectors, the share of manufacturing in GDP of Africa was only 11.5 percent compared with 21 percent for Latin America; 24 percent for South and East

Asia in mid 1990s. Further its share in manufacturing value added of all developing countries was only 5.5 percent in 1995, a decline from the low level of 6.9 percent in the mid-1980s.

A natural question, thus, arises about assessing the validity of exogenous and endogenous factors impacting upon its development process in its post- colonial period. Inarguably, Africa has been rich in both mineral and agricultural resources. For example, Southern Africa alone has nearly 90 percent of known world resources of platinum group metals; 85 percent of chromium; 75 percent of manganese and 50 percent of gold. Nigeria, Libya and Algeria are the major oil producers and exporters, Nigeria alone being the sixth largest producer in the world. In agricultural commodities such as coffee (major producers being Ethiopia, Uganda, Ivory Coast), tea (Kenya, Tanzania and Uganda), cashew (Mozambique and Tanzania) and sugar (Mauritius and Madagascar) occupy important position. Tanzania alone accounts for 90 percent of world's clove production. Cocoa, groundnuts, palm products, cotton, teak and timber are some of the other major farm and forest products in the continent. It remains debatable whether the poor exploitation of its natural resources or over exploitation depressing the commodity prices in general has caused the crisis situation. Except oil, generally the secular trend in primary commodity prices has been southward with adverse consequences for the development processes of these African countries. Insufficient export earnings and rising import bill coupled with debt service obligations forced these countries dependence on ODA; and subsequently aid-fatigued Western countries imposed trade-driven development strategy on these countries. Much of the theorising on the development processes of these countries has been related to their domestic policy failures rather than on exogenous shocks such as deterioration in terms of trade, low price and income elasticity of demand and ever growing threat of substitutes in the importing countries.

Given the widespread onslaught of globalization, this paper seeks to highlight some of the crucial aspects of South-South cooperation in 1990s and positioning Sub-Saharan Africa (SSA) in that conceptual framework. Second, it will be our endeavour to assess broadly India's economic relations with SSA during this period. Importantly, the third section will examine some of the innovative institutional mechanisms to push our exports to hitherto not fully tap or exploited markets, particularly of African continent, drawing some of the lessons from Latin American experience of 1990s. Last but not least, the paper provides summary and main findings of this study.

South-South Cooperation: A Simplified Conceptual Frame

Much of the literature on South-South cooperation had wittingly or unwittingly the imprint of cold war era till late 1980s. Collapse of the Soviet system and emergence of a unipolar world by early 1990s redefined the theory and practice of international relations, particularly the economic relations among developed and developing countries. Globalisation and interdependence emerged the creed for all, replacing the time-worn concepts of dependence, self–reliance, inward-looking development strategies. Importantly, regionalism was also accepted a part of multilateralism/globalism framework. South-South cooperation could presumably thrive provided it embraced 'open regionalism' integrate with the world economy by trade-investment linkages, and reassess its niche in the world economy. Given the resilience of a few major developing countries in Asia, Latin America and Africa, their process of integration with the world economy, although was arduous and somewhat costly, but not an impossibility. However, the crux of the problem was with majority of the small and even medium sized countries to adjust to the new realities with prohibitively high adjustment costs, loss of jobs, shrinking GDP and falling per capita income. The case of Sub-Saharan countries is a pointer in this direction.

In an earlier study, the present author formulated a simple model of economic relations among developing countries ('Indo-Brazil Economic Relations' *Foreign Affairs Reports,* May-June 2003). The assumptions of this model were that economic relations between India and a co-developing country such as South Africa or Brazil do not preclude similar relations between such country(ies) and a developed country or between a developing economy at the lowest ladder and a developed economy. Second, the developing world was divided into groups and sub groups showing marked degree of openness, varying market potential and even magnitude of its economic crisis. The third assumption was that the technology matrix of the newly emerging markets essentially conforms to the factor endowment of less developed among the developing countries.

Based on these assumptions, the model depicted the relationship in the form of a triangle, showing the developed country at the top, newly emerging markets at the mid point of the left and right arms of the triangle and less developed countries at the base of the triangle. The simple process of horizontal division of labour between similar developing countries such as India and South Africa or Nigeria is assumed to facilitate the expansion of trade and resource flows. From these mid points, the vertical configuration promotes the expansion of economic relations not only between unequal economic partners but it also opens the floodgates of mutual cooperation between newly emerging markets in specific sectors. These sectors may be even related to institutional frame, infrastructure, macroeconomic policies and resource allocation, besides trade and investment linkages.

Another analytical framework to discuss international relations relates to the concept of interdependence. Put simply, this implies mutual dependence. Viewed in the context of Indo-African economic relations, one aspect of economic interdependence needs to be examined in terms of sensitivity to price and income trends on both sides and their repercussions on the overall economy of each partner country. However another dimension of interdependence, i.e., vulnerability merits serious attention in the context of economic constraints imposed by exogenous forces on both or one of these countries and their response jointly or singly. For instance, their collective response to the international trading regime can be studied under the dimension of vulnerability, while the sensitivity aspect can be analysed in their trade-investment-aid linkages.

India's Trade and Investment Linkages with Sub-Saharan Africa (SSA)

Comprising of 51 countries in the region, Sub-Saharan Africa presently accounts for less than 4 percent of the world trade. India's trade with this region is largely concentrated in 10 countries—South Africa, Nigeria, Mauritius, Ivory Coast, Tanzania, Kenya, Benin, Ghana, Ethiopia and Senegal. In 2000-01, these countries accounted for more than 80 percent of India's total trade in the region.

A glance on overall trade between India and the region shows that total volume of trade has grown rapidly in the second half of

1990s (except 1997-98). From $1513.9 million in 1995-96, the total trade rose to $3637.25 million in 1996-97, declined slightly to $3603.9 million in 1997-98, again rose to $4664.4 million in 1998-99. With total trade exceeding $7 billion in 1999-2000, India and SSA trade reached its highest level in the same year. This was mainly due to doubling of India's imports from South Africa and Nigeria in 1999-2000 over the preceding year. In 2000-01, the total trade between the two sides nosedived to $3389.6, reflecting a negative growth of 52%. This sharp decline resulted on account of sharp fall in imports from South Africa and Nigeria. Nonetheless, South Africa occupied the top position with bilateral trade of $1312.12 million in 2000-01 and $2432.82 million in 2003-04, followed by Nigeria, Mauritius, Ivory Coast, Tanzania and Kenya. Further in 2000-01, India's exports alone to the above-mentioned group of 10 countries totalling $1367.45 million constituted 76 percent of its total exports to SSA. India's imports of $1003.5 million from South Africa, Ivory Coast, Guinea Bissau, Nigeria, Tanzania, Benin, Ghana, Mozambique and Ethiopia accounted for 92.8 percent of its total imports ($1466.3 million) from the region.

India's exports to SSA constituted nearly 4 percent of its global exports in 2000-01.These exports rose from $1345.06 million in 1996-97 to $1808.93 million in 2000-01, registering a growth of 34.4 percent over the entire period. Based on the disaggregated data of 8 countries (South Africa, Nigeria, Kenya, Mauritius, Ghana, Tanzania, Sudan and Ivory Coast), India's exports to this group of countries increased from $1326.9 million in 2000-01 to $1530.52 million in 2002-03 and $2010.83 million in 2003-04. Similarly, in case of India's imports from SSA, the same grew from $1468.22 million in 2000-01 to $2510.85 million in 2002-03 and $2513.36 million in 2003-04 (South Africa, Senegal, Tanzania, Ivory Coast, Nigeria, Benin, Guinea-Bissau, Kenya and Ghana).

A glance at India's trade balance position during the past 10 years shows that it has been incurring trade deficit with SSA countries (except 2000-01). Importantly, the deficit has been consistently growing in the new millennium.

Composition-wise, major items of India's exports to this region include cotton yarn, fabrics, ready-made garments, drugs, pharmaceuticals, fine chemicals, manufacture of metals, machinery and instruments, transport equipment, primary and semi-finished iron and steel, plastic and linoleum products, inorganic/organic and agro-chemicals. At a country- specific level such as Nigeria, a dozen items-drugs, machinery, manufactures of metals, transport equipment, non-basmati rice, cotton yarn, paper and wood products, plastic and linoleum products accounted for 80 percent of its total imports from India. Such items in case of South Africa reached 60 percent of its total imports from India.

India's major items of imports from SSA have been gold, pearls, precious/semi-precious stones, coal, coke, wood and wood products, cotton-raw and waste, cashew nuts, iron and steel, fertilisers, ores, metal scrap, organic chemicals and electronic goods. In 2002-03, for instance, import of gold, inorganic chemicals, coal and coke accounted for 91.6 per cent of India's total imports from South Africa.

Concern Areas

India has a number of concern areas which need to be tackled while expanding trade relations with this part of the world economy.

First, India faces competition from Thailand, USA and Vietnam in its export of non-basmati rice to SSA countries. Similarly India's wheat exports to Kenya find difficulty in the face of competition from USA, Argentina and Australia. Similarly for spices exports to South Africa, there is potential threat of competition from some Latin American countries. One way to tackle these commodities/ products problem is to enter Preferential Trading Arrangement (PTA) and /or FTA with a single country such as South Africa or a group of countries (SADC).

Second, another variant of problem relates to these countries' competition for India's exports in developed countries of US, EU and Japan. For example, Ghana and South Africa pose competition to Indian exports of manganese ore, chromium ores, ferro-chromium and copper ores in Japanese market. In EU markets, again South Africa is a major competitor for Indian exports in flat rolled iron, non-alloy steel, ferrochromium (alongwith Zambia). Further, South Africa poses competition to Indian exporters in granite and tyres in US market.

South Africa is also a major competitor for India in fruits, vegetables and floriculture products in Western markets. Similarly, for cashew, India faces competition from Mozambique, Ivory Coast and Guinea-Bissau in the Western countries. While commodity agreements can serve the purpose of both side in a mutually beneficial way, this possibility of agreement to supply such commodities market-wise can ensure fair price and income generation from such exports.

Another concern area has been the South African imposition of anti-dumping duties on some of India's exports to that country. Anti-dumping investigations have been instituted by South Africa on exports of paper insulated lead covered electric cables, clear float and sheet glass, carbon black, acrylic blankets, printed and dyed bed linen, aluminium reinforced cable, aluminium steel, reinforced conductor cable from India. Joint Commission Meeting (Dec. 1998) discussed and it was agreed that anti-dumping and safeguard action taken by both sides should be as per principles of natural justice and in conformity with WTO agreement and barriers to trade should be avoided.

Notwithstanding these small irritants, both official and non-official sources have been evincing keen interest to further expand their economic relations. For instance, the Trade Agreements with these countries have served as one of the important tools to expand our trade relations. Presently India has such agreements with 22 countries in the region—three such agreements with Tanzania, Mauritius and Botswana were signed in 2000-01. These agreements cover various issues like the grant of MFN status, specification of payment currencies. safeguard clauses and setting up of Joint Trade Committee to monitor the implementation of the trade agreement. Under investment linkages, there have been investment flows from select African countries, the Indian investment-ODA synergy in Africa has further moved to strengthen our relations with those countries.

Investment Flows and Potential

In the post reform period (1991-2004), FDI approvals of select African countries in India show that Mauritius has been the second largest investor in India. However apprehensions have been expressed that these investment originate from elsewhere but thanks to the liberal tax regime of the Mauritius government, these are routed through that country. South Africa is the second largest investor from SSA, followed by Nigeria, Kenya, Tanzania, Zambia and Sudan. Sectors where Mauritius investors have deployed their investments in India include real estate, BPO, chemicals, polyester film, IT and trading.

Given comfortable foreign exchange position, the Indian government, of late, has been encouraging its investors to invest abroad, more particularly in oil exploration and development, gas projects including pipelines, privatisation projects, M&A activities and green field projects. SSA provides lot of opportunities in privatisation in select African countries (see Annexure). Further India's frenetic efforts to provide energy security to its teeming millions has initiated oil diplomacy with more than a dozen countries. In Africa, on-going projects in hydrocarbon sector are in Sudan, Libya, Egypt, Angola and Ivory Coast. Recently, China has proved a tough competitor for India in Angola where its trade-investment-aid package clinched the oil deal against India. However, a number of Indian public and private enterprises are providing consultancy services to these countries. While RITES is engaged in Angola's Railway Rehabilitation Projects, Telecommunications Consultant India Ltd. is busy in the telecom projects in Angola.

India's Aid Programme for Africa

Over the years, India's aid programme for Africa has undergone a sea-change. In quantitative terms, while Africa received Rs. 4 crore of aid from India in 1999-2000, the same had a quantum jump to Rs. 80 crore in 2003-04. In relative terms, aid to Africa rose from 1 percent of India's total aid to 8 percent by 2003-04. India has also been providing technical assistance in various projects to several African countries. Most recently, areas for such assistance have varied from micro dames and small irrigation projects (Ethiopia), social defence and regional cooperation (Mauritius) to mutual legal assistance in criminal matters (South Africa).

Further, India has agreed to write off the inter-governmental credit outstanding against Zambia, Mozambique; provided fresh credit lines of $10 million and $20 million to these countries respectively in 2003-04. India's EXIM Bank extended a credit line of $10 million to ABSA Bank of South Africa and $5 million to

Angola in the same year. In addition to credit lines, Zambia and Mozambique also received grants, foodgrains and medicines partly on humanitarian grounds and partly towards the implementation of specific projects. Further, the Indian supplies of anti-HIV/AIDS drugs to several African countries have helped them and encourage the exports of pharmaceuticals from the Indian pharmaceuticals firms.

India's focus-LAC strategy, which has paid some dividend in the past few years, stands to test in another area i.e., African continent. Before we chalk out component of such strategic plan for Africa, it would be worth while to have a look at Focus: LAC and some lessons for the African continent.

1990s: An Era of Innovative Export Strategies

India launched its process of economic reforms in 1991. Along with industrial, agricultural, fiscal, monetary, tax policy reforms, trade policy reform was the cornerstone of medium term structural reforms. As a part of the liberal trade policy, the Ministry of Commerce and Industry also formulated several innovative institutional mechanisms to help Indian exports to achieve 1 percent of the global exports. The essential component of the export strategies was to identify growth markets and products for a quantum jump in Indian exports.

Rationale for such strategies was based on the fact that since resources for export promotion activities are limited, concentration on selected products and market segments would provide better return in terms of additional export expansion. Presumably this was considered better than the earlier strategies when the resources were thinly distributed over a large spectrum of products and markets. In this respect, three export strategies merit our serious attention. First, the Extreme Focus Product Strategy with 35 items was introduced with the objective of giving a focused attention to products that have high production capacity in India and potential for export competitiveness. The growth rate of the target products was envisaged around 30 percent per annum in the medium term, and stabilise it around the same level in the subsequent period. A dispassionate analysis of this strategy shows that exports of extreme focus items rose to a level of $16.4 billion in 2000-01 from $8 billion in 1993-94. Their growth rate at 11.1 percent per annum between 1993 and 1996 was higher than that of total exports (8.4

percent). However, share of these focus items in India's total exports hardly increased i.e., 36 percent in 1993-94 to 37 percent in 2000-01. Not only this, 40 percent of these items could show 30 percent or more growth rate in 1993-96, while a majority of items showed lower growth or even negative growth rates. Thus, actual performances of these focus products against their target growth rates was quite lower.

Another innovative export expansion plan was '15x15 Matrix Strategy'. It was launched in 1995. The objective of this strategy was to identify market diversification and commodity diversification. An assessment of that strategy shows that there has been a market diversification towards additional markets, meaning thereby that the share of total top 15 product groups exported to top 15 market destinations in the total exports of top 15 product groups declined to 66 percent in 2000-01 from 71 percent in 1996-97. As regards product diversification, the top three items of India's exports, viz., gem and jewellery, RMG cotton, fabrics and made-ups, continued to remain the same during 2000-01. While USA remained the top market, UK and Japan were replaced by Hong Kong and UAE as the second and third largest markets for Indian exports.

Focus LAC Strategy

Regional focus was first initiated by the government of India in 1997 for the Latin American region, considering the untapped export potential of that region. The thrust of the programme aims at 'sensitizing the organisations such as Export Promotion Councils, Chambers of Commerce and Industry, EXIM Bank, ECGC involved in trade promotion efforts.' The Focus: LAC programme aimed at India's nine major trading partners with special focus and added emphasis, and also three major product groups for expanding its exports to the region. The major product groups include textiles including readymade garments, carpets and handicrafts; engineering products and computer software and, chemical products including drugs / pharmaceutical products.

With 43 countries in Latin American and Caribbean region, it accounts for 5 percent of the total world trade. Despite our best efforts, Latin America has a share of 2.2 percent in India's exports. During 1990s however, Indian exports showed a rising trend, from $166 million in 1992-93 to $982 million in 2000-01.This implied a compound annual growth rate of 25 percent and surpassed the overall export growth rate for this period. While concluding the three export strategies of 1990s, the Medium Term Export Strategy 2002-2007 states:

> ...composition, competitiveness and complexion of world merchandise trade are changing very fast and a dynamic approach with a built in institutional mechanism for constant review is essential for any medium term export strategy in order to achieve a higher share of global exports on a sustainable basis. The focus of the past strategies was on the existing export products of India: what is additionally necessary is to review the import baskets of our current and potential markets and also to examine our export competitiveness, both revealed and real based on our potentialities. The need for a dynamic approach and continuous review are reinforced by the experience of 2001-02 when the slowdown of the world economy witnessed from the beginning of 2001 and aggravated by the September 11, 2001 event led to drastic fall in the growth rate of India's exports during April-November 2001-02.The overall medium term strategy, however, would have to be necessarily evolved on the basis of the perspective of a longer time frame....

Promoting Bilateral and Regional Cooperation with Africa: Thrust Markets and Focus Countries

According to the Ministry of Commerce and Industry (MOCI) Annual Report 2000-01, Kenya, Ethiopia, Mauritius, Zimbabwe, Zambia, Tanzania, South Africa, Ghana, Senegal, Namibia, Ivory Coast and Nigeria have been identified as 'thrust markets' for Indian exporting community. However, the Annual Report 2001-02 of the same Ministry underpins South Africa, Nigeria, Mauritius, Tanzania, Kenya and Ghana (6) as 'Focus Countries' in SSA region. A number of commodities having export potential in these markets have also been identified for special export attention and promotion.

As part of the renewed 'Focus Africa' policy, the Indian authorities have undertaken fresh initiatives to strengthen and deepen existing links with SSA. The Ministry of External Affairs Annual Report 2003-04 aptly summarises these initiatives. For example, high level official delegations exchanges, Joint Commission Meetings, MOUs with regional organisations in SSA have been some of the major steps to forge close relationship with this region. High frequency of visits on both sides has enabled India to put forth its point on issues such as its candidature to the permanent membership of the expanded UN Security Council, cross border terrorism and J&K. As part of India's traditional technical and humanitarian assistance to Africa, large quantity of food aid has been offered to drought affected countries, and also anti-HIV/AIDS drugs to these countries have been donated to lessen the scourge of AIDS. The Ministry of External Affairs has been organising conference of commercial representatives/Heads of Indian Missions in various capitals of SSA countries.

Apart from official efforts, another institutional mechanism has been Apex chambers sponsored Joint Business Councils with their counterpart chambers in SSA. Further, ITPO, FICCI, CII, FIEO have been regularly organizing participation in various trade fairs of SSA countries and also hold exclusive India exhibitions like 'Made in India show' and Indiatech in selected countries for trade promotion.

India-South Africa: A Case Study in Strategic Partnership

South Africa has emerged India's largest trade partner in SSA at the turn of new millennium. According to the Indian Ministry of Commerce and Industry, South Africa is the only market in the category of The Focus 25 Markets, identified on the basis of five major criteria, in African continent. After Mauritius, it has the largest number and volume of FDI approvals in India. It has had and continues to wield enormous economic power in SADC countries which are highly dependent on trade, transport and manufactured goods on South Africa. Both countries are the members of IOR-ARC. Ever since the dismantling of apartheid in South Africa, Indo-South African relations have been growing stronger—politically and economically. In 1998, for instance, both countries established a unique forum known as 'India-South Africa Commercial Alliance (ISACA)'. This forum has the participation of public and private sectors on both sides. In its first meeting, the ISACA identified a number of sectors for cooperation—IT, chemicals, drugs, mining, housing, infrastructure, transport, food processing and engineering equipment. FICCI provides secretarial support for ISACA and follow-up action on the decisions is initiated by the same organization.

Further, following the collapse of Cancun Summit, an era of inter-continental alliances emerged among the developing countries. India, Brazil, China and South Africa were able to protect their mutual interests in agriculture only because they formulated and veered around a common position. Since then, these countries have been engaged in strengthening cooperation in trade, investment and global economic diplomacy.

In early 2003, India, Brazil and South Africa formed a 'trilateral forum' to facilitate economic cooperation. The visit of Brazilian Foreign Minister Celso Amorim, followed by President Lula's visit on Republic Day in 2004 show that both countries are serious about forging closer bilateral relations and to play a leading role in the global economic decision-making process.

The trilateral cooperation arrangement among India, Brazil and South Africa covers not only trade, economic issues, science and technology but also addresses issues such as social justice, freedom from hunger and removal of distortion in the current world order and efforts to set right the adverse terms of trade against the developing world.

The group of three nations was called the 'India, Brazil and South Africa Dialogue Forum' (IBSA) and a trilateral joint commission were set up to coordinate their position on issues of mutual interest. The initiative taken by the three countries (along with China) in organizing the G-20 at Cancun was no less than marvelous. These three, along with China and Argentina, are engaged in discussions on the post-Cancun situation.

The trilateral forum also addresses issues of global concern—socio-economic development, technology and global governance. The forum initiative include combining efforts in order to enhance the effectiveness of the UN General Assembly and its Economic and Social Council; strengthen the sinews of multilateralism; commit the three nations to the pursuit of policies, programmes and initiatives in different international for a to make the diverse processes of globalisation inclusive, integrative, humane and equitable under the Brasilia Declaration of June 2003; remove vulnerability of developing countries from fluctuations in global prices of commodities; and stress on importance of a predictable, rule-based and transparent international trading system.

Future Plan of Action

If selectivity is the criterion, priority areas in plan of action should include:

i) A study on proposed Free Trade Area with South Africa;

ii) A study report for the engineering, chemical and textile sectors for SADC and COMESA and pilot study on South Africa under the field study;

iii) Analysis of SADC's global imports and its imports from India for the year 2003;

iv) Collection and compilation of trade data for SADC/ COMESA countries; institute Focus Africa Export Awards on the pattern of Focus LAC export awards;

v) National Centre for Trade Information should engage its efforts on CD-ROM/ Electronic Book based on an analytical study of global trade of focused SSA countries.

Summary and Main Findings

India's economic relations with African continent have spawned over centuries but their importance in the last decade or so have assumed added urgency. During 1990s, India's exports to Africa displayed 17percent growth rate per annum and India's share in its total exports increased from 2.6 percent to 5.3 percent over the same decade. Nigeria and South Africa contributed significantly to this rapid increase. Despite this, India's share of the continents' total imports remains quite low and there is lot more potential to expand trade with the region. Importantly, India's competitors' strategies is paying rich dividends as their trade-investment-aid package suits more to the requirements and needs of majority of African countries. India faces tough competition from China and Brazil in those countries as well as South Africa within the continent. Certain problem areas have been identified but these are not insurmountable in forging closer relations between the two sides.

The thrust of this study has been to assess and examine the institutional mechanisms by which these relations could be put on sound footing. India's 'Focus LAC' strategy has many lessons for the 'Focus Africa' strategy and plan of action provides important guidelines to achieve the target objectives.

Energy Security Issues: Co-operation between India and African Countries

Aparajita Biswas

The late 20th century has seen profound changes in international relations and the concept of security. A major feature of the change was the conclusion of the cold war, the end of major conflicts in several regions, and the dismantlement of apartheid in South Africa, which paved the way for the current period of democratization, regional co-operation and relative peace. However, despite these changes in international and regional relations, security threats have not been totally eliminated. Non-traditional security threats like environmental degradation, energy security, small arms proliferation, drug trafficking, and piracy, to name a few, have assumed prominence.

This article is intended to address the salient security concerns associated with the issue of energy, which has assumed colossal importance in recent years. An attempt has been made to examine and assess this issue by means of a regional geographical analysis, with the Indian Ocean Region being the focal point. This article will also explore the possibilities of co-operation between India and the African countries in the energy sector.

The energy security issue assumes paramount importance in the oceanic regions of the world which, besides being richly endowed with natural resources, are also a source of a large portion of the world's production of hard minerals like manganese and hydrocarbon. The heightened world focus on the mineral resources of oceanic regions is a result of two distinct trends. First, a steadily increasing demand for mineral resources and petroleum based energy sources, and second, the rapid progress of technology to a point where huge new and unclaimed resources are now at the disposal of modern industry.[1]

In the widest sense, energy security concerns have three facets. The first involves limiting the vulnerability to oil supply disruptions. This is essentially a short-term issue. The second pertains to the long-term concerns of the smooth functioning of the international energy system so as to ensure supplies to meet the rising demand at reasonable prices. Finally, a new dimension that has emerged recently is that production and use of energy must evolve so as to minimize the damage to the environment, and to promote sustainable development.[2]

Since the 1990s, the world has witnessed a significant shift in energy consumption patterns. The share of developing countries in global energy consumption has increased noticeably, compared to 1970s. In 1971, Asia—including the OECD Pacific region—accounted for only 14 percent of the total world demand for energy. Today its share has doubled to 28 percent. In fact, Asia has emerged as the largest oil- consuming region in the world, one percentage point ahead of North America. In 2000, South Asia accounted for approximately 3.9 percent of the world's commercial energy consumption — up from 2.8 percent in 1991. By 2010, the energy use in developing Asia (including China and India, but excluding Japan, Australia and New Zealand) is projected to surpass consumption of all of North America.[3]

According to the World Economic Outlook, Asia's share of oil in the global total will continue to increase and touch 35 percent by 2020. The increase will be evident mainly in China, India and South-East Asian countries. In volumetric terms, this means that demand for energy in Asia, which was 19 million barrels per day (mbd) in 1997, will grow to over 28mbd in 2010 and more than 37 mbd in 2020.[4] However, given the limited and declining production of oil in the region, the incremental demand for oil needs to be met with imports. For example, South-East Asia is already a net importer of oil, in spite of the presence of oil exporting countries in the region, like Malaysia, Indonesia and Vietnam. With regard to South Asia, the region consumed around 2.5 mbd of oil, but produced only 0.80 mbd in 2000, making it a net importer of around 1.7 mbd. India and Pakistan account for most of the South Asian oil production i.e. around 1, 40, 000 mbd.[5] The Middle-East is expected to remain the major source of supply of oil to both South and South-East Asian countries.

Besides oil, there has also been a significant increase in the demand for natural gas in Asia. The Asian gas market splits into that of LNG (Liquefied Natural Gas) and pipeline gas. The International Energy Agency (IEA) projects that the demand for LNG in Asia will be more than doubled in 2020. What is more, of all forms of energy, demand for natural gas in Asia is expected to grow the fastest. Natural gas provides 9 per cent of Asia's total energy needs; when China and India are excluded, Asia consumes 15 per cent of natural gas as a share of its primary energy resources. In South Asia, natural gas reserves are around 58.6 trillion cubic feet or about 1 per cent of the world's total. The region consumed and produced around 1.99 trillion cubic feet of natural gas in 2000. Around 48 per cent of this production is consumed by Pakistan, another 40 per cent by India, and 17 per cent by Bangladesh.[6]

Southeast Asia has also seen a considerable growth in the use of pipeline gas, primarily among the member countries of the ASEAN, with Indonesia, Malaysia, Brunei, Vietnam and Thailand having significant gas reserves. It is important to note that transporting gas is more expensive than transporting oil. Added to it, LNG projects are extremely long term and consist of lumpy, indivisible technology with high upfront capital costs. This is true for both liquefied gas transported in special carriers as well as gas transported through pipelines, since gas has a low thermal density compared to oil.[7]

In recent years, energy pipeline projects have attracted global capital in the Indian Ocean Region. Multinational oil companies like Unocal, Spie Capag, Total Fina Elf of France etc., have made significant investments in the region. However, while the emerging markets have created opportunities for co-operation in the hydrocarbon sector, they have also created conditions for conflict. There is intense competition among oil firms and nation-states to gain control over precious energy resources like oil and gas, especially in today's era of globalization. Due to this competition, political processes - both local and global - are continuously shaping the dynamics and complex inter-relationship between the oil firms and nation-states on one hand, and NGOs like environmental and human rights organizations, on the other. At the core of the politics related to exploration of oil resources are vital issues such as exploration of new oil fields in virgin areas, smooth management of crude oil flows towards refineries through well guarded pipelines, enhanced profit revenues through oil extraction, and their likely impact on environment, development and governance.[8]

There is also important security issues involved in the gas trade. It may be recalled that during the peak of the Cold War, USA had strong reservations about Europe opting to import gas from the former Soviet Union. Europe could secure their agreements only after agreeing to limit imports from the Soviet Union to 70 per cent of total requirements and to develop the giant Troll field in Norway as a fallback measure. Moreover, the security of supplies becomes all the more critical as gas is used mostly in power generation.

Meanwhile, the 'great game' is once again being played in the Caspian Sea Basin and Central Asia, over access to energy and transit facilities.[9] In 1996, the construction of a US$ 3.5 billion pipeline from Turkmenistan's Daulatabad gas fields to Pakistan, was proposed by Cent Gas, a consortium led by Unocal, to construct a 1,635 km long gas pipeline which would pass through Herat, Kandahar, Quetta and Multan, before entering India, to join the HBJ link to Gail (Gas Authority of India Limited). It was originally meant to pass through Mazar-e-Sharief, Kabul and Lahore; however the route was changed to make the extension to India easier.

It is interesting to note here that both USA and Russia are concerned about this pipeline, but for different reasons. Russia's interest is that without the pipeline, Turkmenistan remains hostage to the Russian gas transportation system as a means to access Western markets. This is the leverage Russia is loathed to give up. It has also figured that both in the short-term and mid-term, it would be cheaper to obtain gas from Central Asia rather than make huge investments to develop its own gas fields in Siberia. USA, however, wanted to see the pipeline open for Turkmenistan's gas to reach the coast of Karachi, from where it would be shipped to Western countries as LNG.[10]

Again, there is a decade old Iran-Pakistan-India gas pipeline project. The inability to resolve the Kashmir issues between Pakistan and India has undermined the viability of this project. It may be recalled that a Memorandum of Understanding was signed between Iran and India in 1993 for a 1700 km pipeline. It would pass through 700 km of Pakistan territory. In 2000, the Government of Pakistan affirmed that it would permit a gas pipeline linking Iran's massive gas reserves to India, across its territory. Pakistan would earn transit fees up to US $I billion per year for Iranian gas supply to India, and would also be able to purchase gas from the pipeline itself. Pakistan has also offered security guarantees for the pipeline. India is interested in this project because of its incremental demand of gas, which is expected to reach 400 million standard cubic meters per day. However, it has been reported that US pressure is building up on Islamabad to not to enter into an energy deal with Iran. Thus, an Iran-Pakistan–India gas line project flies in the face of American efforts to isolate Iran regionally.[11]

Again, regional politics also plays a major role in defining the game. As the international gas pipelines have to transit through many countries, it depends on multi-country agreements for smooth and continuous supply of gas. For example, the transit of Russian gas through Ukraine and India-Bangladesh gas pipelines projects had run into difficulties because of regional politics. It may be mentioned here that UNOCAL had long sought to pipe natural gas linking Bangladesh to India, as part of its South Asia Integrated Gas (SAIG) Project. It has also plans to set up a US $ 2 billion integrated pipeline connecting Myanmar to the gas fields of Bangladesh, en route to Haldia port in India. However, all these proposals are continuously held back because of the cold relations between India and Bangladesh. The disagreements between these two countries have slammed the progress for discussions on a natural gas pipeline from Myanmar to India, which will have to pass through Bangladesh territory forcing India to look into the expensive option of creating a deep sea pipeline through the Bay of Bengal that would bypass Bangladesh.

Nevertheless, the trends of co-operation and collaboration between states and global companies have opened up many opportunities in the hydrocarbon sector. The Dolphin project - the world's biggest gas project - was conceived as a joint venture between the United Arab Emirates Offset Groups (UOG), Total Fina of France and Enron. It was an ambitious scheme to transport natural gas from Qatar's huge offshore North Field via an undersea pipeline to UAE, an example of the emerging dynamics of market integration among the neighboring countries. Through the Dolphin project, Qatar - the leading producer of natural gas in the Persian gas region - was able to provide gas to neighboring states like Abu Dhabi and Dubai, which were looking for gas to diversify their economies. At present, the Dolphin project is also supplying gas to countries like Oman, Pakistan and India.[12]

Nevertheless the other LNG project that has attracted a lot of attention is a deal between China and Iran. Through this deal, the Zhuhai Zhenrong Corporation of China has signed an agreement to buy 2.5 millions tons of super- cooled, compressed natural gas per year from Iran, starting in 2008. It is expected to rise to five million tonnes a year from 2013. The Zehrong Corporation, which is also one of China's four major state oil traders, had signed an MOU with the Iranian Ministry of Petroleum, to undertake development and production of three Iranian oil fields as part of the LNG purchasing plan. It may be pointed out here that there is huge pressure on Chinese state oil firms to secure foreign oil and gas assets, to fuel its fast growing economy, especially as domestic oil and gas outputs are declining.[13]

Interestingly, one notices a significant change in the debate on energy security in the 1990s. The energy security calculus today is very different from that of 1970s and 1980s, when oil shocks and fear of global supply shortages determined government resource policies. The notion that conflict may arise over energy competition fueled by a perception of supply shortage, is not the main concern of states today. Rather, the changing patterns in trade, a greater reliance on the Middle-East for oil and therefore, a greater reliance on open access to sea-lanes and shifting strategic relationships are sources of conflict that may have an impact on the region's energy security. In fact, some scholars argue that the common challenge of greater external reliance on energy supplies among Asian states would create incentive to co-operate, not compete.

Traditional and Newly Emerging Regional Security Concerns

Given the dominance of oil as the energy source of Choice and Asia's dependence on the Middle-East for oil, issues like open access to sea lanes and domestic instability, raise concern regarding the security of the sea lanes in the Indian Ocean region. For instance, domestic stability in Indonesia and Malaysia - on both the sides of the Strait of Malacca - is critical to the security of these lanes.

Indian Ocean Sea Lanes

In the Indian Ocean region, access to energy sources is a critical security issue, given the structure of its energy needs and expected future consumption patterns. The region attained enormous importance mainly because of its geographical location and strategic waterways. The first route is around the Cape of Good Hope, onward to Western Europe and the United States, and the other route is eastwards, through the Malacca Strait to Japan. The area is important because the two vital chokepoints lay here, namely the Strait of Hormuz and the Strait of Malacca. These two routes account for more than 60 per cent of oil transits.[14]

The Strait of Hormuz is the world's most critical oil chokepoint, it being the only shipping channel in and out of the Persian Gulf. Over 14 million barrels per day of oil flow through this Strait to Asia, Western Europe and United States. At its narrowest, the Strait consists of 2-mile wide channels for inbound and outbound tanker traffic within the Oman side of the Strait, as well as a 2-mile wide buffer zone. It represents the most important strategic passage in the world, solely because of its access to the oil fields of the Middle East. It forms a strategic links between the oil fields of the Persian Gulf, the Gulf of Oman and the Indian Ocean.

However, the most serious concerns in the region are focused on Iran and Iraq, the greatest long-term threats to U.S. interests in the region. This is because of the strategic location of the Strait which provides a vital connection between the Persian Gulf and the rest of the world. In early 1995, Iran deployed some 6,000 troops in Musa and other islands at the entrance to the Strait. This trade route is so important that any closure of the Strait would trap about 7 to 10 percent of the global very large crude carriers (VLCC) fleet in the Persian Gulf.

The other important strategic passage of the world is the Strait of Malacca, because it supports the bulk of the maritime trade between Europe and Pacific Asia, accounting for 50,000 ships per year (600 per day). The primary sea route from the Middle-East and Africa to Japan, Korea, China, Chinese Taipei and other Pacific Rim countries, passes through the Strait of Malacca. The Strait, which is only 3 km wide at its narrowest point, connects to the

South China Sea, another extremely important shipping lane and a conflict region. Any closure of the Straits of Malacca would mean freight disruption and an increase in sailing time and freight rates.[15]

The other vital issue regarding security of oil supply in the region relates to conflicting claims on the South China Sea. The region has proven oil reserves of around 1.2 km (7.7 billion barrels) with an estimate of 4.5 km (28 billion barrels) in total. Its natural gas reserves estimated at around 7,500 km (266 trillion cubic feet). Contrary to international law, which recognizes only a 12-nautical-mile territorial sea plus a 200–mile exclusive economic zone, this area extends up to 1,000 miles from the Chinese mainland and includes Japan and the Philippines, within Beijing's security range. This area also includes the Spratly, Paracel, and Senkaku island chains, which China claims as its own and which is contested in varying degrees by six other states, namely Taiwan, Philippines, Indonesia, Vietnam, Brunei and Malaysia.[16]

The dispute over the Spratly Islands - 230 islands, islets and reefs comprising a mere 3.1 square miles of entirely uninhabitable land - are the most troublesome, as they lie directly in the path of shipping lanes that converge on the Indonesian Straits. These vital sea-lanes transport oil from the Middle East to Japan and the west coast of the United States. Approximately one quarter of the world's total shipping trade passes through this contested area every year.

Apart from being a leading sea route, the Spratly Islands are rich in fisheries and hydrocarbon resources. It may be recalled that China has aggressively backed its claims in the area, and on a number of occasions, used military force against neighboring countries like Vietnam, the Philippines and Taiwan. Although Indonesia does not make any claim over the islands, it is involved in a dispute with China over the claim of Natuna Gas field. Rich in oil and natural gas, Natuna is believed to be the single largest gas field in the world, with reserves of about 40-45 tcf of methane.[17]

However, apart from the territorial disputes and insecurities about sea lanes of communication, there are also potential concerns relating to energy security in Asia. First, Asia's new relationship with the Middle-East — largely based on Asia's growing energy requirements and the Middle-East's ability to supply them - raises significant considerations. Second, technological innovations and successful private and public sector initiatives have led to improved prospects of natural gas becoming a larger energy resource for Asia in the future.

There are apprehensions regarding the safe export supply of oil because of the history of political instability in the Middle-East. In addition, Asia's increasing dependence on the Middle-East heightens the strategic importance of sea-lanes from the Persian Gulf across the Arabian Sea and the Indian Ocean, through the Straits of Malacca and nearby waterways, and finally across the South-East China Seas to China, Japan and Korea. Moreover, the Iraq war, in particular, has revived concerns over the impact of a disturbance in the Middle-Eastern supplies or a US naval - blockade in this strategic area.

Finally, from a geopolitical perspective, strengthening Asia–Middle-Eastern ties over energy implies new strategic interests for Asia in the Middle-East, which may complicate Asia–USA relations. It has been reported that China is building up bases along sea lanes in the Middle-East to protect its oil shipments. According to the report, titled 'Energy Security in Asia', China is looking at the possibilities of pipelines traversing Pakistan and Bangladesh territory, as part of its 'String of pearls' strategy to bypass the narrow straits of Malacca which experiences 40 per cent of the world's piracy and through which 80% of China's oil import flow. China has also constructed a port in Gwador in the Pakistani province of Baluchistan. The location of Gwador is significant because of its proximity to the Strait of Hormuz. Consequently, the port would compete with a port facility at Chabbar in Iran, which is being jointly developed by Iran and India to access the landlocked states of Central Asia and Afghanistan. China's 'string of pearls' strategy also forms part of a wider Chinese policy to encircle India.[18]

Further, China is looking not only to build a blue water navy to control the sea-lanes, but also to develop under-sea mines and missile capabilities, to deter the potential disruption of its energy supplies from potential threats, including the US navy, especially in the case of a conflict with Taiwan. The report noted that the vast amount of oil shipments through the sea lanes, along with growing piracy and maritime terrorism, prompted China as well as India, to build up naval power at 'chokepoints' along the sea routes from the Persian Gulf to the South China Sea. Iran is also building its bases near the Strait of Hormuz.

There are also signs that China is warming to the idea of a Russian-China-India axis which, in co-operation with Iran, would turn the oil-rich Central Asian region into their domain. It may be recalled that this proposal which would put in place extensive military agreements and pipelines networks, was originally put forward by Russian Prime Minister Yevgeny Primakov. It appears to be gaining ground with the four nations. Recently both China and India have signed 25-year gas and oil deals with Iran, collectively valued at between US$ 150-200 billion. Again, both the countries are also deepening their defence co-operation with Iran.[19]

It is because of the trend of co-operation and conflict in the region that India is working out an elaborate energy procurement plan through its energy diplomacy. One of the challenges to oil diplomacy is to set up enduring engagements through consolidation of existing relationships with foreign countries and companies, as also reaching out to and setting up linkages in new areas. India is stepping up energy diplomacy with states in the South Asian region as well as states further a-field in Central Asia, Russia and the Middle-East as far away as Latin America and Africa. India's oil diplomacy took a giant step forward when India unveiled a multi billion-dollar deal with Iran and Russia that would be crucial to India's long term energy security. India also took the initiative to host the first ever conference on regional co-operation among Asian oil producing and consuming countries.

In its US$ 40 billion deal with the National Iranian oil Company (NIOC), India made a commitment to import natural gas from Iran over a 25-year period, and to develop two Iranian oilfields and a gasfield. As a part of the deal, India's ONGC Videsh Ltd. (OVL) gets a 20 percent share in the development of Iran's biggest onshore oilfield, Yadavaran. The Indian Company (IOL) will also get 100 percent rights in the 300,000 barrel per day and the Jufeir oilfield. The stakes in Yadavaran translates to 60,000 barrel per day of oil in India. Significantly, China also operates in this oilfield and has a 50 percent share.[20]

It is important to note here that these new developments would have serious ramifications in the Asia-USA relationship. Both China and India are locked in an increasingly aggressive wrangle over oil - the issue which has the potential to shape the economic, environmental and geopolitical future of these countries and the world. Recently, during her visit to India, US Secretary of State Condoleza Rice voiced USA's apprehension at the prospects of a US$4 billion gas pipeline bridging the economies of Iran and India. In fact, for India, the Iranian pipeline is only a part of the grander scheme of pan-Asian energy corridors - pipelines crisscrossing Myanmar, Bangladesh in the east and Turkmenistan and Central Asia in the north-west, in addition to the Iran pipeline.

India Africa Co-operation

It may be mentioned here that, although India has significant reserves of coal, it is relatively poor in oil and gas resources. Its oil reserves amount to 5.9 billion barrels, only 0.5 per cent of total global reserves. The majority of India's oil reserves are located in offshore Bombay and onshore in Assam. India imports 70 per cent of its oil, much of it from the Middle East because of the stagnated domestic crude production. What is more, according to the projection of the World Energy Outlook, India's dependence on oil imports will grow to 91.6 per cent by 2020. Thus, in order to enhance energy security, India has undertaken dramatic reforms in the hydrocarbon sector. These include the participation of the private sector, both Indian and foreign, in upstream and downstream activities. The setting up of a de-regulated and market driven oil and gas industry in India was first contemplated by the government in the early 1990's.[21]

Again, India is also exploring possibilities to seek oil from Latin America, South East Asia and Africa. Since 2003, it has been making major efforts to enhance its oil security through accelerated steps for increasing domestic production of oil and gas, and through investing in the oil fields. Recently, the Government of India empowered the state-owned ONGC Videsh Ltd. to invest upto US$75 million in overseas oil and natural gas exploration projects.[22]

It may be mentioned here that the Indian Government launched 'Focus Africa' programme in 2002-2003, to strengthen India-Africa cooperation in the area of trade, investment, technology transfer, information technology, health care, etc. countries. African countries hold 7per cent of the world's oil reserves and account for 11 per cent of world oil production. Of the 8 billion barrels of crude oil reserves discovered worldwide in 2001, 7 billion were in West and Central Africa. According to an IEA projection, the Sub-Saharan African oil production would increase from the current output of 3.8 million barrels per day to 6.8 million barrels per day in 2008. The participation of ONGC Videsh, Ltd (OVL) in South Africa's upstream sector has forged energy ties between the two countries. OVL has also bagged an oilfield in the North Ramadan area of Egypt, expected to have recoverable reserves of US $ 600 million barrel of crude oil. It had also signed a deal to explore oil to Ivory Coast.[23]

OVL also acquired 25 per cent stake in the Greater Nile oil project in Sudan. It decided to invest US$ 750 million in the oil field and acquired for the first time, a stake in a foreign oil field. According to the terms of the deal, OVL's share from the oil field comes to 3 million tones of oil and gas per annum. The first assignment of the crude oil from the oil field was received in May 2003. Moreover, OVL is reportedly in an advanced stage of talks with the Sudan government, to build a 750-km pipeline project from Khartoum to Port Sudan on the Red Sea for transforming petroleum product for the Khartoum refinery. Incidentally, China is investing about US$300 million to increase the capacity of Khartoum refinery.

However there is apprehension about India's aggressive quest for energy security in Sudan, when most of the global players have dumped the country because of the human rights violation in Darfur. It seems that Sudan's ruling party has been using its oil revenues to buy weapons to suppress the opposition in different parts in the country. India's dilemma is that on one hand it has to meet the rising domestic demand for oil and therefore, cannot keep away from its involvement in Sudan's oilfield exploration. On the other hand, it cannot overlook the risk involved in engaging an oil exploration in a country engaged in the civil war. Nevertheless India has taken the stand to go ahead with its energy procurement plan in Sudan.

It may therefore be concluded that the conflict over increasing energy needs is not inevitable. The need to access energy resources on the world stage can be as much a catalyst for co-operation as it can be for conflict. There is a need for continuous contact and dialogue between nations and global actors. It is imperative to continue the process of dialogue between consumers, governments, oil companies and human rights activists, to arrive at a common approach to the security question as well as regional sensitiveness associated with oil exploration. Here, regional organizations in the Indian Ocean region can play a major role in diffusing tensions between nations, and help in bringing about understanding and co-operation between them on the key energy security issue.

Endnotes

1 Leipziger, Danny, 1996. *Seabed, Mineral Resources and Economic Interests of Developing Countries,* Cambridge, Massachussets, Ballinger Publishing company, p. xvi.

2 Paul, Horsnell, 1997. *Oil in Asia; Markets, Trading, Refining and Deregulation,* London: OUP.

3 *Ibid.*

4 *The World Economic Outlook,* 2003. Energy Sector, Paris.

5 International Energy Agency, 2001. 'The IEA's Role in Asian Energy Security Co-operation', 2nd Seminar on Energy Security in Asia, Tokyo, 6 March.

6 International Energy Agency, 1996. *Asian Gas Study.*

7 *Ibid.*

8 See in this context, 'Yadana Pipeline Projects', *www.earthright.org/Burma.*

9 Afghanistan was at the centre the so-called 'Great Game' in the 19 century when imperial Russia and British India vied for influence. Today, its geographical position as a potential transit route for oil and natural gas pipelines, make Afghanistan an extremely piece of global strategy for energy magnets to obtain control over this precious resources.

10 Sanjay Dutta, 2004. 'Gas Pipelines are likely to remain as a Pipedream', *The Times of India,* Mumbai, January, 13.

11 M.K. Bhadrakumar. 2005. 'India Finds a $40 bn friend in Iran', *Asia Times,* January 11.

12 Gerald, D.B. 'The Dolphin Project will set a new standard for the Gulf gas sector', www.ameinfo.com. See also Girijesh

Pant, 2004. 'Globalisation and Co-operation Conflict in the Indian Ocean Region', in V.S.Sheth eds., *Indian Ocean Region: Conflict and Co-operation,* Mumbai: Allied Publishers.

13 China, 2004. 'Iran sign a $200 bn LNG deal', *The Gulf Today,* March 19.

14 Anthony, H, Cordesman, *1999. Geopolitics and Energy in the Middle-East,* Centre for Strategic Studies.

15 *Ibid.*

16 John R. Anderson, 1996. 'Multinational Naval Co-operation into the 21st Century', Halifax Maritime Symposium, Halifax, 22-23 May.

17 *Ibid.*

18 See in this context, Bill Gertz, 2005. 'China Builds up Strategic Sea Lanes', *The Washington Times,* 18 January.

19 *Ibid.*

20 M. K. Bhadrakumar, 'India finds a $40 bn friend in Iran', *op. cit.*

21 Avinash Chandra, 2001. *Overview of India's Hydrocarbon Policy,* Government of India, Ministry of Petroleum and Natural Gas.

22 ONGC, *Report, 2004,* See also Rajen Harshe, 2002. 'Recasting Indo- African Development Co-operation', *Economic and Political Weekly,* 5-11 October.

23 *Ibid.*

India's Changing Engagements with Francophone Africa

Vidhan Pathak

Introduction

This paper focuses on the relations between India and Francophone Africa in the large context of Third World solidarity and within a given framework of South-South co-operation to promote the relations between the two developing regions in the spirit of collective self-reliance. Besides, the focus is also on various suggestions and other inputs, for strengthening the foundations for a long and durable relationship between India and Francophone Africa.

In Africa, there were twenty five French speaking countries and the term 'Francophone Africa' is generally used to denote the countries in Africa which used to speak French even after the Independence. There are nine Francophone West African states namely Senegal, Mali, Guinea, Ivory Coast, Burkina Faso, Mauritania, Togo, Benin and Niger. These countries had diverse ideologies, economic and social structures and political institutions; they did not follow the same system for development and were not uniform in economic development plans. As the economies of Francophone West African countries are fast improving and GDP increasing in real terms in late 1990s, their economies hold immense opportunities of mutually beneficial economic co-operation with India.

The present paper concentrates on India's relations with Francophone West African states. As Francophone West Africa covers the major part of Francophone Africa, it is justifiable to take this study.

French Influence on Francophone Africa

In 1960, majority of French territories in Africa became independent. However, in the post-independence era also, France has been able to maintain in Francophone Africa, a considerable degree of influence, through a combination of cultural, linguistic and economic cooperation[1]. The independence of Francophone African countries did not provoke any radical changes in their relations with France. For France, her former African territories represent a significant sphere of influence knotted together by a complex of socio-economic and military ties. The strength of this linkage is underlined by two interrelated factors, namely close economic relations and military cooperation arrangements.[2] France depends, to a reasonable extent on Africa for its raw materials, while the continent constitutes one of its principal export markets. France developed a special relationship with these African states through a combination of incentives. There was the creation of the Franc zone, which till today allows African member states financial association with France. The CFA Franc guaranteed by France is the currency of international transactions, while foreign exchange earned by exports is kept by the French treasury[3]. Beyond this the economic linkage is consummated by the extent of trade relations. France alone accounts for about 60 percent of the external trade of these countries. This was complemented by a vast programme of economic and technical assistance. More than half of France foreign aid goes to African states making France the continents foremost patron, even ahead of IMF and World Bank. In the same way, French technical assistance has been unequalled[4]. Consequently, French firms have almost unlimited privileges in Francophone Africa. The companies themselves are guarantors of French interests with regard to strategic minerals in different Francophone countries. The companies in fact act as an arm of French foreign policy.[5]

Another display of this special relationship was represented by the French military presence in the continent. The military presence guarantees the perpetuation of friendly regimes and a continuation of that relationship. Within international organizations Francophone votes comforted French policies and increased their significance. The Francophone states gave their political support to France, especially in the UN, and almost on all major issues. France remains the centre of a powerful cultural area based on the French language. Thus, Francophone states have in the past been rather in a class apart in Africa because of the close ties most of them have with France, political, economic and cultural. There was also a loose but effective alliance between Paris and some African leaders[6].

However, today, things have changed dramatically. World have moved rapidly from the cold-war era to trade-wars and fierce economic competition. In the wake of these radical global changes, there is little doubt that Franco-African relationship is no longer what it used to be. France no longer has such a high profile in Africa, where indeed some leaders talk mournfully of France 'abandoning' them[7]. There is some sign for loosening the bond between France and Francophone Africa.

The cooperation between third world developing countries i.e. Francophone Africa, rest of Africa and India is now more expected as it became obvious that Francophone states have far more in common with other African states and India than with France or any other European power especially in their attempts at economic development of the region. Francophone Africa is different due to French culture and the CFA Franc but it is also very much tied with the third world developing countries and has much in common with them.

Political and Diplomatic Relations

Independent India's pursuit of the goal of freedom and self-government for all countries and nations in Africa as well as Asia brought the French dominated territories in Africa within the general ambit of India's Africa policy. India extended its fullest support to all African countries in their struggle for liberty, for race-wise equality and for economic opportunities.[8] India consistently and also constantly championed the cause of the political advance of the African colonies of France in the UN trusteeship council and the UN committee on non-self governing territories.[9] Thus, the increasing cooperation between India and Francophone Africa in all fields is due to India's historical affinities and innate sympathies with the aspirations of the people of Francophone Africa and equally innate desire to assist the development of their personality in all ways possible[10].

Ever since present Francophone African countries were granted independence, India has attempted to establish and strengthen political ties and economic relations with the region mainly through the opening up of diplomatic missions and exploring trading and other economic avenues of cooperation. Diplomatic relations was opened with most of the countries, though mostly through concurrent accreditation. Diplomatic mission were opened in Ivory Coast, Madagascar, Senegal and Zaire. It was also opened in Guinea in 1966 but closed down in 1992.[11] India has currently resident mission in four Francophone African states only, Ivory Coast, Senegal, Zaire and Madagascar, with concurrent accreditation in the remaining countries. There is also an honorary consul in Djibouti. On their part, financial constraints rather than any political considerations have inhibited the opening of mission by the Francophone African states. Only Senegal, Burkina Faso and Zaire have their resident missions in New Delhi. Thus, the diplomatic representation between India and Francophone Africa currently stands at the low level.[12]

High Level Visits and Agreements

Ties between India and Francophone countries were strengthened by a number of visits exchanged by dignitaries at all levels. At the high level, the President of Guinea (Conakry) Sekou Toure was the first Head of state of a Francophone country to visit India in September 1960. President of Senegal visited India in 1977 on a state visit.[13] From Indian side, the external affairs minister visited a number of Francophone African countries like Senegal, Guinea and others. There were also a number of trade-related delegations exchanged between India and individual Francophone African states. A 20-member delegation from the Ivory Coast in 1987 and a sixty-member delegation from the Ivory Coast and Senegal in 1988 visited India. A multi-disciplinary delegation led by the Indian Minister of state for Industry also visited Ivory Coast and Cameroun in 1988[14].

Relations between India and Burkina Faso took a decisive turn when H.E. Mr. Blaise Compoare, President of Burkina Faso, visited India in 1993. On that occasion the foundation was laid for wider cooperation between the two countries. During his visit, a grant of Rs. 15 crore approximately for setting up an agricultural development project in Burkina Faso was announced by India. Following this visit, Mr. Narasimha Rao, the then Prime Minister of India, visited Burkina Faso in 1995 with a high level delegation. In 1997, the President of Burkina Faso H.E. Mr. Blaise Compaore made a second official visit to India along with a delegation of

Ministers of his government[15]. There have been also several bilateral visits between India and Senegal. President Abdou Diouf visited India in February 1997. An agreement on bilateral agricultural project was signed between the two countries. President of Senegal along with Foreign Minister of Senegal visited New Delhi to attend the G-15 summit. He had wide-ranging bilateral discussions with Prime Minister of India. The Minister for Technical Education and Professional Training of Cote d' Ivoire also visited India in October 1997[16]. India's rapidly developing relations with individual Francophone African countries were heightened with the visits of the Minister of State for External Affairs of India in September 1997 to Senegal and Cote d' Ivoire.[17] Sardar Surjit Singh Barnala, the then Union Minister of Fertilisers and Chemicals visited Senegal in November 1998 to attend the foundation laying ceremony of the expansion project of the Industries Chimique due Senegal (ICS). Mr. Omar Abdullah, Minister of State for External Affairs visited Senegal in March 2002.[18] Recently Indian Foreign Secretary Shashank visited the West African region in May 2003; it was the first secretary level visit in last seven years. The Foreign Ministers of Senegal, Cote d' Ivoire, Chad, Burkina Faso, Mali, Ghana, Equatorial Guinea and Guinea-Bissau visited New Delhi on March 1st 2004 to attend a meeting of Team–9 Foreign Ministers.[19]

Since the establishment of diplomatic relations with Francophone West African states after their independence in 1960s, a few agreements have been concluded between India and these countries. Till the mid 1980s, India had bilateral agreements with only two Francophone states namely Senegal and Cameroon.[20] However, in the later eighties and nineties, a significant thrust was given to the promotion of relations with Francophone West African states. In fact more recently bilateral agreements, covering cultural, trade, economic, scientific and technical cooperation have been entered into with the Francophone African states namely Burkina Faso, Cameroon, Ivory Coast, Rwanda and Senegal[21]. Indo-Senegalese bilateral trade agreement was signed in 1974. However, the first session of the joint trade committee took place in Dakar only in August 1995 under the co-chairmanship of commerce secretary. An accord on Cultural Cooperation and another on Commerce, Economic and Technical Cooperation between India and Senegal was signed at New Delhi on 22nd May

1974. A cultural exchange programme for the year 1977 was signed at New Delhi on 14th September 1976 between India and Senegal[22]. India and Burkina Faso signed a cultural agreement in 1984. On 17th February 1993, a trade agreement was signed between India and the Government of Republic of Cote'd' Ivoire (Ivory Coast). India announced a grant of Rs. 15 crore approximately for setting up an agricultural development project in Burkina Faso during the state visit of President of Burkina Faso to India on 22-23 July 1994. A memorandum of understanding on trade cooperation between the two countries was signed in 1995. An agreement on Railways project (protocol for the construction of 240 km railway line) was also signed in 1995. An accord creating the joint commission for cooperation between the two countries was signed in 1995.[23]

A memorandum of understanding (MOU) for establishment of the Entrepreneur and Technical Development Center in Dakar was signed in November 1996 in Harare. The project has since been implemented and handed over to the Senegalese Government in June 2000. A memorandum of understanding on the establishment of a project for agricultural development in Senegal was signed at New Delhi on 16th February 1997, implemented in February 1997, for duration of ten years. The project has been successfully implemented. An agreement on establishment of the Indo-Senegalese joint commission for economic, technical, political and cultural cooperation was signed on 16th February 1997 at New Delhi during the visit to India of the then Senegalese President Abdou Diouf. The first meeting of the Indo-Senegal joint commission held in Dakar in September 1997 agreed on cooperation in the areas of agriculture, transport, mining and training of human resources. The Senegalese side had expressed interest on concluding agreements on Avoidance of double taxation; bilateral investment promotion and protection agreement and Agreement on Technical assistance, whereas India had proposed the signing of a cultural exchange programme. The Senegalese side had immediately sent a draft MOU on cultural exchange to India[24]. As a part of assistance under G-15 cooperation, a MOU was signed between Government of India and Government of Senegal in January 1999 for implementation of a solar energy project under which the villages of Soune and Touly near Dakar were provided with solar energy equipment for home and public lighting. The project has been successfully implemented and the system is functional since March 2000. A memorandum of understanding for cooperation between CII and Chamber of Commerce, Industry and handicraft of Burkina Faso was singed in 1999. A memorandum of understanding was also signed on 26th April 1999 for setting up a pilot agriculture farm in Burkina Faso managed by farmers from Punjab.[25] Recently the 'Team-9 initiative' was launched by India on Monday, 1st March 2004 considering the potential that this region offers. Under the newly launched move, New Delhi announced a credit facility of US$500 million for projects in the economic and social sectors in eight West African countries. India singed MOUs with Burkina Faso, Chad, Cote d' Ivoire, Equatorial Guinea, Ghana, Guinea - Bissau, Mali and Senegal to evolve a mechanism of cooperation under the Techno-Economic Approach for Africa-India Movement (Team-9).[26] 'We have decided to have a long-term and sustained relationship with the eight countries', External Affairs Minister Yashwant Sinha said after holding a meeting with his counterparts from Senegal, Burkina Faso, Chad, Cote d' Ivoire, Equatorial Guinea, Ghana, Guinea-Bissau and Mali.

Thus, these visits and agreements added an impetus to growing bilateral co-operation between India and these countries

Indian Foreign Policy Perspective

India has a creditable record of supporting liberation movements in Africa and the anti-apartheid struggle. The war against colonialism and racism formed, some of the basic ingredients of India's early foreign policy. During the decade of 50s and 60s, more and more countries achieved their freedom from colonial rule. However, these newly emerging countries found a world divided between the communist bloc and the non-communist bloc, the age of the cold war. Under the leadership of Pandit Nehru, President Nasser and President Tito, this community of nations evolved what is known as the Non-Aligned Movement over a period of time, NAM not only acquired a political dimension but also strong economic content. The Group of 77, which consisted mostly of the non-aligned countries, became an important instrument of negotiation and articulation of views of the developing countries in all fora where economic issues were discussed[27].

In changed world scenario and due to recently liberalized and globalize economy, Indian foreign policy gives much importance to Western countries and developed nations. However, the new feature of India's Africa diplomacy during the 1990s was its emphasis on friendly relations with African countries. An integrated programme 'Focus: Africa' was launched from the year 2002-2003 with a view to significantly enhance India's trade with the Sub-Saharan African region. The main objective is to increase interactions between the two regions by identifying the areas of bilateral trade and investment. The Focus: Africa programme was initially focused on Sub-Saharan African region with added emphasis on seven major trading partners of the region viz. Nigeria, South Africa, Mauritius, Kenya, Ethiopia, Tanzania and Ghana.[28] However, with a view to enhance India's trade with Africa the scope of this programme was further extended with effect from 1st April 2003 to all the other countries of the Sub-Saharan African region, where India has diplomatic missions. Therefore in effect, it covers the entire African continent. After 'Focus Africa' India is now turning to West Africa so far neglected in Indian Foreign Policy considerations. With the focus on West African region, the Ministry of External Affairs, Government of India has recently appointed a Joint Secretary for West African region. The emphasis of Indian foreign policy has been shifted to forge beneficial economic relations with these states. Indian foreign policy makers look forward to identify common areas of understanding and mutual benefits in the fields of economy, politics and strategy. India's policy makers are conscious that friendship with this large bloc of African countries will be of considerable value in the future. India's search for new sources of oil and political influence has washed up on the remote shores of West Africa where New Delhi's foreign policy reach has been notable for its absence. Considering the potential that this region offers and our insignificant presence in that market, the 'Team-9 initiative' was launched by India on 1st March 2004. The Team–9 initiative is expected to diversify sources of India's energy security. The endeavour was to put these countries and India together in an economic cooperation framework. Under the newly launched move India signed MOUs with West African states of Burkina Faso, Chad, Cote d' Ivoire, Equatorial Guinea, Ghana, Guinea- Bissau, Mali and Senegal to evolve a mechanism of cooperation under the Techno-Economic Approach for Africa-India Movement (Team-9). Describing Team-9 as a 'wonderful concept', Senegalese Foreign Minister Cheikh Tidiani Gadio said that India and West Africa had opened a 'new path' to take the cooperation between them to a higher level.[29] India's Team-9 initiative points to a renewed focus on the region that offers a huge strategic potential.

For a variety of reasons, these countries are important for Indian foreign policy consideration.

(1) At the level of diplomacy, cultivation of friendly relations to gain support in various international fora for policies, vital to India's national interest, is important for India's foreign policy.

(2) Economically, Francophone West Africa provides vast scope fro mutually beneficial trade and commercial linkages in the spirit of south-south cooperation. The imperatives of India's liberalized and globalize economy make it necessary that third world countries and their markets are more seriously explored. The need for expanded export market and the challenge of the developed and industrialized economies should induce India to develop closer ties with these countries.

(3) India has a stake in NAM, G-77, G-15 and also Africa etc. It has also interest in WTO and restructuring UN, which needs partnership and cooperation with Africa. Thus, the quality and depth of Indo-Francophone West Africa bilateral relations assume even greater significance and a broader canvas of sympathy and support.

It is evident now that India is giving as much importance to Francophone West Africa as was expected. However, India has no media presence in Francophone West African region. It is need of the hour that diplomatic relations should be strengthened and to engage the civil society at large in fortifying and deepening bilateral relations with these countries. There is also a need to install an independent foreign policy planning forum.

Foreign Policy Perspective of Francophone West African States

Francophone West African states in their external relations have maintained close links with the Western World while emphasizing its ties with the developing world. Their domestic imperatives of providing a better life for all, sustainable development and poverty alleviation have become the focus of economic diplomacy in recent years. Their foreign policy is mainly driven by economic imperatives. Indeed, given their dependence on Western markets for investment and trade-essential for domestic economic revival, it is important for them to forge closer links with Western countries. Thus, they have put their own interests first competing, as it must, for Western technology, investment and trade with a host of rival claimants. They remain economically very close to France. France has been most supportive to these countries and has also been generous in its commitment to their economic development. Although they believe that their future is closely linked to the development of the south-south concept, they dare not to ignore certain realities that France, US and other G-7 countries are essential for their economic well-being and they constitute the undeniable economic power base of the world today.

However, they have also shown concern at the uneven impact of globalization on the developing economies and agreed to coordinate their efforts with other developing nations for the development of south-south cooperation. Almost all of them are member of third world Fora's like NAM, G-77, and G-15. Thus, It's confusing to talk of south-south cooperation and the need for full-cooperation with the north in the same breath. There is a contradiction in these countries establishing a strong relationship with third world countries while maintaining its strong ties with the West, particularly France. It is indeed quite a difficult proposition to pursue South-South networking while simultaneously drawing on north-south relations.

It is through the non-aligned and other third world movements that these countries and India have come closer. They have identical views with India on a number of international issues particularly relating to third world development and liberation. Their cooperation in the UNCTAD, the Non-Aligned Movement (NAM), the United Nations, the 'Group of 77' and other international forums is well documented. These countries have now emphasized to develop strong link with India and the potential for mutually beneficial cooperation. They can coordinate and work with Indian economic policy makers to decide which methods are most suitable to cope with the pressure of liberalization and globalization. The new developing partnership between India and these countries reflects their similar worldview and potential for substantial economic cooperation between them. With each passing year, the ties between them are getting stronger, wider and deeper. They are conscious of the fact that any joint action, position, views and partnership they share have wider implications. A strong and positive partnership between India and them is necessary for the growth and development of the region, self-collectivity and south-south cooperation.

Turning dependency theory on its head, Senegal, prominent Francophone state, is pulling away from the 'periphery' of the French 'core' and building a relationship with another 'periphery' of the World economy; India. So pleased are the Senegalese with their new found India connections that they want other West African countries to turn to Delhi for the technology and investment they once sourced from Paris. Senegal has also extended its support to India's candidature in the election to various UN bodies.[30]

Areas of Co-operation

With the end of political decolonization in Africa, economic issues have come to assume greater prominenance and importance. India has been making efforts to enlarge areas of economic cooperation with other developing countries particularly in Africa, which started with the Indian Technical and Economic Cooperation Programme (ITEC) launched in 1964. They now can be partners in the new struggle against global economic apartheid brought about by the uncontrolled globalization and liberalization. In this regard India and Francophone West African countries need to anchor their role in international affairs in the 21st century based on commitment to fundamental principles aimed at promoting and economic social well being of the people of the south. They rightly identified several issues, which deserve solidarity among the developing world.[31]

(1) The important issue where India-Francophone West Africa cooperation can play vital role relates to the reform and the restructuring of the United Nations and its security council. It should truly reflect the diversity of our universe and ensure equity among the nations in the exercise of power within the system of international relations in general and the Security Council in particular. Further, they need to carefully analyze the trends that seem to be

developing at the United Nations. The role of UNCTAD, UNIDO, ECOSOC, UNECA etc. are particularly important at a time when development aid is on the decline and debt-ridden developing countries, particularly in Africa, are struggling for survival. Maybe India and these countries should give support to an idea of building a more representative forum that can provide leadership in economic, social and environmental fields, an economic security council of the UN (ESC).

(2) South-South Cooperation: India and Francophone West African countries together constitute the most vital segment of the developing world. The imperatives of South-South cooperation make it necessary that India-Francophone West Africa cooperation is strengthened and deepened. Increased exchanges between India and Francophone West African countries would help to diversify the pattern of their economic linkages, strengthen multilateral approaches and increase their bargaining leverage with the North, particularly in the present age of globalization. India and Francophone West African countries could be partners in the on-going battle to overcome poverty and underdevelopment.

(3) Revitalizing the Non-Aligned Movement is yet another area in which Indo-Francophone West African countries cooperation can play a constructive role. It is important that NAM must generate new, relevant agenda items to place on the tables of multilateral fora, such as the WTO etc, around the world.

(4) Tackling the debt problem is another issue on which Indo-Francophone West African countries cooperation can play a useful role.

(5) There can be no development without peace and security and no security without economic development and a policy promoting human rights and civil society. Security, peace and human rights form a three-pronged approach in building a common future. Commitment to the protection of environment, prohibition of nuclear proliferation, arms-control, drug trafficking, terrorism, etc. are fundamental.

India and Francophone West African countries can cooperate in this area.

(6) India and Francophone West African countries could co-ordinate their policies to resist extra-territorial legislation being sought to be imposed on developing countries, particularly the social clause. They need to strengthen consultative and collaboration mechanisms with each other in trade and development agencies such as the WTO and UNCTAD.

(7) Strengthening of regional and inter-regional cooperation is vital to counter pervasive globalization. India and Francophone West African countries have to take cognizance of the increasing importance of regional economic blocs.

Thus, India-Francophone West African countries collaboration and cooperation in the 21st century must endeavour to face crucial challenges facing the third world countries, particularly in regard to bringing about functioning democracy, stimulating growth in the economy, developing a strong human rights culture and meeting the socio-economic needs of their citizens.

Economic Relations

Trade Policy of India and Francophone West African States

The trade policies devised by India and Francophone West African countries in order to foster the greater trade cooperation can be understood against the background of the economic diplomacy of these countries, which seeks to serve economic interest through diplomatic means. The trade policy reforms have aimed at creating an environment achieving rapid increase in export and raise share in world trade for achieving higher economic growth.

The Foreign Trade Development and Regulation Act, 1992, which replaces the earlier trade policies in the post-economic reform period, regulate Indian foreign trade. The Act of 1992 empowers the central government to formulate and announce from time to time the export and import policy and to amend it. Prior to this policy, foreign trade of India has suffered from strict bureaucratic and discretionary controls. However, the new government, which took over at the centre in June 1991, soon realized that India's foreign trade policy, must respond to the changes sweeping across the world. To reduce controls, simplify procedures and to create a congenial environment for trade, the government of India made statements on trade policy in Parliament on August 13, 1991, ushering a new trend in the foreign trade policy of India[32]. During this period of analysis, there were two broad policy measures adopted by government of India. The first was the export-import policy for 1992-1997, coinciding with the period of eighth five-year plan. This policy made a conscious effort to dismantle various protectionist and regulatory policies and accentuate India's transition towards a global oriented economy. The second policy was adopted for the period 1997-2002 coinciding with the ninth five year plan, seeks to consolidate the gains of the previous policy and further carry forward the process of liberalization by deregulating and simplifying procedures and removing quantitative restrictions in a phased manner[33]. An outward looking and liberal trade policy is one of the main features of India's economic reforms. The trade policy is characterized by rationalized tariff levels and a drastic reduction in quantitative restriction by introducing a streamlined and simplified system of export and import licences.[34]

Currently the aim of the trade and industry policy of the Francophone West African countries is to create a more diversified expert-oriented production sector that is internationally competitive aimed at realizing socio-economic objectives such as job creation and higher growth rates and incomes. The renewed emphasis on export promotion should be viewed against the background of the changing global economy. Since 1990s, with a renewed emphasis on economic diplomacy, these countries have been able to join hands with like-minded countries in multilateral agreements in the hope of making the global environment a 'friendlier' place for developing economies. These countries like India modulated the trade policy within the boundaries of the World Trade Organization (WTO), to which they are signatories. Therefore, their trade policies formulated in order to orient with the macro-economic scenario of WTO.

There has been rapid growth of interdependence in the world economy over past one decade with particular reference to the growing importance of international trade and capital flows in the era of globalization and privatization. In this regard, the policy instrument is used by the countries for making them greater interdependence. From the analysis of the foreign trade policy of India and these countries, it is observed that there are commonalities of objectives of India and these courtiers, such as firstly, to accelerate the countries transition to a global oriented vibrant economy with view to drive maximum benefits from expanding global market opportunities, secondly, to stimulate sustained economic growth by providing access to essential raw materials and capital good required for augmenting production, thirdly, to enhance the technological strength and efficiency of agriculture, industry and services, generating new employment opportunities and encourage the attainment of internationally accepted standards of quality and finally to provide consumers with good quality products at reasonable prices. Thus, the economic reforms of India in the early 1990s and recently liberalize economy of Francophone West African countries provided congenial environment for forging strong economic ties between the two regions.

Trade

Foreign trade is indeed the barometer of the level of economic relations existing between any two states. The share of Francophone West Africa in Indian trade is rather low. However, this does mean that there was decline in the trade between Francophone West Africa and India. Trade and commercial relations between India and Francophone West African states are flourishing and are definitely on the upswing. This paper attempts to trace and analyse trade relations between India and Francophone West African countries in twenty-five year period (1975-2000).

Exports

India's exports to the nine Francophone West African countries in the 1976-77 amounted to Rs. 16.17 crore which gradually increased to Rs. 47.31 crore in 1980-81 and Rs. 85.15 crore in 1991-92. However, the highest increase in exports occurred during the late 1990s from Rs. 111.82 crore in 1992-93 to Rs. 460.97 crore in 1995-96 and Rs. 647.42 crore in 1999-2000. With exports jumping to Rs. 1055.1 crore in 2000-2001, India's trade relations with Francophone West African countries indeed entered a new phase. Evidently there was a very sharp increase in India's exports to Francophone

West African countries from Rs. 16.17 crore in 1976-77 to Rs. 1055.1 crore in 2000-2001. However considering the potential that this region offers, ours presence is still insignificant.

During the period of 1976-77 to 1981-82, India's export to the Francophone West Africa increases from Rs. 16.17 crore to Rs 55.54 crore. However, there was decline in the exports from Rs. 31.52 crore in 1982-83 to Rs. 12.93 crore in 1985-86 due to the deepening economic crisis in Francophone African states like in the rest of Africa which adversely affected their capacity to import.[35] In 1982-83, Francophone African states had a negative rate of growth of GDP over the previous year. In Ivory Coast, one of India's important trading partners, the negative growth rate was as high as - 4.4 percent in 1982-83.[36] However, there was reversal of trend, and India's export again started rising in the following years with this region. It increased from Rs. 20.7 crore in 1986-87 to 29.23 crore in 1989-90 and again from Rs. 45.96 crore in 1990-91 to Rs. 460.97 crore in 1995-96 and finally touching the figure of Rs. 1055.1 crore in 2000-2001. This is indeed a remarkable achievement in promoting exports in a region where a good numbers of barriers had to be crossed.

Benin, Senegal and Ivory Coast are relatively important client of India in this region. Benin with the import of Rs. 15.08 crore from India in 1976-77 was the India's top client and with the import of the value of Rs. 25.78 crore in 1994-95, it remains the top client of India in the region. However, Ivory Coast became the top client of India in this region with the import of value of Rs. 129.13 crore in 1995-96 and Senegal second leading client with the import of the value of Rs. 126.16 crore from India in 1995-96. Ivory Coast with the import of the value of Rs. 149.93 crore in 1999-2000 and Rs. 209.76 crore in 2000-2001 from India is the largest importer of Indian goods from this region. Benin with the import of the value of Rs. 122.89 crore in 1999-2000 and Rs. 206.20 crore in 2000-2001 from India is close second. Senegal with the import of the value of Rs. 86.90 crore in 1999-2000 was the third largest client of India. But with the import of the value of Rs. 108.59 in 2000-2001, it is well behind the Togo which imported the Indian goods worth value Rs. 180.71 crore in 2000-2001 and Niger with export of the value of Rs. 119.55 crore in 2000-2001 from India. The five leading clients of India in this region are Ivory Coast, Benin, Togo, Niger and Senegal. The Indian exports were in excess of Rs. 100 crore in five countries of this region namely Ivory Coast, Benin, Togo, Senegal and Niger and more than Rs. 200 crore in two states, Ivory Coast and Benin.

Imports

India's import from the region decline from Rs. 8.77 crore in 1976-77 to Rs. 6.72 crore in 1980-81 and further to Rs.5.48 crore in 1982-83. However, it started to increase from Rs. 27.14 crore in 1983-84 to Rs. 84.7 crore in 1986-87 to Rs.177.45 crore in 1990-91. It increases to Rs. 310 crore in 1991-92 and then started to decline from Rs. 306.52 crore in 1992-93 to Rs. 159.12 crore in 1994-95 and again to increase from Rs. 273.54 in 1995-96 to Rs. 1161.58 crore in 1999-2000 and Rs 1197.72 crore in 2000-2001. Thus, this is evident from the trend that there was an enormous increase in the imports from this region in period of 25 years as a whole.

India's imports from Francophone West African region are confined to limited number of countries. During the period of 1976-77 to 1983-84, Senegal, Ivory Coast and Guinea were the leading suppliers to India from this region. In 1984-85, Togo with the import of the value Rs. 10.92 crore emerged as another important supplier to India. During the 1990s, Benin and Mali emerged as new suppliers to India. Burkina Faso with the export of the value Rs. 55.24 crore in 1999-2000 and Rs. 48.02 crore in 2000-2001 also emerged as substantial supplier to India. Ivory Coast was the leading supplier to India with the export of the value of Rs. 422.39 crore in 1999-2000 and Rs. 562.39 in 2000-2001 to India. Senegal was the second leading supplier to India in1999-2000 with the export of the value of Rs. 378.34 crore to India. But Benin became the second leading supplier to India in 2000-2001 with export of the value of Rs. 237.93 crore to India ahead of Senegal's Rs. 202.55 crore.

Thus, there is indeed a significant development in the trade relations between India and Francophone West African states. India's trade with these states could be taken as a general trend of India's trade with the Francophone African states. In conclusion, it can be stated that overall trend in trade between India and these states augurs well for the development of India's trade with Francophone West African region.

Trade Balance

During the period of 1976-77 to 1982-83, India had trade surplus in its trade with Francophone West African countries. It was Rs. 7.30 crore in 1976-77, Rs. 44.54 crore in 1981-82 and Rs. 26.04 crore in1982-83 in India's favour. This was due to considerable increase in exports to Ivory Coast. However, the trend was reversed after 1983-84. It was Rs. 8.92 crore trade- deficits for India in 1983-84 and Rs. 35.69 crore in1985-86. It was Rs. 123.92 crore in 1989-90 and reached the figure of Rs. 224.85 crore in 1991-92 with a sudden rise in imports from Senegal.

The trend was reversed again with the trade surplus for India in 1993-94 of Rs. 59.94 crore. Except for the year 1994-95 the next four years it was in India's favour, with the trade surplus of Rs. 187.43 crore in 1995-96, Rs. 81.53 crore in 1996-97, Rs. 10.23 crore in 1997-98 and Rs. 149.87 crore in 1998-99. However, again it was trade deficit for India in 1999-2000 with the figure of Rs. 514.16 crore and Rs. 142.62 crore in 2000-2001.

Trading Commodities

During the 1980s the sluggishness of India's export performance was partly attributed to the narrow base of India's export mix to Francophone West Africa. This is perhaps no longer the case now and is abundantly clear from India's commodity pattern of exports to Francophone West African states. The important items of export from India to this region are Cotton; Vehicles other than Railway or Tramway rolling stock, and parts and accessories thereof; Articles of apparel and clothing accessories knitted or crocheted; Articles of iron or steel; Cereals; Other made up textile articles; sets; worn clothing and worn textile articles; rags; Pharmaceutical products; Miscellaneous chemical products; Rubber and articles thereof; Nuclear reactors, boilers, machinery and mechanical appliances; parts thereof; Articles of stone, plaster, cement, asbestos, mica or similar materials; Tools implements, cutlery, spoons and forks, of base metal; parts thereof of Base metal; Special woven fabrics, tufted textile fabrics, lace, tapestries, trimmings, embroidery; Man-made staple fibres; Man-made filaments; Tanning or dyeing extracts; tannins and their deri. Dyes, pigments and other colouring matter; paints and ver; putty and other mastics; inks; Electrical machinery and equipment and parts thereof, sound recorders and reproducers, television image and sound recorders and reproducers and parts; Essential oils and Resinoid, perfumery, cosmetics or toilet preparations; Glass and glassware; Optical, photographic cinematographic measuring.

In return, India's imports from the region are fairly heavily concentrated in a narrow range of commodities. India's major imports from the region are Inorganic chemicals; organic or inorganic compounds of precious metals, of rare earth metals. elem or of isotopes; salt; sulphur, earths and stone; plastering materials, lime and cement; Edible fruit and nuts; peel or citrus fruit or melons; wood and articles of wood; wood charcoal; Cotton; Cocoa and cocoa preparations; Oil seeds and olea. Fruits, misc. grains, seeds and fruit; industrial or medicinal plants; straw and fodder; Mineral fuels, mineral oils and products of their distillation; bituminous substances, mineral waxes; Fertilizers; Lac; gums, resins and other vegetable saps and extracts.

Ivory Coast and Senegal has emerged as relatively important trading partner of India in this region. The five leading products exported from India to Senegal are (1) cotton textiles, clothes and fittings, various textiles, ready to wear etc. (ii) metallurgy (iii) organic/inorganic/agricultural chemical products (iv) pharmaceutical products and (v) iron and steel. While the five leading products imported by India from Senegal are phosphoric acid, phosphates, cashew nuts, hides and skins and Arabic gum. India was the key buying client of Senegal in 2001. It bought 100% phosphoric acid (56 billion CFA F) and 70% phosphates (10 billion CFA F). The main exports from India to Ivory Coast consists of cotton; vehicles other than Railway or Tramway Rolling Stock and parts and Accessories thereof; articles of apparel and clothing accessories, not knitted or crocheted; other made up textile articles, sets, worn clothing and worn textile articles, rags; and rubber and articles thereof. The main imports from Ivory Coast consists of Edible fruit and nuts, peel or citrus fruit or melons; Wood and articles of wood, wood charcoal; Cotton; Oil seeds and olea, fruits, misc. grains, seeds and fruit, industrial or medicinal plants, straw and fodder; Cocoa and coca preparations.

Francophone West African States Potential Items of Export to India

Senegal is one of the largest producers and exporters of phosphate and phosphoric acid in Africa. India is a large importer of these items. There also exist opportunities for Francophone West African states to export agriculture produce like cocoa, cocoa preparations, edible fruits, nuts (cashew nuts) and rubber, cotton raw and waste, wood and wood products, fertilizers (crude), leather and fruit juices etc to India. India can also import items like gold, precious metals, inorganic and organic chemicals, Iron & Steel and Petroleum, crude and products etc from these countries.

Potential for Enhanced Trade

There is an opportunity for enhancing trade between India and Francophone West African region because of

(1) Liberalized and growing economy of India as well as this region.

(2) Though the markets of these countries on their own are not big, the regional trade agreements like ECOWAS and UEMOA have enabled them to have a wider reach with re-export possibilities and transshipment facilities to even land locked countries like Burkina Faso and Mali. Meanwhile it is not the size of the market that matters but it is the sweep and the reach that counts, and in that respect Francophone West African countries present an expanded market with enhanced opportunities.

(3) Use of French language should not be a major handicap. One has to remember that though other Asian countries like China, South Korea and Japan too, have faced the same problem but they have overcome this disadvantage and in fact, are able to reach a dominating position in this French speaking market. If China can do, not doubt, India too can do. Language problem can be overcome with the help of software available for quick translation of business correspondence between English and French or other prominent African Languages.[37]

(4) High freight rates and longer shipping times also do not seem to be a major constraint. It is pertinent to note that the nearby African country Nigeria is topping the list in the import of engineering goods from India by African countries. If India is competitive in Nigeria and can ship the goods to them in time, there is no reason why we cannot do so with Francophone West African countries.

(5) The potential for expansion in trade and investment is great since Francophone West African region is rich in natural resources.

(6) There is huge shortage of skilled manpower leading to poor manufacturing activity in this region while India has largest skilled manpower.

(7) Activation of regional trade arrangements like ECOWAS provides ample scope fro enhanced trade with this region. The principal objective of ECOWAS is the establishment of a customs union and a common market for promoting the free movement of goods and people within West Africa. The treaty also provided for the harmoninization of regional policies in several sectors, including agriculture, industry, energy, transport and communications. In 1994 Francophone members setup their own Union Economique et Monetaire Oust-Africiane (UEMOA) to work towards a custom union and other aspects of economic convergence.

However, the real issue is attractive credit terms offered by competitors from European Union which Indian exporters are unable to match. Basically Francophone West African Countries are credit-oriented market where payment terms like 'LC' and 'Advance Payment' turns away business opportunities. Therefore this issue needs to be addressed to in a business like manner. Either the government of India or the Export-Import Bank of India should extend a line of credit, the terms of which shall be tuned to take care of the demanding perspective in these countries to facilitate Indian exporters to supply capital goods and machinery on equal terms on par with their competitors. In fact, the Exim Bank has decided to extend the line of credit to the tune of $2.2 billion to Senegal along with other African countries like Mauritius, Uganda, Egypt, Botswana, Tanzania and Zambia as part of India's recent commitment to promote and encourage trade with them.[38]

Armed with this attractive armour Indian exporters can confidently approach the Senegal importers to source from India.

Economies of India and Francophone West African States are Complementary

The term complementarity between the developing regions such as India and Francophone West Africa was considered with reference to two essential characteristics:[39]

(i) Two regions can be considered to be complementary to each other, in economic terms, if certain items or products produced in one region could fruitfully be inducted as import in the production activity of the other region by increasing or without affecting, the level of production and

(ii) The term can also be applied if the substitution of one set of relations by another set helps in affecting structural modification or transformation by generating, or by raising the expectation of generating greater, indigenous autonomous capacity.

Examining the plural economic features of the Francophone West African economies, on the one hand, and the Indian economy, on the other, it was evident that there was an built in complementarities aspect in the very structuring of the two economies. The production complementarities attained by India, since her independence, were found to be remarkably suited to providing the 'missing middle' in the African economies.[40] India is one of the countries, which has not only the required expertise and experience in the technological and management fields but also is in a position to help other developing countries in the process of their development in a variety of sectors, such as agriculture, industry, trade, joint ventures, consultancy etc.

India has been making special efforts to enlarge areas of economic cooperation with other developing countries. The imperatives of India's recently globalize and liberalized economy make, it necessary that African and other third world countries are more seriously explored. The need for an export market and the challenge of the developed economies should induce India to develop closer ties with these countries. The economies of India and Francophone West African countries are complementary and therefore they stand to gain from increased trade and greater economic cooperation. Francophone West African states are growth oriented emerging economies and they have all the potential to become a strong trade partner of India in the African region. For India, they can be both, a good market for export of product and services as also good partners for joint ventures and collaborative ventures. They offer tremendous business opportunities to Indian entrepreneurs.

The scope for economic cooperation between India and these countries is, indeed, vast. This is due to several reasons, firstly India and these countries are moving on the path of economic liberalization and are encouraging foreign investment. Secondly, India is at comparable level of industrial and technological development and has much to offer to these countries. Thirdly, controlled inflation rate and comparatively self-sustained economy of India and growth oriented economies of these states. Fourthly, Francophone West African States are developing in terms of infrastructure and healthy financial sector. All these factors are able to raise the Indo-Francophone West African states economic relations to a new height.

An important modality of India-Francophone West Africa production cooperation could be the agency of joint industrial ventures. But, it was found that Indian-Francophone West African states joint ventures, compared with India's worldwide spread, Indo-Asian joint ventures and even other regions of Africa, had as yet just scratched the surface. Despite unmistakably growing production complementarities between India and several Francophone West African countries, the economic relations between the two regions did not reflect full potential of such complementarities. This was mainly due to well structured 'dependency syndrome' of the Francophone West African economies[41]. The situation was further compounded by the economic crisis and political instability. Most of the Francophone West African countries have so far been relying heavily on tied aid and credits from developed countries. The foreign debt is increasing and they have not been able to obtain adequate aid from IMF and World Bank. Thus, in the light of acute shortage of foreign exchange, faced by most Francophone West African countries, the only way out is production cooperation between India and Francophone West Africa.

Investment and Joint Ventures

Joint ventures are now receiving increasing attention in the collaboration efforts of developing countries to promote trade and industrialization. Joint ventures are a comparatively flexible instrument in that they can assume many different modalities concerning initiative for establishment, ownership, sources of management and technology and market arrangements for the provision of inputs or sale of their products.[42]

India has, in fact a long history of setting up joint ventures in developing countries of Africa and Asia. Evidently, the scale of Indian collaboration projects in Francophone Africa was negligible during 1970s. And it was only in the mid 1980s that India opened her JVA account in Francophone Africa with the setting up of a project in Senegal. An efficient Indian company in public sector is collaborating with the Senegalese government in the field of fertilizers and phosphoric acid[43]. There are 3 joint ventures in Senegal, one in Guinea and one Wholly Owned Subsidiary in Ivory Coast. However, there is ample scope for collaboration for a variety of products. Paper and pulp, mineral processing, agro-based industries etc provide ample scope for Indian joint ventures in these countries. One can think of establishing a big joint venture in respect of a textile complex in Burkina Faso or Mali which could cater to the requirements of the neighbouring land locked countries like Niger and Chad as well.[44] Indo-Francophone West African joint ventures will necessarily lead to larger trade between India and Francophone West African countries. There is thus an urgent need to set up more joint ventures in Francophone West Africa. India infact should take concrete steps in identifying the projects in consultation with Francophone West African states so that this useful area of collaboration is extended further, both in width and depth.

Sectors in Francophone West African Countries for Indian Investment

India in its experience of over fifty years industrial growth, attained expertise in certain important sectors and has comparative advantage to do investment business anywhere in the world. These sectors are agriculture, infrastructure like communication, irrigation, housing, health and small and medium scale industry. Thus, in the matter of production cooperation, a number of areas were identified.

1. Food and Agriculture:[45] In the field of production cooperation, top priority should be given to agriculture. Agriculture is not confined just to production of agricultural products but includes supply of fertilizers, irrigation, storage, communication etc. It can also provide

lots of employment opportunities. Francophone West African countries have a lot of fertile land, untapped, undeveloped and not harvested, which could be utilized for food production to enable them to attain self-sufficiency in food. India is in a position to offer appropriate technology and training to the agriculturists in these countries. Diary farming is another such area. India's experience in setting agriculture related institutes and universities could also be very useful for establishing such institution in some higher countries and regional institutes in the smaller ones.

2. Rural and small-scale industries:[46] The rural and small-scale industries sector is another area of Indian specialization. SMEs could not only strengthen the industrial base of these countries but also provide employment and income generation opportunities to the active working population, which is at present unemployed. India could assist these countries in establishing small-scale industries (SSI) in the field of agro-processing like sugar cane, forestry products, consumer durables and the light electrical and electronics industry, other sectors such as oil refining, food processing and preservation, hotel, mineral processing, small cement plants, granite and marbles. India could help in prospecting, exploration and development of mines and could provide a good market for many of the minerals, as well.

3. Most of the Francophone West African countries are interested in improving their basic infrastructure in the transport sector, shipping and port facilities. India with her experience of not only developing her own infrastructure but also of completing a number of turnkey jobs in this area in the middle-east can do a lot to help these countries.

4. India has an internationally recognized and growing expertise in the Information Technology (IT) sector. The IT is one major specific sector in which there is a huge scope for expansion in terms of co-operation between Indian and Francophone West African companies. India has

offered technical trainings to these countries under the ITEC. This has involved technical training, consultancy services and project assistance.

5. Housing has emerged as a promising area of cooperation between the two regions. India has proven expertise in low-cost housing.

6. Indians could provide assistance in the field of techno-economic surveys, planning, preparation of feasibility and detailed project reports, entrepreneurship development and managerial assistance. Recognizing the fact that most African countries lack capital resources and entrepreneurs, it might be useful to think of starting many industries on a joint venture basis with Africans and Indians joining together. Joint ventures could be established in the field of consumer industries especially because most African countries are importing all types of consumer goods. This cooperation could then be extended from production to marketing and export as well.

7. In the following sectors also India has the opportunity for investment: Setting up of Industrial Training Institutes (ITIs) to train manpower; Drugs, pharmaceuticals and the chemicals; Banking, insurance and communication sectors; Hotel management; Engineering and equipment; Construction and infrastructure development; Transport including automobile, rail, vehicles etc; Coal washing and Service sectors with emphasis on hotel and tourism, health care, computer software and the institutions to provide basic education. Processing of various produce like timber and local forest products.

Technical Cooperation

ITEC: India has offered technical training to Africans under the Indian Technical and Economic Programme (ITEC)*. These covers short and medium term training courses in various disciplines ranging from diplomacy, media studies, legal drafting, water management, computer software, wildlife management, defence policy, agriculture, small-scale farming, SME entrepreneurship and low cost housing. The ITEC programme now also includes opportunities in information technology (IT), jewelry manufacturing and the arts and crafts. In India, both education and training is comparatively cheap than Western countries and the standard is also high, so they are interested in sending their citizens to India.[47]

India has provided technical and financial assistance to these countries under ITEC programme, SCAAP and ADR. Several projects in Senegal, Burkina Faso and Benin under ITEC projects were completed in 1997-98. Under SCAAP slots were utilized by Senegal (26), Ivory Coast (3), Burkina Faso (2) and Benin (2) till January 1998. Under ADR, diesel water pumps and sewing machine were provided by India to Ivory Coast.[48] In recent years, growing demands have been made on Ministry of External Affairs of India through ITEC programme to transfer knowledge and skills gained under India's green revolution, by developing countries, especially in Africa. The first experiment in transferring such technology was launched in Burkina Faso. The pilot farmers' project started in October 1999 for a period of three years was successfully completed whereby Burkinabe farmers were being taught and trained in mechanized farming to increase there per hectare yield. There is request for agricultural assistance from other countries of Africa like Tanzania and Namibia.

However, this programme certainly deserves a fresh look with a view to further widen its coverage and funding provisions. At multilateral level, too, the programmes such as SCAAP and Colombo Plan need further supplemental inputs. For instance, India's membership of Economic commission for African Development Bank calls for a thorough examination to see how India could further widen economic and technical cooperation base within African countries in Africa based developmental programmes and projects.

Multilateral Cooperation

The regional cooperation through NAM, G-77 and G-15 in south-south cooperation framework or interregional cooperation like through ECOWAS provides India and these countries with newer opportunities and challenges. The regional groupings are working to promote sustained growth and balanced development of the region and of the member states and have added a fresh impetus to growth of South-South cooperation.

The formation of the WTO throws challenges and opportunities to developing countries in the new global trading system. Acceptance by the WTO of regional trading bloc's as effective institutions to facilitate global trade has made the situation vulnerable for those countries, which do not belong to any effective regional trade blocs. The factors endorse the need for the establishment of a comprehensive and effective regional forum. The only way for many developing countries in the south to avoid economic marginalization is to seek membership of a key, trading group. The regional groupings like NAM, G-77 and G-15 offers the potential for it.[49]

A strong and positive partnership between India and Francophone West African countries could prove beneficial to the whole range of Indo-African relations and south-south cooperation. India and these countries are hoping to give a new dimension to south-south cooperation by bringing the economies of Asia, Africa and Latin America closer together. Thus, it is important for India and these countries to work out adequate policy packages, institutional structures, technologies, and inter-regional development schemes etc. to develop mutually beneficial and effective linkages in the spirit of South-South cooperation.

South-South Cooperation : South-South cooperation has come to assume an important role in third world diplomacy in recent years. The countries of the third world have come to increasingly recognize the need for closer cooperation among them. In order to become more independent and less reliant on the north, the south-south cooperation is vital for third world countries. Starting with the NAM, UNCTAD-I, formation of 'Group of 77' and the creation of the 'Group of 15', the least developed countries (LDCS) have moved a long ways and means to contribute to each others economic and social progress by effective utilization of complementaries between their respective resources and requirements. The trend towards south-south cooperation has provided a strategic dimension to the concept of economic cooperation among the LDCs. This would also increase their bargaining strength and countervailing power in the negotiations with the developed countries and would at the same time serve as a valuable complement to international economic cooperation. Thus, today south-south cooperation is an economic necessity and is based on equality and free will of the third world countries.

While the struggle for NIEO goes on, south-south cooperation was regarded as a first step towards reduction of their dependence on former colonial powers. With this spirit, the regional, formations have already come up in South East Asia (ASEAN) South Asia (SAARC) Africa (OAU), West Africa (ECOWAS) and Latin America.[50] Thus, the agenda of south-south cooperation has increased manifold and has become broad based during course of its development, which covers not only economic issues but also all issues of social concerns. These include cooperation in agriculture, trade, banking, eradication of poverty and social injustices, human resources enhancement, regional and multilateral cooperation, technical cooperation etc. and many more.[51]

Now it has well defined targets to be achieved in a specified time schedule under definite programme of action. It has also developed its institutional arrangements like south commission and its secretariat, task force, expert groups for effective and successful coordination among various agencies in the world for successfully achieving its goal.

NAM: The replacement of political agenda by economic issues was natural outcome of the international situation where political differences have disappeared with the end of cold war situation. The new developments in international scenario have limited meaning and the third world crisis remains the same. The new actors in international relations have emerged with definite ethnic characteristics, facing grave economic crisis and are being constantly shattered by domestic violence and internal problems. The NAM states supported the idea of increasing the south-south cooperation in this situation. Thus, the south-south cooperation has remained a major plea for NAM. The developing countries faced even more serious problems of economic development and economic situations under these compulsions. The agenda of NAM has also to reflect the changes.

The sustainable economic growth and development can be pursued within the context of the NAM and within the axis of south-south cooperation. NAM addresses the asymmetries and imbalances of the global economy and it developed strategies to promote the economic and social empowerment of the south. The non-aligned nations have adopted economic cooperation among themselves as an alternative means to reduce their dependence on the industrially advanced countries. The concept of south-south cooperation has emerged as a universal principle, both as a strategy in support of the development efforts of the developing countries and as an instrument for promoting collective self-reliance in order to ensure their effective participation in the international economic system. It is realized that strengthening of south-south cooperation was necessary to create a more truly interdependent global economic order. It is in this context that role of industrially more advanced countries like India has become more crucial. The issues which have concerned the NAM after the end of cold war appeared to be in nature of economic, technological and more in the direction of cooperation and became less ideological and political. The issues, which concern the developing world, including the NAM, remained the exploitative nature of natural resources by industrial and developed world. The deprivations and backwardness among the developing states were their major concerns. The NAM showed greater unity on these issues. NAM demanded that multilateral debts of low-income developing countries be written off.[52] The issue of cooperation among south-south states has been further increased when various regional group formations have taken place both at international and regional level. Many of the issues with which the NAM has been concerned, poverty and the gap between rich and poor, global security, environmental conservation have assumed even greater significance. There is consensus within NAM on a number of challenges, which developing countries are facing. These include the nuclear disarmament, fighting against international terrorism, the marginalisation of developing countries in the process of globalization, the critical economic situation in Africa, the promotion of democratic participation at the national and international level as well as new challenge - such as, transnational crime, international drug trafficking and HIV/AIDS. NAM also recognized the need for constructive dialogue with the north, aimed at the resolution of global problems.[53] Thus, the need for wider, powerful and effective international fora remains essential and from this point of view NAM attains more urgency for developing states belonging to Asia, Africa and Latin America.

India and other members of NAM are trying to give a new direction to the movement (NAM). It is imperative therefore, that India and Francophone West African states take into consideration the changed international scenario. The focus should now inevitably be on trade and economics. NAM can be revitalized by the cooperation between India and Francophone West African states. It will further enhance the prospects of more genuine south-south cooperation. The need for UN reforms and expansion of Security Council to provide a constructive voice to the aspirations of the developing countries and the need for reforming the World Bank and International Monetary Fund attend significance in changing world scenario. The decisive international and coordination of both India and Francophone West African states on the ongoing debate about the reform and expansion of the UN Security Council well as World Bank and IMF is critical. This may add momentum to the emerging Afro-Asian Cooperation and consultations. With Africa functioning as a bridgehead to expanding ties with Latin America and the Caribbean, a necessary critical mass in multilateral negotiations might be created. This will benefit the countries of the South.

Group of 77: The Group of 77 has become principal forum and instrument respectively of the non-aligned countries in the UN for achieving the required changes in the international economic relations. The non-aligned nations constitute the majority of members of the Group of 77 (presently 134 members including some aligned states) continuously exert pressure on the international community to reform the prevailing economic and monetary systems. Policy guidelines for the reinforcement of collective self-reliance have been concretized by the NAM since the formation of the Group of 77.[54] To secure economic and trade cooperation among them, the developing countries are trying to coordinate in their policies over different issues to be pursued with the G-77. The economic and technical cooperation (ECDC and TCPC) among developing countries soon evolved as a central thrust area of the 'Group of 77' and 'NAM'. The G-77 conferences on 'ECDC' in 1976 and 1981, identified many subjects and assigned them to a large number of meetings of 'Expert Group', 'High level Group', 'Head of agencies' and other governmental fora. Thus, the basis for Third World political solidarity on international economic issues was laid.[55] India had been playing a prominent role in sponsoring economic cooperation as an integral programme among the G-77 and non-aligned countries. India had laid greater stress on mutually beneficial economic relationship to under score the significance of south-south collective self-reliance. The economic and technical cooperation among developing countries had thus evolved as a central concern of the G-77 fora and NAM. The third world countries have undergone a change during last few years and most important of all was the new emphasis on economic diplomacy. South-South Cooperation had by now become the new mantra of the G-77 and NAM.

G-15 : At the initiative of India, a summit level group for south-south consultation and cooperation known as G-15 was established by ninth NAM summit at Belgrade in 1989. Since 1990 the G-15 (now includes 17 members) has been organizing its summit level meetings on annual basis. The goals of G-15 include fruitful debate on economic issues among developing countries which aims at increasing the level of contacts among themselves; to bring comprehensive and intense cooperation in the economic sphere; to develop economies of member countries by exchange of information, technology, to forge unity and solidarity among themselves with a view to change the intransigent and hostile attitude and policies of developed nations and also to pressurize them for aforesaid all objectives.[56] G-15 reflects the quest of the developing countries to find ways and means of cooperation among themselves to mutual advantage. G-15 insists on an equitable economic order, which will help combat unemployment and poverty. The main thrust of G-15 remained to develop trade contacts and also to promote technological know—how among the member states. This group opposed to trade barriers among the states, which hamper the free flow. The G-15 is committed to play a catalytic role in fostering south-south cooperation. It is now clear that the G-15 has became action-oriented in promoting south-south cooperation.

ECOWAS : ECOWAS is a regional organization of 16 West African states consisting of Burkina Faso, Benin, Cote d'Ivoire, Cape Verde, Guinea, Gambia, Guinea-Bissau, Ghana, Liberia, Mauritania, Mali, Niger, Nigeria, Senegal, Sierra Leone and Togo. It is the largest common market accounting more than 250 million consumers. With the emergence of regional groupings like ECOWAS, it is worthwhile to consider bilateral trade as a part of the larger arrangement of intra and inter-regional levels. ECOWAS constitute an important initiative for regional and global cooperation, through facilitation of free trade and investment flows.

The need for an export market and the challenge of the developed economies induce India to develop closer ties with members of ECOWAS and its 250 million peoples[57]. India can have wide ranging cooperation with these countries in areas related to trade, joint ventures and human resources development projects and can be in addition to the facilities already being offered bilaterally to member countries of ECOWAS. India and these countries can support each other efforts to cooperation in their respective regions and mutually consult on matter relating to regional and global security. The regional groupings have potential to boost India-Francophone West Africa economic interaction.

Constraints on India's Relations with Francophone West Africa

There are shadows as well which may stand in the way of promoting trade and economic relations between India and this region. They are

(1) French language:[58] use of French language in these countries for business correspondence, government administration and in technical standards is considered as a big constraint by Indian businessmen in approaching the market of these countries since Indian businessmen mainly use English in their communication. Further, there is a perceived notion in their minds that the small size of the market and the commercial gains that will come from the modest volume of business may not be commensurate with the cost involved in translation of various details and communication in French.

(2) Keen international competition: A number of developed countries including France, Belgium, Italy, USA, Germany and Netherlands have a strong foot hold in these countries. A rapid survey of India's potential exports to these countries shows that India may face stiff competition from France and China. China in fact, is having an aggressive trade drive in this region China is expected to offer competition to India in this region market for a wide range of goods from textiles to engineering goods.

(3) Slow pace of reforms and political instability in this region: Higher incidence of civil strife, macro-economic instability, modest progress made both in liberalization and

privatization have affected Indian trade with this region; Limited purchasing powers and costly domestic credit of these countries: High freight rates and longer shipping times; Inadequate after sales service and lack of durable arrangements for ensuring supply of spare parts.

(4) Attractive credit terms offered by the European firms, especially the French firms, who have historical links with these countries in contrast with the tendency of Indian firms to insist on LC Terms of payment and their reluctance to supply on credit terms of payment.[59]

(5) Indians prefer short-term supply contracts rather than long term joint ventures with local partners. No serious studies exist about this region: To formulate a proper policy for fruitful relations with this region, there is a need to build up data banks and teams of experts.

Due to the absence of Diaspora factor (PIOs) in these former French colonies, the information outlets, both direct and indirect, have been relatively fewer thus inadequacy of information about business opportunities. A more high-profile publicity for India seems an imperative need. The only media exposure of India to the Francophone African States seems to be through the cultural journal Rencontre avec l 'Inde, brought out by the ICCR[60].

Conclusion

Traditionally, India and Francophone West African states have close and cordial relations. However, political, diplomatic and cultural relations along with commercial relations have not grown commensurately due to several reasons. However, with a significant thrust for mutually beneficial economic collaborations, the relations between them are definitely on the upswing.

The new collaborative links that are being forged between India and Francophone West African countries are free from any friction or misunderstanding. On the contrary, they are based on immense mutual goodwill and clear understanding of each other problems. On several issues concerning conflict situations in the world, India and most of the independent Francophone West African countries have often stood on the common platform, strictly adhering to the policy of non-alignment and peaceful co-existence. India's relations with Francophone West African states have acquired greater significance, mainly because a number of areas have already been identified in which they share common interests. However they have to solve their own internal contradictions, conflicts of their respective societies and increase their capacities to deal with their own resources to stabilize their life. India seems to perceive a certain commonality of interests and aspirations with Francophone West African states, be it in the bilateral context, in NAM or the UN. Francophone West African states along with India can be identified with the Non-aligned movement. Francophone states not only have a numerical strength in the UN but they also give a firm anti-racial and anti-colonial content to the movement. They also gave impetus to the demands for a new international economic order. They are aware of the tremendous prospects of their economic cooperation and have already taken several strides in that direction. New patterns of development are emerging both in India and Francophone West African states and a new economic order is taking shape. Essentially it initiated cooperation between India and Francophone West African states to act as one voice in matters of common concern. The scope for economic cooperation between India and these countries is very vast. As India and countries of Francophone West Africa are moving on the path of economic liberalization, their economies hold immense opportunities of mutually beneficial economic collaborations in the changing global environment.

India and Francophone African states were conscious of the fact that a strong and positive partnership between them is necessary to safeguard their joint interest in economic, social and cultural development and in international co-operation. The new initiative by India the 'Team-9' has opened a new path to take the cooperation between them to higher level. In the changing world scenario, new challenges and opportunities are emerging due to globalization and liberalization and thus this is the time for starting a more concrete and meaningful relationship between India and Francophone West African states.

Endnotes

1 Olusoji, Akomolafe A. 'Francophone Africa into the 21st Century'. *Africa Quarterly*, vol. 34, no.1, p. 96.

2 Mathews, K. 2004. 'Francophone Africa Today'. *Africa Quarterly*, vol. 41, no. 4, p. ix.

3 *Ibid,* p. xii.

4 Olusoji. *op. cit.,* pp. 96-97.

5 Mathews. *op. cit.,* p. ix.

6 Taliyarkhan, Homi J. H. 1980. 'India and African Liberation Movements and Economic Growth' in R.R. Ramchandani, eds. *India and Africa.* New Delhi: Radiant Publishers, p. 71.

7 Ramamurthi, T.G. 'India's Relations with Francophone African States' *Africa Quarterly,* vol. 34, no. 1, p. 38.

8 *Ibid,* p. 40.

9 Taliyarkhan. *op. cit.,* p. 71.

10 Ramamurthi. *op. cit.,* p. 38.

11 Ramchandani, R.R. 1995. 'India and Francophone Africa: A Study in Economic and Political Relations'. *Asian Studies,*vol. XIII, no. 1 p. 7..

12 Daleep Singh, 1992. 'India's Economic Relations in the Francophone Africa', in Virinder Grover, eds., *International Relations and Foreign Policy of India,* New Delhi: Deep & Deep Publications, p. 347.

13 *Ibid.*

14 Ramamurthi. *op. cit.,* p. 42.

15 *Burkina Faso for Business.* 2000. Embassy of Burkina Faso: New Delhi, p. 10.

16 Government of India. 1999. *Annual Report, 1998-99.* Ministry of Commerce: New Delhi, pp. 61-62.

17 *Ibid.*

18 Mathews, K. & Veena Sharma. 2001. 'Senegal'. *Africa Quarterly,* vol. 41, no, 4, p. 160

19 *Outlook,* 8 March 2004, New Delhi, p. 53.

20 *Ibid.,* p. 23.

21 Government of India. 1999. *Annual Report, 1998-99.* New Delhi: Ministry of Commerce, p. 5.

22 Government of India. 2001. *Current Status of Various Bilateral Agreements, A Report.* New Delhi: Ministry of External Affairs, Africa Division.

23 *Burkina Faso for Business.* 2000. New Delhi: Embassy of Burkina Faso, p. 10.

24 Government of India. 2001. *Current Status of Various Bilateral Agreements, A Report.* New Delhi: Ministry of External Affairs.

25 *Ibid.*

26 *Hindustan Times.* 2004. New Delhi, Tuesday, March 2.

27 Foreign Policy statement by Shri Yashwant Sinha, 2002. Minister of External Affairs, Government of India. on 18 Nov, at National Defence College, New Delhi.

28 *Hindustan Times.* 2004. New Delhi, Tuesday, March 2.

29 *Times of India.* 2004. New Delhi. Wednesday, March 3.

30 *Times of India.* 2004. New Delhi. Monday, March 1st.

31 Mathews, K. 1997. 'India and Africa in a Changing World' in N. N. Vohra & K. Mathews, ed. *Africa, India & South-South Cooperation.* New Delhi: Har Anand Publications.

32 Government of India. 'Export and Import Policy (2002)'. New Delhi: Ministry of Commerce, pp. 1-70.

33 *Ibid.*

34 Government of India. 1996-97. 'Indian Economic Survey'. New Delhi: Ministry of Commerce, p. 89

35 Singh, Daleep. 2001. 'India's Economic Relations with Francophone Africa 1965-2000: Hope and Scope'. *Africa Quarterly.* vol. 41, no. 4. p. 17.

36 Singh, Daleep. 1990. 'Indo- Francophone African Economic Relations: Retrospect and Prospect' in R. R. Ramchandani. ed. *India-Africa Relations.* New Delhi: Kalinga Publications. vol.1, p. 248.

37 Government of India. 2002. *Focus Africa,* External Affairs Ministry : New Delhi.

38 This was announced by E. Barwa, Joint Secretary, Ministry of External Affairs, at an Assocham Seminar on 17 March 2004, *Times of India,* 18 March 2004.

39 Ramchandani, R.R. 2001. 'India Africa Economic Cooperation in the Context of Changing Global and Regional Relations', in V.S. Sheth, eds., *Globalization and Interdependence: Africa and India.* Mumbai: Allied Publishers Ltd. p. 323.

40 *Ibid.*

41 Economic Trends. 2002. *Africa:, South of Sahara.* London: Europa Publications, p. 14.

42 Mathews, K. 1997. 'A Multi-Faceted Relationship: A Synoptic Views'. *Africa Quarterly,* vol. 37, no. 1-2, p. 2.

43 Singh, Daleep. 1992. 'India's Economic Relations in the Francophone Africa' in Virinder Grover. eds., *International Relations and Foreign Policy of India.* New Delhi: Deep & Deep Publications, p. 343.

44 Singh, Daleep. 2001. 'India's Economic Relations with Francophone Africa 1965-2000: Hope and Scope', *Africa Quarterly.* vol. 41, no. 4, p. 23.

45 Ramchandani, R.R. 2001. 'India Africa Economic Cooperation in the Context of Changing Global and Regional Relations', in V.S. Sheth, eds., *Globalization and Interdependence : Africa and India,* Mumbai: Allied Publishers Ltd. p. 329.

46 *Ibid,* p. 329.

* The ITEC was launched in 1964 to extend bilateral assistance and cooperation to different countries.

47 *Government of India.* 1998. *Annual Report (1997-98).* New Delhi: External Affairs Ministry.

48 *Ibid.*

49 Mathews, K. 1997. 'India's Africa Policy: A Perspective', A paper presented at Seminar on 23 May, 1997 at New Delhi, p. 8.

50 Tripathi, Sudhnshu. 2003. 'NAM and South-South Cooperation'. *World Focus.* No. 279. March 2003, p. 12.

51 *Ibid,* p. 14.

52 Chaturvedi, Arun. 2001. 'Understanding NAM in Post Cold War World' in V.S. Sheth, ed. *Globalization and Interdependence : Africa and India.* Mumbai: Allied Publishers Ltd. p. 366.

53 Matsila, Jerry M. 1998. *UBUNTU,*. vol. 3, no. 3, July-Sept. pp. 3-4.

54 Tripathi, *op. cit.,* p. 12.

55 *Ibid.*

56 *Ibid.*

57 *Burkina Faso for Business,* Embassy of Burkina Faso, New Delhi, 2000. p. 13 *Ivory Coast: Potentials and Prospects for India,* 2002. EEPC Report. New Delhi, p. 94.

58 Singh, Daleep. 1990. 'Indo- Francophone African Economic Relations: Retrospect and Prospect' in R. R. Ramchandani, eds., *India-Africa Relations.* New Delhi: Kalinga Publications. vol. 1, p. 248.

59 EEPC Report, 2002. *Ivory Coast: Potentials and Prospects for India.* New Delhi, p. 94.

60 T.G. Ramamurthi, 'India's Relations with Francophone African States'', *Africa Quarterly,* vol. 34, no. 1, p. 43.

Indo-African Relations: Revitalising ties with North Africa

Jagdish P. Sharma

Introduction

India has offered an ambitious $50 million programme to connect all the 53 nations of the African Union by a satellite fibre optic network. The offer of a 'connectivity mission' for the African Nations was made by the former President, Dr. A.P.J. Abdul Kalam, in his landmark address, the first by a non-African head of state to the second session of the Pan-African Parliament in Johannesburg. After rounding off his four-day visit to Tanzania and Zanzibar, Dr. Kalam was in South Africa for five day leg of his tour to Africa. It was the first visit by an Indian President to South Africa. 'We have prepared for this visit a long, long time and coming at this time, it is a pilgrimage for any Indian leader', said Indian High Commissioner to South Africa Shiv Shankar Mukherjee.

Dr. Kalam's African visit was significant as it took place in the year in which South Africa was celebrating a historic decade of democracy and freedom after shedding the rule by a white minority. The visit was aimed at taking India's Afro-Arab Policy forward. It was a boost to India's Developing World Policy. This is in continuation of our Africa policy. The visit is not ceremonial but a substantial one with huge content", Secretary (West) in the External Affairs Ministry, Shashi Kant Tripathy said. A few months after the President's visit, a novel programme for agricultural development was launched for the African water-deficient crop cultivation, to help African farmers improve their harvests. The agreement was signed by representatives of Andhra Pradesh Government and the Governments of Kenya and Uganda.

The MOUs on information communication and technology and another on a waiver of a loan of Rs.40 Crores were signed during the President's visit to Tanzania. India and Tanzania have decided to set up a task force to identify and implement projects to utilize the $200 million credit the extended by New Delhi. A suggestion to form the task force was mooted by Dr. Kalam during a one-to-one meeting with his Tanzanian counterpart Benjamin William Mkapa. The largest and most politically stable among the East African Troika - with Uganda and Kenya - Tanzania has shared common goals and aspirations with India ever since its late President Julius Nverere bonded with Jawaharlal Nehru and his non-aligned vision. Nyerere was conferred the Jawaharlal Nehru Award for International Understanding in 1974 and the Indira Gandhi peace prize in 1995. Both countries have had regular exchange of visits at the highest levels since the 1950s. Indian dignitaries who have visited Africa include Dr. S. Radhakrishnan in 1956, President Venkataraman in 1989 and Prime Ministers Indira Gandhi, Rajiv Gandhi, I.K. Gujral, and Atal Bihari Vajpayee. President of Ghana, John A. Kufuor and the Tanzanian President Mkapa visited India in 2002, followed by visits of President Thabei Mbeki in 2003 and the Zanibar President in 2004.[1]

These visits underline the importance accorded by India to the development of friendship and socio-political, economic and diplomatic ties with the wider comity of Arab and African nations with many of whom a common bond existed during the independence struggles. India values its close historical ties and traditional cultural affinities with the countries of the region. The trade and cultural links between India and the Afro-Arab region go back to ancient times. For thousands of years, the Indian Ocean has served as a great highway for commercial and cultural interaction between them. The Afro-Arab region continues to occupy a special place in India's post-independence diplomacy and foreign policy. The countries in the region have become a main source for energy imports and amongst the most important trade, investment and joint venture partners for India. One of the main goals of India's foreign policy under Jawaharlal Nehru was to secure for the newly independent Afro-Arab and Asian countries the voice and influence to which they were entitled in the councils of the world. Nehru was critical of all forms of domination and exploitation of one country by another on the ground that it was contrary to the national interest of all states. He held that freedom and world peace were indivisible and elimination of colonialism and imperialism was an essential precondition for the realization of world peace. [2] India is vitally interested in the peace, prosperity and stability of the region. India's core strength of a vibrant democracy, steady economic growth, a large pool of scientific, technical and academic manpower and a diversifies experience in development, provide a functional framework for a sustained partnership with individual Arab and African countries as well as with regional groupings in the continent.

Algeria

A look at the interaction with individual nations gives the following picture.

Algeria is one country in Arab Africa with which India has had cordial relations although Algeria along with Egypt acted as the bastion of revolutionary nationalist movements in Africa.[3] India-Algeria relations date back to the days of the Algerian liberation struggle (1954-1962) when India advocated the cause of Algerian independence at the United Nations and other international fora, following Algerian independence, the ruling party Front de Liberation Nationale (FLN) favoured a radical, socialist ideology and an active foreign policy based on third world solidarity and the creation of a new international economic order. This policy orientation brought India and Algeria closer. India-Algeria relations have been characterized by a convergence of approach on major issues of international concern. Active partnerships within the Non-Aligned Movement and agreement on issues of basic importance to developing countries have been cementing factors over the years in this relationship. The year 2001 witnessed a high point of Indo-Algerian relation. The then Indian President K.R. Narayanan and Algerian President Abdulaziz Bouteflika together called for increased cooperation between the two countries for mutual economic benefit and for restoration of peace in the region torn by conflicts, when the Algerian President made a state visit to India in January 2001. President Bouteflika was the first Arab-African leader to be invited as chief guest to witness the Republic Day Parade.[4]

It has been noticed that there is a strong political will on the part of India and Algeria to grow and develop relations in a holistic manner. Many Indian companies are actively involved in the developmental process in Algeria. Companies like Videocon,

Ispat and ONGC Videsh are already reaping the rewards of their investment in Algeria. A Cyber Park on the lines of the ones set-up by India in Nepal and Mauritius is in offing in Algeria.[5] The 8th session of the Indo-Algerian Joint Commission for economy and trade took place in Delhi from 8-10 October, 2003. The Algerian delegation was led by Minister of Transport Mr. Abdelmalek Sellal. Issues relating to trade, finance, energy, mining, fertilizers, small and medium scale enterprises, railways and shipping, culture and information and consular matters were also discussed. An MOU on cooperation in the field of small and medium enterprises, the Cultural Exchange Programme (CEP) and an agreement between the news agencies of the two counties, viz. PTI and APS, were signed. The third joint Business Council meeting between the two countries business organisations also took place simultaneously.[6] The continuing process towards political pluralism and full democracy, along with Government's efforts to contain violence and terrorism in Algeria were noted with interest and encouragement.

Egypt

The Indo-Egyptian relationship dating back to the dawn of history is sustained by common traditions and struggles, ideals and values. This relationship forged by commercial, cultural and civilisational contacts over centuries[7] is today a major factor in the stability of the fluid political situation of the Afro-Arab and Asian world. Bilateral ties of friendship, mutual understanding and cooperation with Egypt have been strengthened in recent times by building upon the momentum imparted by the Indian Prime Ministers visit to Egypt in October 1995. The meetings between the Indian Prime Minister and President Hosni Mubarak at the G-15 Summit at Harare, and between the Minister of External Affairs and Egypt's Foreign Minister at the U.N. General Assembly in New York, sustained the ongoing high level dialogue. The Grand Sheikh of Al Azhar (Cairo) visited India in October 1996. The visit served to add a new dimension of mutual understating at intellectual, academic and cultural levels. The visit of Minister of State for Planning and Science and Technology to Cairo, to the Middle East and North Africa Economic Conference in November, 1996 afforded opportunities to explore additional measures of cooperation in economic and technology fields. A high level inter-ministerial delegation led by Dr. Hamdy Al Syed, Chairman of the Health Committee for People's Assembly (Parliament) visited India in August 2003. They studied meat exports' facilities throughout the country. A Ministerial delegation led by Dr. Hassan Al Khedr, Minister of Supply and Internal Trade and including Mr. Fayza Abou El-Naga, Minister of State for Foreign Affairs visited New Delhi in October 2003. Talks were held with the Ministry of Consumer Affairs, Food and Public Distribution and other concerned Ministries and agencies with a view to conclude an inter-governmental agreement to enable supply of Indian wheat to Egypt and import of various Egyption Ministry of Foreign Trade, led by First Under Secretary Mr. El-Said Kassem visited India in April, 2003 for the 3rd round of discussions on a Preferential Trade Agreement (PTA) and the Joint Working Group on Bilateral Trade.

Secretary, Small Scale Industries, Mr. S.K. Tuteja visited Cairo in October 2003 with 4-member delegation to review the implementation of the Joint Action Plan concluded between the Egyption Social Fund for development and the Indian Ministry of. Small Scale Industries. The Third Round of Talks on the Preferential Tariff Agreement (PTA) with Egypt, under the auspices of the Indo-Egyption Joint Committee on Trade, was held from 8-10 December, 2003 in Cairo. Indo-Egyptian trade and economic interchanges continued to expand. Similarly, India continues to be one of the major investors in Egypt with investments of about US$ 350 million. In September 2003, the Aditya Birla Group decided to set up a plant for manufacturing acrylic fibre near Alexandria. More Indian investments are in the pipeline. Egypt is a trading partner in Africa and occupies a prime place insofar as India's exports are concerned. India shares with Egypt a common desire for peace, stability and security in the region and for safeguarding the independence, sovereignty and territorial integrity of the Arab African nations.[8]

Libya

Compared to its potential significances and in the context of friendly political relations that India and Libya have developed over the years, economic cooperation and trade between them are still far too limited. Even though there has been pressing realisation on both sides that political amity and cooperation should be strengthened by dynamic and growing trade relations and economic collaboration between the two sides, this has not come about to the necessary extent and on the scale desirable. India's relations with Libya were characterized by efforts to strengthen economic cooperation in recent times. Secretary (North Africa) visited Libya from 20-22 March 2004 and held talks with Foreign Minister Mr. Abderrahman Mohd. Shalgam, Energy and Trade Minister Dr. Fatehi Omar Ben-Shatwan, and a number of senior government officials in Oil, Energy and Foreign Affairs Ministries. Various areas of cooperation were identified during the visit. He also called on Mr. Suleiman Sassi Al-Shahoume, Chairman of Foreign Relations Committee of the Libyan Parliament and Mr. Salem Ben Amer, Special Envoy of President Col. Gaddafi for South Asia. Libya has invited participation from Indian Companies for cooperation in the field of road construction, maintenance and repair of Airports, maintenance of hospitals and management of hotels. During the visit of Libyan Minister of Industry and Minerals Dr. Muftah Azzouzah in November 1997 the two sides identified petroleum, steel and power-generation as new areas of bilateral cooperation.[9] Indo-Libyan economic relations registered progress with BHEL and ONGC Videsh Ltd. Bagging fresh contacts BHEL secured a contract for the US$ 215 million Western Mountain Gas Turbine Power Project in Libya. This was followed by ONGC Videsh Ltd. (OVL) securing oil and gas exploration contract worth US$ 30 million in Libya in collaboration with the Turkish Petroleum Oil Co. (TPOC) in August 2003. In the cultural field, a 12 member Bhangra Group visited Libya from 1-11 April, 2003 in connection with Tripoli International Trade Fair.[10]

Morocco

The Organization of an exclusive 'Indian Trade Expo' in Casablanca, Morocco, in April 1996, was a major initiative to promote bilateral commercial exchanges. Deputy Chairperson of Rajya Sabha Dr. Najma Heptullah visited Morocco on this occasion. The visit of Morocco's External Commerce Minister to India in December 1996 ensured that the momentum of growing bilateral trade would be maintained. Minister of Textiles, Mr. Syed Shahnawaz Hussain visited Morocco on 23-24 June 2003 to inaugurate the Textile Festival in Casablanca. King Mohammed VI paid a private visit to India in October 2003. The Second Indo-Moroccan delegation while the Indian delegation was led by

Secretary, North Africa. Bilateral and regional issues were discussed during the consultations. An MOU for interaction between the two Foreign Service Institutes was signed during the visit.[11] Morocco along with other Arab African countries looks to India as an important leader of the Developing World.

Sudan

In the current context India has also offered humanitarian assistance to the people of Darfur region in Sudan. Sudan is keen that the Darfur refugee problem should not be politicized and exploited to whip up anti-Sudanese sentiments. During my visit to Khartoum recently officials and intellectuals explained to me that the problems of the region were being exploited by interested powers. They wanted to stir trouble for the government with an eye to securing a foothold in the region, which is rich in oil and other mineral resources. Indo-Sudanese relations had never been high profile earlier. But of late the situation has been changing. President Abdul Kalam's October (20-22) 2003 visit to Sudan was a major landmark in the strengthening of Indo-Sudan ties.[12]

President Kalam held talks with the Sudanese President Mr. Omar Hassan Ahmed Al-Bashir and addressed the Sudanese Parliament. He also interacted with academicians and students at the University of Khartoum and held a meeting with the Sudanese alumni of Indian Universities. During the visit of the President to Sudan, the Bilateral Investment Promotion and Protection Agreement (BIPPA), the Double Taxation Avoidance Agreement (DTAA), and the MoU on cooperation in the field of Information Technology were signed.[13] Sudan came out strongly in support of a permanent seat for India in the United Nations Security Council and both sides agreed to closely coordinate positions in the international fora. The two nations shared the view that there was an imperative need for a comprehensive reform of the UN system including an expanded Security Council to make it more representative and responsible to the needs and aspirations of the developing countries.

Following the historic State visit to Sudan by the President in October 2003 there was an upward momentum in bilateral interaction. Several Ministers, in different fields, paid separate visits to India during December 2003. Mr. Al-Jaz, Energy and

Mining Minister visited India from 5-9 December 2003. Similarly, Minister of National Defence Lt. Gen. Bakri Hassan Salih, accompanied by Defence Secretary, DGs for Training and Military Industry and other senior officials visited India from 12-15 December 2003. The transportation Minister, Mohd. Elsamani Elwasile, accompanied by State Minister of Finance, Dr. Hassan Ahmed Taha, visited India from 22-29 December 2003. Sudanese Minister of State for Defence Mr. Ahmed Mohammad Ali led a five-member delegation to the DEFEXPO INDIA 2004 from 3 to 6 February 2004. The above visits indicated appreciation of our sensitivity and interest in Sudan.[14]

Tunisia

India and Tunisia have had contacts with each other since the Pre-independence period. Tunisia has consistently pursued a balanced policy of openness and moderation in its international relations.[15] Delegations were exchanged with Tunisia in several fields, including trade, agriculture, science and technology, and environment. An Indian textiles exhibition was organised in Tunisia in June 2003, which was attended by Textiles Minister, Mr. Syed Shahnawaz Hussain. Tunisian Industry Minister, Moncef ben Abdallah visited India in April and the Minister of State for Foreign Affairs Madame Saida Chtioui visited India for bilateral consultations in October 2003. Minister of State for Information Technology and Internet Mr. Montassar Ouaili visited India from 8 to 14 February 2004. A MoU on Cooperation in Communications and IT was signed during the visit. A new $ 10 million credit provision has been made by EXIM Bank of India to promote investments.

Tunisians have invested in the Godavari Fertilisers and Chemicals Ltd. Bilateral trade between India and Tunisia is now touching US $ 200 million.[16]

Western Sahara

It is sad and surprising that the government of India withdrew the recognition it gave during the Rajiv Gandhi period to the Sahrawi Arab Democratic Republic (SADR). It goes against the spirit of our 55 years of foreign policy of supporting genuine liberation struggles in the Afro-Arab-Asian continent. By de-recognising SADR India has undone its decision to recognise it in 1985.[17] It is attributed to the pressure from Morocco.

Conclusion

When India got independence in 1947 there were only four independent countries in Africa (Ethiopia, Liberia, South Africa and Egypt). By 1957 Libya, Morocco, Sudan, Tunisia and Ghana had gained independence swelling the number of independent nations to nine. Between 1957 and 1966 another 31 countries (17 in 1960 alone) became free. With the independence of Namibia in 1990 and Eritrea in 1993 the number of independent countries in Africa increased to the present 54. The historic dismantling of the brutal system of apartheid in South Africa and the inauguration of the Nelson Mandela government there in May 1994 marked the full liberation of the Afro-Arab world, with the sole exceptions of Palestine and Western Sahara.

India's trade and economic ties and technological collaboration with Arab and African nations have widened to a great extent in recent years. From oil exploration in Sudan and Libya, to defence cooperation with South Africa and supply of Indian wheat to Egypt to collaboration in information technology, health, medicine and agricultural research ties with many countries, it is a wide canvass. All along, India has enjoyed warm relations with the struggling and independent countries of the Afro-Arab region. In the international fora India and the Arab and African states have pledged to keep up the unity displayed by developing countries at the recent World Trade Organisation talks. They have reaffirmed their commitment to promote the formation of an equitable multi-polar world order based on equality of states, principles of rule of law, territorial integrity of both Iraq and Sudan and non-interference in the domestic affairs of states with a view to removing threats to stability and international security. Both feel that the United Nations should be 'equitable' and 'represent a just world order'. They have expressed grave concern over the expansion of international terrorism, religious intolerance, international crime, drugs and arms trafficking. On the West Asian Peace, India and the Arab and African states have reiterated their support to the existence of two states, a Palestinian and Israeli state, living side by side in secure and internationally recognised borders. The traumatic passing away of the father figure of Palestine Liberation Organisation PLO, President Yasser Arafat, has given a new impetus to the international efforts to resolve the Palestinian – Israeli conflict and hasten the liberation of Palestine. Both India and Arab African states have much to offer to each other for their mutual benefit. Conditions must be created to achieve the full potential of the interaction. With efforts and commitments from both sides, our cooperation will be strengthened for mutual benefit and lead to the social-economic development, progress, peace and stability of the people's of India and the Arab and African region. During his African visit Dr. Kalam has offered technical and financial help to meet one of the continents gravest health problems, that is, HIV/Aids. The historic ties of India with this region should logically lead to expanding interaction in economic and political fields in keeping with the rapid changes taking place in the world in various spheres particularly in science, technology and economic cooperation.

Endnotes

1 Sharma, Jagdish P. 2004. 'Kalam's Africa Pilgrimage' *National Herald.* New Delhi. 23 September.

2 Sharma, Jagdish P. 1997. 'Nehru, Nasser and the Afro-Asian People's Movement' in *Nehru and the People's Movement. eds.,* New Delhi: Manak Publishers.

3 Sharma, Jagdish P. 2003. *Foreign Policy Challenges: India and the Afro-Arab World.* New Delhi: Anamika Publishers, p. 30.

4 Sharma, Jagdish P. 2001. 'Great Potential for India-Algeria Trade' in *Algeria- 2001.* New Delhi: Embassy of Algeria, p. 21.

5 Belarbi, Abdelkrim. 2001. Ambassador of Algeria to India and Benchikh Mohamed, Former Councellor, Embassy of Algeria, 2001. 'Algeria–47th National Day' *The Indian Express.* New Delhi, Mumbai, 1 November.

6 *News from Algeria.* 2003. Embassy of the Democratic and People's Republic of Algeria in New Delhi. Issue no. 11, November, p.6.

7 For details see Sharma, Jagdish P. 1995. *Peace Policy of Nations: Egypt, Palestine and India.* New Delhi: Manak Publishers and Sharma, Jagdish. 2003. *Afro-Asia and Contemporary Politics.* New Delhi: Anamika Publishers.

8 *Egypt in Focus.* 2004. New Delhi: Embassy of Egypt. 23 July. pp. 20-29.

9 *Embassy of Libya.* 2004. 'India-Libya Socio Economic Relations' quoted in *Kayadat* .New Delhi.16-30 September, p. 30.

10 Government of India. 2004. '*Annual Report,* 1st January 2003-31 March 2004', Ministry of External Affairs. p.59.

11 *Ibid.* p.59.

12 Quoted in *Press Trust of India.* 2003. Khartoum. October 21.

13 *Ministry of External Affairs, op.cit, p.60.*

14 *Ibid.*

15 *Tunisia Today.* 2004. New Delhi: India -Tunisia Friendship Association, p.12.

16 Government of India, *Annual Report, op.cit,* p. 60.

17 For details see, Sharma, Jagdish P. 2003. *op.cit.*

Indo-African Relations with Special Reference to Sudan

Jaffar Mirghani

Sudan and India show many facets of resemblance. However, until recently, all that one could have, respecting Indo–Sudanese relations are but fragmented comments and isolated case studies by single-handed students of knowledge. Russell (1833), for example, in his book entitled: '*Nubia and Abyssinia*' dwells on the striking resemblance, which (says he) is known to subsist between artefacts of the ancient inhabitants of West India and those of the first settlers of Upper Nile (i.e. Sudan).

Harit Krishna Deb identifies among some names of rulers mentioned in the *Satapatha-Brahmana* (an 8thC. B.C. Vedic work) *Tarksya* with *Tirhaga* the name of a Cushitic (i.e., ancient Sudanese) king. (*Journal of Asiatic Society* of Calcutta; Letters Vol.XIV, 2, 1948).

Suniti Kumar Chatterji, in his monograph: '*India and Ethiopia*' (1968), applies Russell's comparative approach; but, building on Deb's findings, drops in time from the age of *ancient inhabitants* and *early settlers* to the 7th century B.C. Short of sources he abandons Sudan to Abyssinia.

In ancient Greek literature the lands extending from the Atlantic coasts of Africa to India were referred to by the generic name: *Ethiopia.* Strabo (1st.C,B,C) traces the idea back to the 10th century B.C., quoting Homer who in his famous Iliad says:

The Ethiopians utmost of mankind
These eastward situate, those to the West

With Homer's, well echoes the following verse in an old patriotic Sudanese song:

That I love most
From Berno (Nigeria) to India
My beloved Sudan

A very ancient literary romance attributes to Alexander the Great the designation of an ambush tactful plot set for Candace, his foe and contemporaneous queen of Sudan; to discover in the end that he was led all the time by the wily queen's stratagem to his own trap. In this interesting piece of ancient Sudan extant literary works, the author depicts an Indian princess, tied in marital bond to Candace's elder son, who swore to avenge his father-in-law (Poor King, killed at the hands of Alexander).

In the oldest extant Islamic history book entitled *Sera*; (i.e. Biography of the Prophet) Seyf, prince of Yemen, addressing the emperor of Persia, is related to have said: 'We have been conquered by the *Sudan*'. Hearing that the emperor inquired: 'Whom do you mean by *the Sudan*, the Indians or the Abyssinians'? It is interesting to note here that the term (*Sudan*) in Arabic corresponds to (*Ethiopians*) in Greek.

In *Tubdawe*; (a language spoken in eastern Sudan towards the Red sea) the word *Hindi* refers, literary, to green, but green in Sudanese usage refers also to dark complexion.

Meagre comments and scattered finds as coated above may have, uptill cold war end times, served to add some nice flavoured citations to statements addressing bilateral relations. The editors of '*East Africa and the Orient*'; (1973), justifiably state that: 'for too long the civilizations of the lands bordering the Indian Ocean and East Africa involvements with the wider world had been studied from a series of parochial perspectives, and within the traditional categories of particular disciplines. There had been few attempts to relate the concerns of different disciplines to each other or place them in a cross cultural context'.

Today, the whole world arena is restructuring in accordance to globalization, much needed, for better understanding and future well-being, is a sober holistic perspective of past experience in concert with a critical approach to present world affairs. Full coverage of evidential instances, reflecting age long intercourse in continuum, studied from a series of perspectives within diversified domains of concerned disciplines; related to each another and placed in a cross cultural context.

Observing that the cultural and economical aspects of our world have much differed since the European advent of discovery and colonization it is intriguing to phase out, reasonably, our eventful, age long relations into: *Pre-colonial; colonial and postcolonial.* Inclined first to adopt it, I refrained. Important as it is, political history should by no means shadow the most important environ-geographical element of history. Nature rather than events furnish first our socio-cultural makeup. Sudan northern and southern extremities fall under latitudes, which respectively traverse north and south India; a fact indicating climate similarities. Topography and other natural conditions are also comparable. Similar environs must have had conditioned ancient human life, here and there, molding their first inborn cultural choice.

A truth of human social history, mostly ignored is that seas, even oceans, are the oldest and best means of strong contact. Wherever there is a sea, wide or narrow, you are sure to find that peoples occupying the lands bordering its coasts have age old intercourse and even ethnical ties. Thus, as an example, the Mediterranean African coasts were from early times in contact with the Mediterranean European coasts. Phoenician vessels used to traverse it from times immemorial. History tells us it was they who built ancient cities all around its coasts; such as Beirut, Tyr, Cartage, Cordoba, Madrid and Venice. It was they who in the days of the Pharaohs sailed all around the coasts of Africa starting from the delta coasts of the Mediterranean and ending in Red sea.

The widest water basin is the Pacific Ocean; yet it did not severe human societies from contact and ties going back to prehistoric times. Anthropology tells us that the so called Red Indians and the aborigines of Australia have racial relations with the peoples of East and Southeast Asia.

The Indian Ocean is not an exception. Witnessing the fact that the oldest habitats of the human race are to be found scattered over lands surrounding its coasts and those of seas and gulfs linked to it, we may conclude that these are the waters in which humanity in its earliest infancy first learned sailing and sea faring.

Allusion to trade and intercourse handed down from ancient times reveal the necessary steps of advancing civilisation, as William Cooley, justifiably, stated in his treatise: *Claudius Ptolemy and the Nile.* Civilisations interconnected by those water tracks, escalated their shared experience to the level of real learning and enlightenment

Getting aware of development sustainability for every better morrow, planning for economic growth became inevitable. Sea liners of the Indian Ocean and water courses open to it were linked by caravan roots to those of the Mediterranean. The Great Wall of China, as a citadel of security measure, maintained by successive dynasties bear witness that the southerly water route was by far more safe and sustainable at every point of time than the northern land route. Caught in active currents of far distant trade and worldwide transactions lands of warm climates extending from East Asia to West Africa became so intermingled to such a degree of familiarity as depicted in the book of Ibn Batuta Travels. Prehistoric contacts and the ever growing commercial conduct evolved common trends of culture and a profound bond felt between all these nations of warm climates in different phases of their back history.

The natural division of the world into cold North and warm South, hence variety in resources, demand and exchange founded the basis of mercantilism upon which world economy used to depend. It has Influenced now and then, strategic planning, political decisions and military actions.

The idea of North-South division well figures in ancient Greek natural philosophy, physical geography and classical literature. Strabo (1stCent.B.C.) spurs many pages of his work on geography reviewing different opinions of his predecessors over this matter. From the level of physical geography, Greek scholars pursuit their argument; building on grounds of natural philosophy and human social life analysis, an overall division of the habitual quarters of the globe known to them. Eratosthenes, among others, draws meticulously the line of division, which according to him runs straight from the straits of Gibraltar to the ridges of the mountains, which bound the northern extremities of India. Subsequently and naturally enough a generic names were fetched. All nations living south of that line in-between the tropics or on the near reach to them were styled Ethiopians, while those on the North were styled Scythians or Celtics. The Ethiopians occupy most of the habitual earth; the whole of Africa and a vast track of Asia extending from the red sea to India.

In old Arabic literature the notion of a whole integrated Afro-Asian world of warm climates is to be found. In his book titled: *The Glory of the Sudan*, Gahiz, a renowned old Arab writer, who lived twelve centuries ago, entertained the idea of a completely integrated Afro-Asian world of warm climates elaborated on it. Under the generic name (*Sudan*), he counts the Chinese, Indians, Abyssinians, Nubians, Copts, Berbers and all other nations living in-between.

The generic name, *Ethiopia* in Greeks, *Sudan* in Arabic, given to all this Afro-Asian world in-between, or within the near reaches of the tropics, can be, in a modern coinage style, phrased into: *Pan-Sudan, Pan-Ethiopian*, or, even better, *Pan-Tropical.*

Thus, stemming from natural environs at the infrastructural level, the division North-South developed at the super structural level into a universal geopolitical thought. It had always been, as it still is, behind strategic planning, political decisions and defence measures.

Analysis of history reveals recurrence of analogous situations and the authors of (*Thinking in Time: The Uses of History for Decision Makers)* were right when they pointed out that Marshall Plan was an outcome of a habit, he developed of 'seeing time as a stream' rather than seeing every problem in isolation and thus as new and unique. That well perceived, it would help to sketch a master plot around which evolve worldwide human activities and in the light of which socio-economical, political or military strategies can be interpreted.

Responsibility towards their Third World, or better, *Warm South,* collective problems, on the part of the countries gathering in the Afro-Asian conference of Bandung 1955 was not incidental; nor was it stimulated only by a shared fate, or common ground situations created by colonialism, cold war or underdevelopment. It springs from that profound bond which ties up these lands and peoples of warm climates extending from the seas of East Asia to the Atlantic coasts of West Africa. Alienated for long by colonialism, once emancipated, the *Pan-tropical* world re-inspired its age long feelings of natural alignment. Enthusiastically received over the warm *South,* the event aroused a jealous alert criticism in the *West* or *cold North.*

Awakened by the move, which lead to the Bandung event, F.W. Fernau grasps the case. In his: *Moslems* on *the March*(1955) he states: 'The emancipation of the peoples of Asia and Africa seems to be treated as of secondary interest. Only at times of crisis is it given wider attention for the moment. The upheavals in the near and Far East cannot be judged simply with reference to their bearings on the Cold War though that element is obviously important from the stand point of the West. Such one sided consideration would run the risk of obscuring the longer view and confusing temporary expedients with genuine solutions. What is happening among those alien people is a process *Sui generic* of world wide historical importance and not merely incidental to conflict between the Soviet Union and the West. It raises questions that call for at least as much resourcefulness and vigilance as broad and imaginative treatment, as that with the Soviet Union, failing that, this chapter of history might one day call irrevocably for the comment: Too little too late. For the very reason of this intermediate position, may become of critical importance to the future development of the whole world'...

The above coated statement reflects a deep insight on the reality of North-South natural division and its bearings on geopolitics. In referring alternatively to the peoples of Asia and Africa, thence the peoples of Islam, F.W. Fernau is resonating complicity; coupled with his phrase *(intermediate position chosen by the peoples of Islam*) which expresses an act of deliberation? If so; then many crucial thoughts, from a western perspective, can be here inferred.

First, we are met here with quite a seldom, yet very true interpretation of the strategy behind the early Islamic invasions. The strategic goal was to occupy and bring under a unified political domain the whole of this intermediate position between South and North extending with,and falling right south to, the demarcation line of their division as drawn by Eratosthenes and other ancient Greek scholars. Alexander, the Great, endeavoured to bring under his sway an empire of the same extent, over the very same *position*; but, he himself shortly outlived, his generals failed to realize his plan. The Moslems, long after succeeded where the Greeks failed; bringing under the sway of the old Islamic political domain the whole of this divider *path*, whereby all trade roots between North and South had to cross. Occupying ideal positions on the frontiers of this intermediate domain India and Sudan had the best chance to host the most frequented sea ports inroads for transfers and exchanges, getting more in touch the one with the other.

It is of great significance to note that this *intermediate position,* as defined in Fernau's work, is nothing but the *Middle East* of today in its widest geopolitical definition, except that featured here a divider between two, he appropriately substitutes (*intermediate)* for (*Middle).* Was it then that the concept of *Middle East Command* kept lingering in the strategic thought of the East and West since the days of Alexander and Prophet Mohammed?

Related by definition and placement to the South, and serving as its protective frontiers, Alexander's march against this divider path, or any part of it, should have been counted an aggression against the whole South. Herodotus admits this fact where he traced the reason behind the Greeco-Persian wars; and the Sudanese ancient romance coated above alludes to it. On the other side, the composite Islamic power of the past, arising from within and commanding this intermediate path, kept alert vigilance on the North, and developed peaceful strong commercial ties with the vast hinterlands of the South; thus build capacity and confrontation ability. This situation had been attested and checked by the European advent of discovery and Colonisation. The West, having opened the Atlantic Sea route up to India, successfully by passed the siege, managed to colonise one after another the hinder regions of the South, cut trade veins and ultimately, subdue the frontiers.

Overwhelming hot issues imposed by the two opponent super power poles and the haunting threat of nuclear weapons during cold war times, have much blurred our vision and drew away attention from the real seed of the problem. Rivalry over resources and markets of the South and incessant expansion intent remains always the cause behind polarisation in the cold North. In less than a quarter of a century it cost humanity two bloody world wars resulting in a dual polarisation, which left little choice to the once prosperous, consolidated Pan-Tropical world except to try to accommodate itself in a movement with a newly coined name of passive notion, the (*Non-Alignment*). A label which blocked our thoughts and vision to the extent that when the cold war was over the Non-Aligned Movement could do little in its aftermath situations.

Anticlimax the West, or better the cold North, focusing only on its own wellbeing, is unifying and consolidating. NATO is expanding, East Europe is in the process of joining in and even former soviet Russia has been approached. The cycle is set back, and the cold North can see no better remedy to its economy in post cold war situation but to try to exploit once again the warm South; rich in natural resources yet haunted by poverty and torn by fights.

Counting for consequences of Cold War, in my opinion, was actually Third World War (*fought in cold*). Using economy exhaust as its most destructive weapon, one of the two rivalry super power poles, (NATO) won decisive victory over the other; which latter, (Soviet Union and its Warsaw Pact) as a result, had to withdraw its weapons, dissolve its league. Even the very existence and or unity of some of its member countries were checked. What more could have been achieved by direct *hot war*? If it had to have massacres and human victims, a third party, the Non-Aligned, paid for that. During decades of cold war times disastrous hot fight went on all over the Third World, by highly advanced conventional weapons, triggered by (*sometimes directly fought by*) one or the other of the opponent super power poles.

Post Third World War situations are not much unlike those in the aftermath of Second World War. WTO is actually (GATT) update. Prerequisite for sustainable traffic is World Peace and World Justice. Much needed is Worldwide soberly worked out healthy model plan of positive economic diplomacy fitting an era of globalization. Donators should neither use donations to hinder the advancement of developing economic powers, nor help any shape of dominance over the underdeveloped. Donations capped by sanctions and limited mostly to humanitarian aids help very little in any kind of sustainable development.

Post cold war measures, decidedly taken by the victorious campaign, capped by VITO and manipulated majority in the security council rendered the once esteemed forum of multilateral diplomacy almost handicapped in peace making and peace keeping.

African and West Asian countries rarely had a chance to economic independent growth as achieved by South and East Asian countries. On the other hand the latter mentioned could help the former through investment in large schemes of development, which are sure to help building reliable infrastructure; by and by create a situation of a healthy independent economy. The unwise policy of aggression, sanctions and economy squeeze adopted by the mighty powers of the cold North is apt to revive the lost bond. African and Asian nations will see no way out but to rewind the bond. Shall the cold North then welcome fair free competition with Asian growing economic powers in Africa, or resort to a feeling of jealous rivalry?

Indo-Ethiopian Relations: Emerging Trends

K. Mathews

'I do not want my house to be walled in on
all sides and my windows to be stuffed.
I want the cultures of all lands to be
blown about my house as freely as possible.'
(Mahatma Gandhi)

It is in the communion of ideas
that nations express their greatest affinities.
(Nelson Mandela)

Introduction

India's contacts with Africa go back to over two thousand years. This is particularly true of India's contacts with Ethiopia. Ethiopia is the oldest political entity in Africa. It has a recorded history, which stretches back to the biblical times. Ethiopia is mentioned a number of times in the Bible. It is also the only country in Africa, which was never colonized by the Europeans and thus it is a symbol of independence and freedom in Africa. India pioneered independence struggles in Asia and thus symbolizes Asian liberation. India and Ethiopia are two ancient civilizations well known for their glorious histories and cultures. These two countries, though located distantly in the heart of Asia and the Horn of Africa, from time immemorial maintained close commercial and cultural contacts. Despite the divergence in size, population and power, both countries, have much in common. Their economies are complementary. Both are multi-cultural, multi-lingual, multi-ethnic, multi-religious and face identical problems and challenges of nation-building. Both are engaged in the struggle for democracy and development. While India is the largest and older democracy, Ethiopia is in the process of consolidating its democratic institutions and practices since the overthrow of the Derg regime in 1991. With the adoption of the new Constitution of Ethiopia in 1994, the country has adopted a federal and democratic structure like that of India. The main assumption of this paper is that a historical and holistic understanding of the development of relations between these two unique civilizations is essential for the healthy development and strengthening of relations in the future. What is attempted here is to show that there is a proud historical legacy and profound cultural basis on which the diverse bilateral cooperation arrangements could be strengthened and promoted in the years to come. However, before tracing the evolution of these relations, it may be appropriate to provide, by way of setting the stage, a brief background sketch of the two countries.

A land of kings and legends Ethiopia is an ancient state with a new constitution and a new beginning in Africa. The home of 'Lucy', Ethiopia is said to be the cradle of human race. The discovery of the fossil of the earliest hominoid in Hadar, in the afar desert of Ethiopia in 1974, has accorded it an uncontested place in human history. Myth and legend are blended in the history of this ancient land. Its recorded history goes back to more than 1000 years BC. Its thriving civilisation had once reached its apex during the famous Axumite Kingdom (1st to 6th Century AD) and the legendary Queen of Sheba (or Saba) is said to have ruled the country from her domain in Axum. She visited Biblical King Solomon in Jerusalem and got a son named Menelik-I from King Solomon. Christianity was brought to Ethiopia during the 1st century and during the reign of Emperor Ezana, in the fourth century AD became the first country to adopt Christianity as a state religion in the region. Islam, which is the second religion in Ethiopia, was brought during the 7th century AD. The peaceful coexistence of these two religions in Ethiopia is something unique and remarkable. Ethiopians are ardent followers of their religious faiths. Religion is a powerful factor in politics in Ethiopia. The country's historical and cultural relics are the manifestations of the living symbols of its civilisation to the present day. The famous obelisks of Axum, the Rock-Hewn Churches of Lalibela, the Castles of Gondar etc. attest to the fact of Ethiopia's being the nurturing place of civilization in Africa dating back to thousands of years.

The land of legendary King Prester John, of Emperor Menelik-II who soundly defeated the Italians in the historic battle of Adowa in 1896, Ethiopia became the symbol of independent Africa. The international borders of the 20th century Ethiopia were negotiated with the neighbouring colonial powers during Menelik-II's long reign (1889-1913).

The modern Ethiopian state was created in the later half of the 19th century. Ras Tafari Mekonen became ruler as crown prince in 1916 and was enthroned as Emperor Haile Selassie in 1930. He was driven into exile by the invasion of fascist Italy in 1936. Following the country's liberation by Allied forces in 1941, Haile Selassie returned. Eritrea was federated with Ethiopia in 1952. In 1962, Ethiopia annexed the federal Eritrean state, provoking a protracted war. In January 1974, a series of strikes and mutinies in the armed forces led to a *coup d' etat* by army officers. Haile Selassie was ousted from power in September 1974 and the Derg began 17 years of military rule. The military government proclaimed Ethiopia a socialist state. By November 1977, Colonel Mengistu Haile Mariam had established control of the Derg. A coalition dominated by the Tigray People's Liberation Front (TPLF), together with Eritrean forces, defeated Mengistu's army in 1991. Eritrea gained *de facto* independence and a transitional government of Ethiopia was formed under TPLF leader, Meles Zenawi. The constitution of 1994 has symbolized the new reality in Ethiopia. Following a series of elections, the Federal Democratic Republic of Ethiopia (FDRE) was proclaimed in August 1995. Relations between Eritrea and Ethiopia deteriorated and a full-scale war was fought between 1998 and 2000. The second general elections were held in May 2000 and the ruling Ethiopian People's Revolutionary Democratic Front (EPRDF) was returned to power under Meles Zenawi. The next multi-party general elections were held in May 2005.

India, like Ethiopia, is an ancient civilisation with a long and chequered history. More than 4,000 years ago there flourished , in the North-western part of the Indian sub-continent, the Indus Valley Civilization. The classical civilization of India developed from the earlier Vedic civilization, and the Vedic civilization was the creation of the Aryans, a invading race, whose first arrival in the sub-continent is probably dated around 1500 BC. The Indus Valley Civilization flourished roughly at the same time as the Nile

Valley civilization in eastern Africa. India has a long and chequered history and prides of great Emperors and Empresses like Ashoka, Akbar and the Queen of Jhansi. Unlike Ethiopia India was a victim of multiple invasions and conquests starting with the Aryan invasion around 1500 BC, the Turkish and Mughal invasions and was colonized by Great Britain for nearly 200 years from 1757 to 1947. In 1857 India was brought directly under the British rule ending the rule of the East India Company. British rule brought about great changes in India in many fields. A historic struggle for liberation was waged which finally brought independence to India in 1947. For the past 57 years (1947-2004) India has been involved the task of nation building through democracy.

In a world where nations, big and small, are breaking into micro-entities, often with disastrous consequences, India has demonstrated its inherent resilience. This strength comes from its composite culture that has made India a truly vibrant democracy - a country where unity thrives on diversity. India's independence struggle was an epic struggle for democracy, freedom and liberty, not only for her own people, but for the people all over the world suffering from the yoke of colonialism, imperialism and fascist rule. While Ethiopia, as the only country not colonised by the Europeans, symbolised the spirit of independence of Africa, India which pioneered independence of Asia symbolised Asian liberation. India like Ethiopia is a multi-cultural, multi-ethnic and multi-religious country. Religion is central to Indian culture and its practice can be seen in virtually every aspect of life in the country. Hinduism is the dominant faith in India, serving over 80 percent of the population. Ten percent embrace Islam, and five percent are Sikhs or Christians and the reminder are Buddhists, Jains, Bahai, among others. In its quest for modernisation, India has preserved its ancient civilisation and never lost sight of the ideals that gave her strength through countless centuries. There is much that India and Ethiopia can lear from each other. We may now turn to a brief overview of the historical development of Indo-Ethiopian relations.

The Route through History

It is difficult to establish when exactly contacts between India and Ethiopia started. A number of scholars of ancient Indian history has noted that in olden times large numbers of people migrated from the west coast of India in search of new lands and settled in Egypt, Nubia (the Sudan) and Ethiopia. In those days the famous Nile Valley and Indus Valley civilizations interacted with each other. The Nile and the Red Sea provided well known routes to Indian traders and visitors. Commercial and cultural contacts between the two countries, which were facilitated in earlier times by trade winds blowing between Africa and Asia, dates back to thousands of years. The mass migration of the Hamitic people from Asia to Ethiopia is generally believed to have reached its zenith around 3000 B.C. and the Semitic migrations followed 2000 years later, both arriving through the regions of Tigrai and Eritrea. These Hamitic people had a long history of commercial links with the regions on both sides of the Red Sea. It is believed that the arrival of Semitic settlers from Asia to Ethiopia was only the last decisive phase of the long intercourse between the Ethiopian region and the other side of the Red Sea. Many historians have noted that ancient Indians came into direct touch with the Egyptians and Ethiopians through the intermediary of the Iranian rulers and organizers of the great Persian empire from the 6th Century B.C. Some classical historians have pointed out that Ethiopians were originally an Indian race. They also provide ethnological grounds which support the assumption that the ancient Ethiopians are of Indian origin. The physical similarities, both in colour and shape of the body, for instance, between South Indians and Ethiopians, are presented as an additional proof. Well known Afro-American historian William Leo Hansbury, for example has stated: 'Ethiopia in the Middle Ages as well as in ancient times was frequently called India and its inhabitants were often designated as the *Indi* or the *Indians of Africa*.'

Furthermore, these historians have pointed out that it was on record that during the days of Marco Polo, Africa was called 'Greater India' and Ethiopia was 'Middle India'.

There is a mass of evidence, both Indian and Ethiopian, with respect to exchange of commodities between the two countries in ancient times. During the Auxumite Empire (1st to 6th century A.D.) in Ethiopia, Indian traders flocked to the ancient port of Adulis (now called Zula near Massawa) in the eastern part of Ethiopia for trade. The port of Adulis, had become a meeting point for maritime trade and served as an outlet for Axum, itself a main collecting centre for ivory from various regions. The position of

Axum in commerce was further evident in the minting of its own gold, silver and copper coins. The importance of India's trade relations with the Axumite Empire was brought to light by the discovery of 103 Kushana gold coins around 230 A.D. in Axum. The Auxumite period witnessed the expansion and intensification of trade contacts between the two countries and vividly showed that some of the products exported to India from Ethiopia were of a high value. Ethiopia was a great source of gold, ivory, rhinoceros horn and slaves, all of which were in great demand in India at the time. India in turn supplied cotton and silk, pepper and other spices which were equally in great demand in Ethiopia. Indian spices greatly influenced Ethiopian cusine.(It is so even today!) Another important dimension of the Indo-Ethiopian trade relations in the earlier periods was the slave trade. Auxum at that time represented the global commercial significance of Ethiopia and its trade with India was a factor of supreme importance in the evolution of India-Ethiopia relations in the past. The strategic location of Auxum at the heart of series of trade routes made it suitable for international commerce and human settlement.

The existence of flourishing trade and commercial intercourse at the time was further supported by archaeological evidences. These evidences were mainly gold coins used for exchange of commodities between the two countries. These coins were later discovered in several parts of south-west India and northern Ethiopia. The Axumite trade with the East was an on-going affair in ancient times and it traded with India, Ceylon as well as Arabia and Persia. It is an established fact that Indian maritime presence in the Red Sea, had by the 6th century A.D. impressed Axumites sufficiently for Emperor Kaleb to commission nine Indian ships in his retaliatory expedition to South Arabia. That the Indian silk trade, as distinct from traditional cotton, was also highly prized in the region is evident from the records of Byzantine historian, Procopious, who relates how the Roman Emperor Justinian tried to persuade the Ethiopians to directly purchase silk from India and sell it to the Romans in order to break the monopoly of Persians, their enemy. Adulis was destroyed in 710 when Islam spread along the trade routes to the Ethiopian interior. But Indo-Ethiopian economic relations survived the vicissitudes of history. There was continuing import of great variety of Indian textiles, including silks and brocades. Many literary works of the early 14th

century have revealed the deep Ethiopian interest in India. By this time Ibn Battuta, the great Moroccan traveler in Africa and Asia, was also making several references to the presence of 'Habshis' in the slave trade during his visit to India (1333 - 1342).

Slave Trade and Ethiopian Diaspora in India

The flourishing trade relations between India and Ethiopia that began during the ancient period continued in the subsequent centuries with the added dimension of slave trade. According to well known historian, Richard Pankhurst, the coming of Ethiopian and other East African slaves to India a millennium or so later is abundantly documented in various historical records. Western India, from the 13th to the 17th century, witnessed massive forced migration of Ethiopians and other East African slaves. Such slaves were known mainly by three alternative names: 'Habshis', 'Sidis' and 'Kaffirs'. The term Habshi was a corruption of Habbash, the Arabic name for Abyssinia, now Ethiopia. The word Habshi was later used more widely for all Africans. However, most slaves from Africa to India would, for geographical reasons, have originated on the eastern coast of the continent, particularly, Abyssinia. The term 'Sidi' by contrast was a corruption of the Arabic word 'Sayid' or 'master'. The term 'Kaffir' was derived from the Arabic 'Kafir' originally an infidel, or Unbeliever in Islam. The word tended to be used in India for any non-Muslim, and was in many cases applied to African immigrants and their descendants.

'Habshis' (Ethiopian Slaves) are known to have arrived in India as early as the 13th century. Many of them subsequently rose to very high positions. The first prominent 'Habshi' of whom we have record was a slave called Jamal al-Din Yaqut, a royal courtier in the kingdom of Delhi. A handsome and most likable individual, he is reported to have won favour of then reigning sovereign Queen Razzia. This incurred him much jealousy at court, on which account, he was eventually murdered by his rivals. Habshis, it is evident from 14th century records, were then also prominent in several other parts of India. The largest concentration of slaves was apparently found in the north-west, facing Africa, in Gujrat, and immediately to the east, around the Gulf of Cambay. Both areas had long been in close commercial contact, across the Arabian and Red Seas, with Ethiopia and the Horn of Africa. Evidence of an Ethiopian slave presence in the Indian sub-continent is provided by the famous Moroccan traveler Ibn Battuta in the 14th century. These Ethiopian slaves were also used as famous guarantors of safely on the Indian ocean against pirates and idolators. A sizable number of Habshis were also found much further south, at Calicut (now Kozhikode), which also faced the African continent and traded with Ethiopia. Habshis were also reported in the interior of northern India. Ibn Battuta recalls that at Alapur, north of Delhi, the governor was 'the Abyssinian Badr..., a man whose bravery passed into a proverb'. He was 'continually making raids on the infidels alone and single-handed, killing and taking captive, so that his fame spread far and wide and the infidels went in fear of them'. Later in the century a slave called Malik Sarwar, described as a Habshi, was appointed further north as Governor of Jaunpur.

Numerous Habshis and other foreign slaves were likewise politically very prominent in 15th century Bengal, which also enjoyed extensive trade with Ethiopia and other parts of Africa. The then Bengali ruler, Sultan Rukun al-Din (1450-1474), reportedly had no less than 8,000 African slaves, some of whom rose to positions of considerable importance. Such slaves were particularly influential during the ensuing reign of Jalal al-Din Fath Shah (1481-1487). Habshis were in fact so powerful in Bengal that a group of them, conspired to overthrow Jalal al-Din Fath but later killed. Thus from protectors of the dynasty, the Habshis became masters of the kingdom. There are many such stories of protectors becoming masters. The Habshis who had shown themselves so formidable in the bloody struggles of the time, were subsequently banished from Bengal. Many sought refuge further north, in Delhi and Jaunpur, after which they drifted to the Deccan in the south and Gujrat in the west, were many of their number had earlier lived.

The Deccan, in the south-western India, was another area in which the Habshis gained prominence, and, as elsewhere, became involved in many conflicts of the day. At the beginning of the 15th century the local Bahmani ruler, Sultan Firuz (1397-1422), had many Habshi slaves as his personal attendants, as well as his bodyguards and *harem.* Indeed many notable Habshis feature in the Deccan annals of the time. Ethiopian and other African slaves were at this time probably arriving in India in large numbers. Though most Habshis came to India as slaves, their faithfulness, courage, and energy often raised them to positions of high trust in the Bahmani court. So they were exalted to highest employments in the state. Several Habshis became prominent during the ensuing periods. The importance of Habshis of this time is also evident from the fact that a hill outside the capital city of Bidar, where once they had their stronghold—and where many of them were buried–is to this day known as 'Habshi Kot'.

Habshis at this time were also prominent at several points along India's western coast, particularly at the island fort of Janjira, and in the nearby creek of Danda-Rajpuri, where they were almost invariably referred to as Sidis. There are different stories as to how the Sidis established themselves strongly at Janjira. The Sidis remained in effective control of Janjira for the next two hundred years. Further north at Daman, on the coast of Ahmadnagar facing Africa, the governor at the time of the Portuguese occupation in 1530 was a Habshi chief called Sayf al-Mullk Miftah, who had a force of 4,000 fellow Habshis. To the south meanwhile, at Goa, Habshis were also prominent. In 1493, the Bahmani admiral Sidi Yaqut is said to have been sent with a fleet of 20 vessels against the Gujrat fort of Mahim near Bombay, and succeeded in capturing it. Habshis were likewise came to the fore at Calicut, the populaltion of which, according to the modern Indian historian, K.M. Panikkar, continued to include many people from Abyssinia (Ethiopia).

Cambay, to the north-west of the sub-continent, also had considerable Habshi population. Some made their way into the interior, including Mandu, whose sultan, Shah Khalji (1469-1500) reportedly had 500 Abyssinian slave girls dressed in male attire. In the 15th and 16th centuries with the advent of the Red Sea and Gulf of Aden region and the rise of the Muslim state of Adal, in the East of what is now Ethiopia, bordering Gulf of Aden, and the increase in slave raiding in the interiors of Ethiopia resulted in considerable expansion in the slave trade, and in particular to the export of numerous Ethiopian slaves to Arabia, India and elsewhere. It is said that Ethiopian slaves, serving in India as soldiers, were 'strong and valiant to such a degree that there was a proverb throughout India that good soldiers, or *ascaris* or servants must be Abyssinian'. It is said that there were, no less than 5,000 Habshis at Ahmadabad, and 1,500 in Baroda, in 1561-62. When the Mogul Emperor Akbar (1556-1605) subsequently entered Gujrat in 1572, there were likewise, 700 Habshi horsemen on the scene. The best known Habshi of the early 17th century was said to be Malik Ambar (1549 –1626), an 'Abyssinian' slave purchased in Baghdad, who became chief Minister in the shrunken kingdom off Ahmadnagar. He won fame in 1601 by defeating the Mogul forces in south-west Berar. Several other Habshis held important positions later in the century. It is said that there was at least one prominent Habshi named Rahut Jung (died 1796) in the 18th century Hyderabad, in the interior of central India.

Though the influence of the Habshis in India was on the whole declining in the later years, they continued to hold power at the island of Janjira, on the west coast, where they were almost invariably referred to as Sidis. The Sidis played a notable role in the struggle between Emperor Aurengzeb and the Maratha leader Shivji (1674-1680). It is said that no less than three of the principal provinces of Bijapur, were then controlled by Sidis. The Sidis, were said to be at this time rich, and reportedly gained as much from their trade as from a stipend from Aurengzeb. It is said that the Sidis besides possessing many vessels of force, carried on considerable trade. It is said that the Habshi admirals of the Mogul Empire also enjoyed an influence far beyond Janjira. After the advent of the British in Bombay, in 1773, they concluded an offensive and defensive alliance with the Sidis.

Indian trade with Ethiopia and the Gulf of Aden etc. continued to flourish in the 17th century and beyond and was accompanied by many further shipments of slaves. The importance of Habshis in the Indian political affairs diminished subsequently. It is noted that slave exports from Ethiopia and the Horn of Africa in the first two-thirds of the 19th century was by no means inconsiderable. Such exports (which were destined for Arabia, India and other places) were then running at close on ten thousand a year, i.e. almost a hundred thousand per decade, or nearly a million per century. These figures suggest, as far as the Indian sub-continent is concerned, there was a significant influx of slaves from Ethiopia and the Horn of Africa, and that they would have at least partially replenished the ranks of the long-established Habshi population in India. Habshis, or their descendants, continued in various parts of India. Most of the Habshis largely lived a life of near anonymity and scarcely feature in the records of the time. The first marriages of the Habshis, were said to be with natives of India, but later ones were largely among their own families, which preserving their nationality, in time, formed a numerous community, distinct in figure, colour and character from all the other races of Mohammedans in India.

The export of Ethiopian slaves to India, apart from helping to sustain the long standing trade ties between the two countries, provided an opportunity to ancient Ethiopians to contribute significantly to Indian history. They made contributions in many fields particularly architecture and masonery among others. Regarding the Ethiopian architectural influence in India during the medieval period, in particular their ability in designing and construction in general, I.M. Muthanna has noted that the Habshis who were the chiefs of governments, army commanders and politicians, had an interest in the Muslim architecture and they continued to build great structures during the reign of the Bahmini Sultans and the Mughal chiefs in the north. The greatest Habshi construction in India was that of an Abyssinian noble, Sheik Sa'id Al Habshi, Sultan of Ahmadnagar, who got the Sidi Sa'id Mosque built. This Sidi Sa'id Mosque is now a leading tourist attraction in Ahmadabad. The same writer has noted that little is known about this gifted Abyssinian master-mason who created this marvel of stone in perfect workmanship. He was in India originally as a slave and then rose in the service of the Sultan Muzaffar Ali, and later became a big landlord. It is also very much evident that Ethiopian stone masons, craftsmen and architects had a hand in the building of not only this famous Sadi Sa'id Mosque in Ahmadabad but also in the construction of the same kind in other states in India, particularly the Deccan, Gujrat, Khandesh, Oudh and Bengal. Ethiopian war prisoners of Ahmed Grangn (the left-handed), who invaded Ethiopia in the 16th century, were also sent to India as slaves, but later educated to become soldiers, palace guards and traders. The important role Ethiopians played in India in the Medieval times thus continued by their holding different positions of high rank close to Indian rulers. We may now turn to examine the role that Indians played in Ethiopia.

Indian Influence in Ethiopia

It is noted that in Ethiopia, after the defeat of Ahmad Grangn by Emperor Leba Dengel (1506-1546), with the support of Portuguese military, Indian technicians (commoners, builders, blacksmiths, carpenters, masons, shoe-makers and other craftsmen) went to Ethiopia from Goa when Portuguese Missionaries and travelers were shuttling between East Africa and India in the 17th century. It is in record that the contributions of Indians in Ethiopia were significant, especially in the fields of construction etc. To quote the report of the Jesuit Priest Almeida: 'some masons come from India, brought by the patriarch were employed by the Emperor to build a palace of stone and lime, a structure that was wonder in the country.' It is said that the Indians played an innovative role, particularly in the building of bridges and introduction of lime and mortar construction. By the 17th and 18th centuries, trade continued to dominate the relations between the two countries. Ethiopian products, especially gold continued to be exported to India to buy cloths from India. Commercial contacts led to more visible contacts in the field of culture and arts. The impact of Indian influence, according to Richard Pankhurst, can also be seen from the 18th and 19th century Ethiopian Christian arts. In this regard, Pankhurst has stated:

> Contacts with India, in this period seem to have had interesting, though by no means, exclusive, influences on eighteenth and early nineteenth century Ethiopian Christian art.... *The Virgin Mary* is thus occasionally depicted in an unmistakably Indian posture; guardian archangels in the interior of churches are often seen wearing Moghul-type clothes; some manuscript illustrations of buildings seem of Indian inspiration.

There are also many other areas where Indian influence is clearly evident in Ethiopia. This includes all aspects of culture and calls for separate study. I may mention only some aspects here. In 1868 for the first time, Indian soldiers then under the British, came to Ethiopia, under Robert Napier's expedition against Emperor Tewodros of Ethiopia. The expedition at the time had 12,000 troops out of which more than 8,000 were Indian soldiers from Bombay and Punjab Regiments and artillery from Bengal. Later, following the defeat of the Italians by King Menelik in March 1896 at the famous battle of Adowa, the British attempted to win the friendship of the Emperor, by dispatching a Mission. It is interesting to note that this Mission, in addition to British officers, included Indians and an Ethiopian surgeon, Dr. Workneh, who studied in India. He had an important official post in India before he returned to Ethiopia to become later on a personal physician to the Emperor. Towards the end of the 19th century many Indians such as merchants, workers and artisans came to Ethiopia and some settled in the country by establishing business shops and trade firms. It is estimated that by 1909 there were about 150 Indian businessmen in Addis Ababa with established business enterprises. Leading trading houses, with headquarters in Bombay, exported coffee, pulses and wheat to Ethiopia while they imported items such as cotton, rayon, yarns, gunny bags etc. Before Ethiopia was invaded by fascist Italy in 1935, the number of these business firms in Addis Ababa increased to 3,000.

While discussing the role and influence of Indians in Ethiopia, it is also pertinent take note of the Indian response to the Italian invasion of Ethiopia in 1935. When Ethiopia was invaded by fascist Italy, there was vast sympathy and solidarity from the people of India to Ethiopia. Indian nationalist leaders like Jawaharlal Nehru, Mahatma Gandhi etc. vehemently condemned the aggression and gave total political and moral support to Ethiopia. Jawaharlal Nehru declined to accept the invitation extended to him by the fascist leader Benito Mussolini to visit Rome while he was visiting Europe in 1936 because it 'would inevitably have led to all manner of interferences and would be used for fascist Italy propaganda'. Besides, shortly after his return to India, the Indian National Congress, organized a mass demonstration under the Banner of '*Ethiopia Day*' to show India's full solidarity with Ethiopia against Italian atrocities in the country. Mahatma Gandhi, also expressed his deep sympathy to the Ethiopians and revulsion against this barbaric act. The total moral and political support extended to Ethiopia by the wide section of the Indian intelligentsia , including the Press was indeed striking and constant. The late Indian President Dr. S. Radhakrishnan, who was then Professor at Oxford University, added his voice to the moral support Ethiopia enjoyed in India by saying that 'events in Abyssinia constituted a betrayal of moral values'. The famous Indian poet, philosopher and Nobel laureate, Rabindranath Tagore, vividly conveyed in his poetry the friendly sentiments and sympathy that prevailed in India in the following words:

> The savage greed of the civilized stripped naked its unashamed inhumanity. You wept and your cry was smothered, Your forest trails became muddy with tears and blood, while the nailed boots of the robbers left their indelible prints along the history of your indignity.

Evidently the then colonial situation in which India found itself was a major contributing factor to the unanimous solidarity India demonstrated to Ethiopia. Both India and Ethiopia at the time were waging their independence struggle against colonial rule and fascism respectively. In that sense Ethiopia and India were co-sufferers of colonial oppression.

It was during this time of Italian occupation that the Indian troops, for the second time, after almost seven decades, came back to Ethiopia again under the British flag, but for different purpose, that is, to join the Allied Armies to fight against Fascist Italy's occupation forces. During the Second World War it is estimated 5,000 Indian soldiers lost their lives in the decisive battle of Karon alone, where in the famous fortress the Italian forces were entrenched. The Italians surrendered after five years of grim guerilla warfare and the heroic liberation campaign of 1941. The short lived Italian African Empire (including parts of Somalia) collapsed. Following the ignominious defeat of fascist Italy and the re-entry of Emperor Haile Selassie into Ethiopia, the Ethiopian Emperor on several occasions expressed gratitude to Indian troops who along with the Ethiopian patriots fought hard against the aggression. India also supported Emperor Haile Selassie's measures in integrating Eritrea with Ethiopia in a federal arrangement.

Post-Independence Scenario

When India achieved independence in 1947, it sent a goodwill Mission to Ethiopia led by Sardar Sant Singh who became India's first Ambassador in 1950, Ethiopia established diplomatic relations with India at the legation level earlier in July 1948. Both the countries maintained close and cordial relations during the long reign of Emperor Hailse Selassie and afterwards. The Emperor himself visited India twice - in 1956 and 1968. Indian President V.V. Giri visited Ethiopia in 1973. Even after the 1974 Revolution in Ethiopia, India was perhaps one of the few countries with which its relations were never hostile, unlike with most of the Western, Arab or even other Asian countries. President Mengistu Haile Mariam visited India in 1983 (NAM Summit) and in 1985. The current Ethiopian Prime Minister Meles Zenawi visited India in 1997. There were many other exchanges of high level delegations between the two countries. It may also be noted that India and Ethiopia hold identical views on international issues and on issues of concern to developing countries. Both support each other within the United Nations (UN), Non-Aligned Movement (NAM), etc. on policies and postures on disarmament, North-South dialogue,

South-South Cooperation, the Indian Ocean and numerous other issues. India's sympathetic attitude towards problems of liberation and economic development of African nations and its sensitivities to their needs are viewed by Ethiopia with much appreciation. Ethiopia considered India's experience in grappling with the problems of economic reconstruction after independence as more relevant and modeled its development and institutions after India's. Ethiopia learned from India's experience and expertise in many areas particularly, sugar technology, textiles, small-scale industries, engineering industries, agriculture, water resources management and the like.

India has also been providing modest economic and technical assistance to Ethiopia. Such assistance has mainly been in the form of training facilities and scholarship to Ethiopian nationals in academic and technical institutions, deputation of Indian experts, donations of food grains, medicines and handlooms, agricultural equipment, books and publications, and the conduct of techno-economic and feasibility studies. This continued from 1965 under India's Technical and Economic Cooperation Programme, known by its acronym, ITEC Programme. After the visit of the then Ethiopian President Mengistu Haile Mariam to India in December 1985, assistance under this Programme was expanded considerably. India also has cooperation arrangements with Ethiopia in the field of defence since the early 1960s, when it set up a Military Academy at Harar for training officers. The Harar Military Academy which was originally designed and established by the British was later run by the Indian Army Officers delegated by the Indian Military Academy, Khadakhvasla, near Pune, India.

Trade and Bilateral Cooperation

Since 1991 with the coming to power of the new EPRDF regime in Ethiopia and liberalisation of both the Indian and the Ethiopian economies, political and business ties between the two countries have grown significantly. After liberalization, the Indian economy is now on the verge of sustained increase in domestic demand due to rising per capita GDP and the increasing globalisation of India's capital markets. These, coupled with the availability of low-cost, high quality man-power, offer attractive opportunities for business in India. India is one of the largest emerging market economies in the world, with a GDP of over US$ 2.9 trillion. Its improved macro-economics, trade and investment friendly initiatives, and low-cost, high-quality manpower base offer significant opportunities for business. Ethiopia also has introduced rapid political and economic changes and reforms since 1991. From 1974 to 1991, the Ethiopian economy was run on the basis of a Central Command System. After the collapse of the Derg regime in 1991, the Government of Ethiopia endeavoured to steer the economy from the central command system to a decentralised market oriented economy, by adopting a new economic policy both at the macro and the sectoral levels. Ethiopia has been receiving considerable financial and technical assistance from multilateral and bilateral donors. Indo-Ethiopian economic cooperation has also intensified. A new Trade Agreement between India and Ethiopia was signed on 6 March 1997 at New Delhi during the visit of the Ethiopian Prime Minister Melez Zenawi to India. Among others, a Joint Trade Committee (JTC) was constituted which held a number of fruitful meetings subsequently. The volume of trade, though small, has grown gradually and in 2001- 2002 has crossed the US$100 million mark with exports from India valued at US$ 90.4 million and imports from Ethiopia at US$ 18.4 million. Bilateral trade stood at mere US$ 12.9 million a decade earlier, in 1992-93. India is Ethiopia's sixth largest trading partner for merchandise exports. The main items of exports from India are Iron & Steel (approx 50 percent), manufactures of metals, drugs and pharmaceuticals, machinery and instruments, paper/wood products, yarn and textile fabrics, auto parts, plastic and linoleum products and food items among others. The main items of export from Ethiopia to India are pulses (41 percent), raw hides and skins, raw cotton and leather. Raw cotton and pulses are the new items of exports to India. We notice that India's trade with Ethiopia has virtually been a one sided affair with the balance of trade heavily in India's favour. I am told more recently (2002-03) there has been a decline in India's exports to Ethiopia on account of increase in price of steel in the international market which is the major Ethiopian import item from India, a general gloomy market sentiment in the country due to severe drought, low purchasing power and penetration of cheap Chinese goods into the Ethiopian market.

However, there is vast potentialities of expansion of bilateral trade. There are many areas in which new and mutually beneficial initiatives can be taken. The development of small-scale industries is one of Ethiopia's thrust areas and a major part of the purchase is left to private entrepreneurs. Ethiopia has also introduced a New Investment Code in July 2003. The private sector is encouraged to invest in most areas of the economy. Even those economic areas reserved for the governments, namely defence industries, hydropower generation, telecommunications are now open to private domestic and foreign investors. A foreign investor may team up with a domestic investor for a joint investment. This offers India vast new opportunites. On account of a number of recent trade and investment liberalization measures initiated in Ethiopia, the latter now provides many opportunities for increased Indian exports. It should be stressed that Indian products do not suffer from any discriminatory barriers whether tariffs or non-tariffs. There has also not been any case of countervailing duties imposed on Indian goods as anti-dumping measures.

There is great scope for enhanced trade and bilateral cooperation between India and Ethiopia in such areas as agro-based industries, leather and leather-products, knowledge-based industries including pharmaceuticals and drugs, information technology etc. Other areas having potential are iron and steel, engineering goods and machinery, textiles and yarns, plastic and paper products etc. Potential areas of India-Ethiopia joint ventures are garment industry, mineral and mining, tourism, machinery for light industry, foundry shops, processing of oil seeds, commercial farming, processing and packaging of coffee, assembly of tractors, among others. There are also ample scope for cooperation in the production of solar energy and supply of solar equipments. It is pertinent to mention here that 28 Indian enterprises have received investment permits in Ethiopia in the past decade (1992-2003) as per the information provided by the Ethiopina Investment Authority.

In 2002, the Government of India launched a new 'Focus Africa' Programme with a focus initially on seven countries of Sub-Saharan Africa, namely, South Africa, Nigeria, Mauritius, Tanzania, Kenya, Ghana and Ethiopia. This has been subsequently expanded to include all other sub-Saharan African countries. Under this programme, the government of India extends assistance to exporters, Export Promotion Councils etc. to visit these countries, organize trade fairs and invite African trade delegations to visit

India. The initiatives taken under this programme have received an encouraging response from the Indian exporting community. It is likely to further boost bilateral trade in the coming years, including trade between India and Ethiopia. It is however, important to point out here that the quantum of trade between the two countries still remains much to be desired. India's share in Ethiopia's global imports except in iron and steel remains largely insignificant. A glance at figures relating to India's imports from Ethiopia and her exports to Ethiopia provide a dismal picture. Between 2002-2003 there was steep decline in India's imports from Ethiopia (- 43.14 per cent). Similarly, there has been considerable decline in India's exports to Ethiopia (-33.40 per cent) (Figures from GOI, Ministry of Commerce and Industry.) It is worth examining how this situation can be reversed.

However, there has been increasing cultural interaction between the two countries in recent years. These included the visit of an Ethiopian Folk Dance troupe to India in 2001, the exhibition of Indian contemporary paintings in Addis Ababa in June 2002, the Indian Film Festival in Addis Ababa in March 2003 and the tour of the Cultural Troupe from Rajasthan, India to Ethiopia in November 2003. The presence of a strong Indian community in Ethiopia, particularly in Addis Ababa, possibly the largest foreign resident community in the country, is yet another indication of the strength of growing Indo-Ethiopian cultural relations. They numbered more than 9,000 at one point of time. The number reduced during the communist Derg regime and they numbered over 3,000 at the end of the 1980s, made up mostly of businessmen, and teachers. The number of professionals and technical personnel has been steadily on the increase in recent years. In 2003 alone the Ministry of Education, Government of Ethiopia, recruited about 250 Indians for teaching at the University of Addis Ababa and other Universities in Ethiopia (the author being one of them). There are also a couple of Schools run by the Indian community in Addis Ababa. The Mahatma Gandhi Hospital in Addis Ababa, was equipped and commissioned by the government of India and the Indian community.

Emerging Trends and Prospects

India and Africa, particularly India and Ethiopia, share much in common in terms of history, culture, socio-economic characteristics and common political aspirations. If we look towards the past, it becomes evident that India and Africa have been part of a common struggle for freedom. Today, it is significant that Africa and particularly Ethiopia is changing. A new Africa and a new Ethiopia is coming into being. The new millennium could well see a new resurgent Africa and Ethiopia. It is clear that existing relations between India and African countries, particularly in the economic field, do not reflect the full potential. This is particularly true of India-Ethiopia relations. It should be stressed that the economies of India and many African countries, particularly Ethiopia, are quite complementary and, therefore, they stand to benefit from increased trade and greater economic cooperation in a variety of fields. Thanks to the success of the Indian economy over the past decade and a gradual process of economic reform in the world's most populous democracy, firms from the sub-continent are setting up ventures in Africa in various sectors. Textile is an obvious preference. It may be noted that the first ever Indo-African joint venture was in the textile sector. The Birlas set up the first Indo-Ethiopian Textile Mill near Addis Ababa in the late 1950s. The IT sector is another prospective area. Drugs and AIDs treatment is another possible area where Indo-Ethiopian economic cooperation can be of great relevance. Joint ventures may be the best option from a tariffs point of view. For Ethiopia, like most other African countries, industrialization and modernization is the path ahead and not perpetuating the raw material economy.

Africa has also been promoted as an attractive investment destination by the Export-Import Bank of India (EXIM bank) Since 1999, the EXIM bank has cooperated closely with the African Development Bank (ADB) on projects in Africa aimed at promoting the growth of medium and small scale enterprises and encouraging investment in Africa by Indian firms. This has much relevance to Ethiopia. The increasing interest of Indian firms in selling to African markets and in setting up factories on the continent marks an important step in the maturity of global economy. Unlike in the past, the arrival of large scale south-south trade is an encouraging sign. In that sense, at long last Africa may be seeing some benefits from globalization. The consolidation and strengthening of India-Ethiopia economic linkages can go a long way to usher in a new era of meaningful South-South Cooperation.

Conclusion

In conclusion, it may be said that traditionally, relations between India and African countries, particularly Ethiopia, have remained close and cordial. Over the years Indo-Ethiopian relations have grown steadily. The civilizational and cultural influences of both the countries have gone beyond their frontiers and have produced a lasting impact on their relations. Their ancient merchants, through trade and commercial intercourse, and masons and craftsmen carried with them elements of their art, architecture and paintings, which are still evident today in both countries. They can learn a great deal from each other beyond trade and commerce. As Nelson Mandela has rightly said, '*it is in the communion of ideas that nations express their greatest affinities.*' The sharing of knowledge, ideas and values is the noblest way to transcend national barriers. In sum, it may be said that the prospects for further strengthening Indo-African and particularly Indo-Ethiopian relations in the future appear brighter.

Endnotes

1 Endeshaw, Assafa. 2002. *Ethiopia: Perspectives for Change and Renewal.* Singapore: Senglee Press.

2 Basham, A.L. eds. 1975. *A Cultural History of India.* New Delhi: Oxford University Press.

3 Zewde, Baharu. 2002. *A History of Modern Ethiopia, 1855-1991,* (2nd Edn.). Oxford: James Curry.

4 Barker, A.J. 1968. *The Civilizing Mission: The Italo-Ethiopian War,* New York: Dial Press.

5 *Embassy of India.* 2003. *India and Ethiopia.* Addis Ababa, October.

6 Nahum, Fasil. 1997. *Constitution for a Nation of Nations.* New Jersey, Asmara: The Red Sea Press.

7 Muthanna, I..M. 1995. *Indo-Ethiopian Relations for Centuries.* Vancouver: James Waix.

8 Harris, Joseph E. eds. 1974. *Pillars of African History,* Washington D.C.: Howard University Press.

9 Negash, Kebret. 2001. 'Ethiopia-India relations: A Historical Perspective', *Africa Quarterly,* vol. 41, no. 3.

10 Abraham, Kinfe. 2001.*Ethiopia: From Empire to Federation,* Uppsala: NINA Press.

11 Markakis, John. 1974. *Ethiopia: Anatomy of a Traditional Polity,* London: Oxford Press.

12 Mathews, K. 2001. 'Ethiopia: A Country Profile', *Africa Quarterly,* vol. 41, no.3

13 Gudina, Merera. 2003. *Ethiopia: Competing Ethnic Nationalisms and the Quest for Democracy* 1960-2000, Addis Ababa: Chamber Printing Press.

14 Ottaway, Mariana. 1990. *The Political Economy of Ethiopia,* New York: Praeger.

15 Roy Choudhuri, P.C. and Dutta, K. K. 1956. *An Advanced History of India,* London: Macmillan and Co.

16 Pankhurst, Richard. 2002. 'Ethiopian Diaspora in India', in Richard Pankhurst ed. *African Diaspora in the Indian Ocean,* Prenton N.J: Africa World Press.

17 Pankhurst, Richard. 1990. *A Social History of Ethiopia.* Addis Ababa: The Red Sea Press.

18 Pankhurst, Silvia. 1955. *Ethiopia: A Cultural History,* London: Lalibela House.

19 Ali, Shanti Sadiq. 1980. *India and Africa Through Ages.* New Delhi: National Book Trust of India.

20 Chatterjee, Suniti Kumar. 1968. *India and Ethiopia from the Seventh Century B.C.* Calcutta: Asiatic Society.

Restructuring Development Identities in a Globalised World: Zambia-Indo Relations in Science and Agriculture

Euston K. Chiputa

Introduction

Although there are both positive and negative sides to the globalization phenomenon, the negative effects of globalization can be quite intense among developing countries like Zambia and India. Anwar Tilak argues that 'while globalization is viewed as a key for higher growth and poverty reduction, it is also argued that it reduces growth rate, increases poverty and threatens employment in developing countries'.[1] Developing nations have to respond appropriately to the many challenges posed by the effects of the globalized economic landscape. This can be done particularly through economic bonds amongst themselves. The points of emphasis should shift more to sharing skills and experiences and investment opportunities. Zambia and India stand to benefit more if they exploit the benefits that lie untapped in these fields because the fruits of science and particularly the use of science in agriculture are only limited by limited ability to exploit them to the benefit of mankind. The poverty of nations is basically due to lack of resources or the willingness and ability to utilize such resources.[2]

This paper presents an attempt to reconstruct the transition of the Zambia-Indo relations in the related fields of science and agriculture. Science and agriculture are cardinal ingredients in national reconstruction and overall national development. India stands out as a developed among developing countries in the fields of science and technology, and in agriculture. Post-colonial India's outstanding ability to transcend the vagaries of famines and starvation prevalent in colonial India, and her overall ability to rise above most developing countries in the fields of science and technology and agriculture are cardinal experiences that ought to be engaged to see how other nations can traverse similar roadmaps and achieve similar scores. The Zambia-Indo relationship stands to gain greatly from such bilateral collaboration.

Restructuring Links among Developing Countries: A Historical Overview: Trans-national technology transfer mechanisms were seen to exist only from developed Northern hemisphere countries to the Southern hemisphere ones. Even the mindsets of the peoples of the Southern hemisphere were for a long time tuned to that effect. In the recent past this has come to be challenged as an erroneous and anti-development perception. The negative effects of the global world system to stifle the south-south cooperation, which had succeeded in the past, are no longer able to hold complete sway on the developing countries' vision on science and agriculture and other fields. A number of factors in the recent past have led to this changed scenario. The fact of the failed policies of both the multilateral Breton Woods Institutions of the International Monetary Fund (IMF) and the World Bank (WB) have had quite negative feelings among developing countries that borrowed from and have been struggling to repay loans to these institutions. The failure to repay and the consequent inability to borrow to finance development agendas have together tended to *inspire* these countries into looking for alternative development paradigms. One of the emerging paradigms has been the need for developing countries to overcome the arrogance[3] of these institutions by looking to fellow developing countries for *economic solace* in terms of changed perceptions about loans from the Breton Woods Institutions as well as those borrowed on bilateral terms from developed countries. Moreover, it has been established that:

> Contrary to popular belief, very little external assistance has actually gone to Africa and what little does go is not used effectively. The donors are very good at magnifying their contributions.[4]

The emergence of developed/developing countries has also boosted not only the ability of the developed/developing countries to assist the struggling counterpart countries, but it has raised a realisation in the less developed countries that development can be had without necessarily traversing the path long travelled by the developed Northern hemisphere countries. It also seems to have begun to raise the confidence among developing countries that overall human development can actually be achieved by sharing skills and experiences amongst developing countries.

Further, resource development in the West-dependent mono-commodity economies promoted only those commodities favoured by and useful to the West. Science and agriculture were thus skewed towards the realisation of these desires. The resulting lopsided economic *development* was more beneficial to the West than to being mutual, as should all such economic relations. It left the developing world without any economic partners within the developing world; whatever existed had to be via the West. There is a realisation that in the present globalized world economic arena there is need to find economic partners especially among fellow developing countries without cocoons like those that encapsulate the West and barricade them from mutual economic relationships. The World Trade Organisation (WTO)'s protectionism of the West and the double standards on products of developing countries is a pointer in this direction. This was yet another eye-opener to the developing countries about the need for economic relationships amongst themselves. The Zambia-Indo economic relationship is one such product of this realisation. Although this does not entail a supplanting of the relations with the West, it does amount to a rediscovering, but on a higher scale, of the early thinking about South-South relations in the economic sphere.

Background to the Zambia-Indo Relations

The *Periplus of the Erythrean Sea,* one of the earliest books to have been written about trade across the Red Sea talks about the trading activities of the Arabian, Indian and the East African coastal peoples. It is recorded that:

> The Hindus became the dominant commercial nation of the Indian Ocean long before the great development of Arabian sea power, and later shared the trade of the East African coast with the merchants of Oman and Yemen.[5]

It is also noted that the Hindus from the kingdom of Kalinga in Orissa must have traded with the East coast of Africa. This is concluded from the inscriptions of a giraffe, domiciled only in Africa, being presented to the king of Kalinga. The thirteenth century inscription is a reflection of trade contacts between India and Africa having flourished long before Zambia and India were both colonised by the British. Benudhar Patra contends that:

> The representation of a giraffe, purely an African animal, not seen anywhere else, in the sculpture of the Konark temple only proves that Kalinga had commercial relations with Africa... (It) suggests that in ancient days either some people of Kalinga might have gone to Africa and seen the giraffe or one live giraffe must have been brought to Orissa by some merchants...[6]

The Indian traders had mastered the Monsoon winds and known how to utilise them for trade purposes. The Indian trade goods mentioned in the p*eriplus of the Erythrean Sea,* and the iconographic evidence presented by Patra together show that the East African coast was a trade destination for Indian merchants long before the Arabs, and later the Portuguese and the British ventured there. The Indians, like other Indian Ocean traders to the East African coast, used their geographical knowledge of the seasonal direction of the Monsoon winds to travel to and from the East Coast of Africa. The existence of a large Indian Diaspora on the Eastern coast of Africa was partly a consequence of this and, especially later, the British government's use of Indians as indentured labour.[7] The British later encouraged many of the indentured labourers to migrate further into the hinterland as traders. Many found their way into the then British interior colonial territory of Northern Rhodesia. Asian peoples of Indian origin had begun to arrive in colonial Zambia as early as the first decade of the twentieth century through East Africa. These were the first Indian traders to reach Zambia, shortly after the British had annexed the region. These traders were brought by the British to provide trade services in the various administrative stations that the British were setting up in the North Eastern Rhodesian territory particularly after the First World War. By the time the Second World War broke out many Indians had set up shop in the Eastern part of the territory. From there many spread out to other parts of colonial Zambia basically as retail and wholesale traders. Others had established themselves in Livingstone, colonial Zambia's first capital city before the capital was moved to Lusaka in 1935. Therefore, the Zambia-Indo relationship is now more than a century old. Today the Indian Diaspora in Zambia forms the majority of the Asian population that forms about 0.2 per cent of the national population.[8]

Prior to the decolonisation and consequent independence of Zambia the Second World War had provided the first opportunity for Zambians to visit the Indian part of the Asian continent. Colonial troops had been drafted to Myanmar (Burma) to fight the Germans and Japanese, and India, especially North-eastern states, was the obvious passage route and rearguard zone to the troops fighting in Burma. To this day names like Kohima, Chindwin, Arakan, and Burma are common among Zambian institutions and roads. These are reminders of the Zambians who fought side by side with Indians and other colonial peoples to maintain the status quo of the British Empire in Asia. That was the first contact Zambians physically made with the Indian subcontinent.

Although the local Indian community in Zambia did not seem to offer much overt help to the decolonisation campaign, the Indian government led the former colonial states in rendering material, morale and training support to the independence movement of Zambia. Zambia's first President Kenneth Kaunda drew great inspiration from the Indian National Congress party and especially from Jawaharlal Nehru and Mahatma Gandhi. Kaunda's admiration for both Nehru and Gandhi was always openly stated. The fact of both Kaunda and Nehru having had profound influence from the Fabians of Britain was one factor that endeared Kaunda to Nehru for whom the former had profound respect. Mahatma Gandhi greatly inspired Zambia's freedom movement as regards his *non-violence* campaign in the fight for decolonization. Kaunda equally admired Gandhiji's simplicity of life and respect for the dignity of the human person.[9] India provided skills training facilities for would-be leaders in various countries. Zambia benefited through scholarships, even before Zambia's independence, to such people as Simon Mwansa Kapwepwe, Nalumino Mundia, Munukayumbwa Sipalo and later Daniel Lisulo and many others studied in India.[10]

On the other hand Africa's contribution to the Indian decolonization struggle came by way of the inhuman treatment that Mahatma Gandhi suffered as a young lawyer in South Africa at the hands of the racist white minority government. This provided the impetus for Gandhi's philosophical and spiritual transformation. It aided the non-violent freedom crusade that the

Indian people carried out against British colonial rule. Zambia's support for India's quest for a seat at the United Nations Security Council has never wavered since Zambia's independence despite the change of governments and presidents over the years.

Why Zambia-Indo Relations?

Admitting the inadequacy of manpower in Zambia at independence in 1964, the *Transitional Development Plan (January 1965-June 1966)* stated that:

> Of the 1800 personnel needed to fill the vacant government positions, many of the posts are for professional and technical men—architects, engineers, statisticians, geologists, economists, surveyors, agricultural specialists, veterinary officers, graduate teachers, mine inspectors, biologists, doctors, pharmacists—to mention but a few... In addition there would be heavy demands outside the civil service, for graduates in teaching service, technicians, qualified artisans, foremen and master builders in private firms of the construction sector.[11]

The scenario depicted above arose because at independence in 1964 Zambia had only 1200 Africans with a Cambridge School Certificate, a figure obtained in Kenya back in 1957, Uganda in 1955, Tanzania in 1960 and Ghana in 1943, while barely 100 of the population were University graduates.[12] Therefore, reliance on expatriate labour became inescapable. The *First National Development Plan* reported that:

> The absence of managerial and technical personnel in all fields necessitates a heavy reliance, at least for some time, on expatriate skills... The use of a large number of expatriates may be the only alternative, but it is also the most costly manner of developing a poor country.[13]

Therefore, expatriate personnel were sought in all fields from such countries as Egypt, India, Pakistan, Czechoslovakia, Sweden, Yugoslavia, Japan, Denmark, Israel, Norway, Ireland and Finland. The fact that India was one of the first countries to respond, together with Egypt and Pakistan, in the first instance points to the eagerness that the Indian government had in contributing to the post-colonial development efforts of Zambia.[14] The need to recruit expatriate labour, especially in the fields of education, science and technology, agriculture and medicine was boosted by

India's ability to supply the necessary expertise. Therefore, at the height of President Kaunda's rule 'about 6000 expatriates worked in Zambia and Zambia became the biggest recipient of Indian Technical and Economic Cooperation (ITEC) assistance'.[15]

To understand how Zambia and India can optimise mutual benefit from their relations in science and agriculture, it is salient to cast into the picture some outstanding aspects of Zambia's underdevelopment and poverty so as to see how her maginalisation can be overcome. In the Foreword to Raj Sharma's book *The Missing Middle in Sub-Saharan Africa: Role of South-South Cooperation,* V.R Panchamukhi states that:

> Mounting debt burden, continued dependency on external resources, growing inequities in the distribution of income and wealth, structural distortions due to backwardness of agriculture and lopsided industrialisation coupled with highly inadequate human resources development have added to the maladies of the African crisis.[16]

In spite of Panchamukhi's reference to the Sub-Saharan African situation in general, it does quite neatly fit the Zambian situation. Zambia's economy does suffer from the described economic maladies. In fact what Raj Sharma calls Africa's 'Missing Middle', that is, the 'dash' for modernisation via copied but not adapted Western technology does fit Zambia into this mould. Even though Zambia suffers from inadequate financial capital it has abundance of labour, but lacks managerial capacity and technical expertise to design and maintain sophisticated equipment.[17] Moreover, spares, no matter how trivial, have had to be imported from the parent company that manufactured the respective machinery or equipment. This is because Zambia has not been able to produce her own intermediate appropriate technology. This lack of entrepreneurship in micro- and medium term technologies between simple traditional implements and sophisticated modern machinery is a cause for much of Zambia's underdevelopment. The Zambian economy has been too dependent on a mono-primary commodity export base with copper as the main source of the country's foreign exchange. When copper prices shrank on the international market from 1975, Zambia's economic fortunes slumped with them.[18] This is in contrast with Asia's, and particularly India's reliance on small-scale or cottage produced hand-held tools, especially for rural use. In Zambia the investment and operating costs are prohibitive and the end products are even more costly. This in turn pushes the majority of the population into deeper realms of poverty instead of getting them out.

Further, the use of inappropriate technology directly contributes to the creation of an abundance of unemployment and underemployment in Zambia. This is partly, as Pranab Mukherjee states, because:

> Development models borrowed from the industrialised countries are inadequate to effectively address our specific needs and have only increased our dependence on foreign aid and technology... The dependence syndrome has complicated the task of nation building.[19]

The use of appropriate technology protects the local economy from too much reliance on foreign investments in which most production and service industries are bound to pander to the dictates of such investors, especially multinationals which have the ability even to strangle the local economies if their demands are not met sufficiently. Appropriate technology helps propel the economy beyond reliance on primary exports production. Yet, as Utsa Patnaik puts it:

> When the exports are from the primary sector, then it is possible to have an export-led worsening of welfare for large segments of a developing country's population and indeed (this) has been taking place in a number of developing countries since the eighties.[20]

However, heavy reliance on foreign investment is a consequence of low levels of domestic savings, which in turn, in Zambia's case, has been fuelled by Government's over borrowing in the domestic financial market. The resultant high interest rates crowd out the small investor from borrowing. The end result is perpetuation of inadequate domestic savings, under-investment by the indigenous investors and consequent unemployment and underemployment. This in turn creates a spiral of problems that feed on one another and thus sustain the poverty cycle. Hans-Otto Sano says that 'since the copper prices started to slump in 1975, a growing level of unemployment has characterised the Zambian Copperbelt towns and Lusaka'.[21] There then develops limited, if any at all, domestic inter-sector linkages. This induces other externally determined linkages between local extractive industries and foreign manufactures.

The outcome of the imbalances discussed above is lack of mastery of both the technological innovations and the resources needed to generate human development that is able to sustain itself. Zambia's liberalised economic structure in post-1991 reveals a paucity of support to small-scale producers. Instead the state went heels-over-head in pampering foreign investors with all sorts of *tax holidays*.[22] The results of the pampering have been very disastrous, as many companies quit after the tax holidays came to an end. However, for the local producer policy changes became even more stringent and therefore unfriendly. The state shifted protection from local state industries (which were being sold) to foreign investors. Tanzania's first President, Julius Nyerere once stated that 'we thought we could develop without involving the people... We tried to build socialism without socialists. We tried to build capitalism without entrepreneurs'.[23] Nyerere's words sum up two of Zambia's problems: lack of democracy, from 1972 to 1991, and lack of indigenous capitalist investors in the Zambian economy, traceable to the pre-independence period.[24]

Zambia's reliance on the multi-lateral lenders' *advice* imperilled the economy in total. One state enterprise after another closed down or scaled down its productive capacity to such low levels that it became uneconomic to keep them running, but for political expediency. These problems, coupled with deterioration in the international terms of trade in which Zambia relied on copper sales for most of its foreign exchange earnings, meant that the little earnings had to be spent on servicing the multi-lateral and bilateral debts. In Jomo's view the inception of the World Trade Organisation (WTO) regime entails losses for Africa, through the loss of preferential treatment from its erstwhile colonial masters and the European Union under the Lome Convention.[25] Given the ever-escalating interest accumulations it was impossible for Government to leave any foreign exchange to the private sector to access for their own growth and expansion. Overall, the Zambian economy suffered significant financial, material and human resources drain over the years. The country suffered a contraction of the productive sector: industrial, agricultural and employment generation too. The negative impact of all these factors was quite ghastly.

Zambia-Indo Relations in Science and Technology

In Julius Nyerere's words, Africa is 'trying to begin to develop by increasing their "value-added" components by more local processing and more conversions into consumer goods'.[26] However, for this to be sustainable, it can be suggested that developing countries generally, and Zambia in particular, should learn from both the successes and mistakes of fellow developing countries, trade with one another and even lend to one another. This is because developing countries understand one another's problems and their experiences are similar in terms of such developmental problems and their possible solutions. On this score the Zambia-Indo relations in science and agriculture come into focus.

The reality of India's comparative advantage, which she has built up over the years, means that her road from being an underdeveloped to a scientifically and technologically developed developing country can be used as a yardstick of development by Zambia. Even then Zambia has to avoid the pitfall of merely shifting her dependent status in science, technology and agriculture from Western countries to dependence on fellow developing countries like India that have a scientific and technological edge over her. Shifting dependency cannot achieve much substance besides perpetuating and aggravating the dependency status. What is needed is the development of mutually beneficial collaborative efforts in science and technology. The concept of merely learning from fellow developing countries cannot just do. Learning is one thing and using productively the knowledge so acquired is yet another. Zambia has to adapt the knowledge so learnt from the collaborative efforts to suit her own local circumstances, environment and conditions. It is through adaptation of acquired technology that India has been able to harness science out of which she has developed a niche for herself in the fields of science, technology and agriculture. The development of village industry and technology has enabled India to produce goods and services relatively cost-effectively. Persistent belief in her abilities and the resilience of her people has produced an industrial base that is able to rival even those in the industrialised Western countries in many respects.

Another advantage India has had over the years is consistency in policy formulation and implementation. Firstly, these policies have been Indian generated and owned. Their implementation by Indians themselves has not aroused any alienation resulting in antagonistic feelings among citizens so as to render the policies difficult to implement. India's patience with her 'self-reliance' policy, even in the face of being considered a backward economy unable to race with neighbouring and economically robust China, finally began to yield the desired results, aided by an internally formulated and controlled liberalisation programme that began in 1991, having had the launch pad set back in the 1980s and earlier.[27] She already joined the *developed countries club* in terms of information technology, agricultural, pharmaceutical and medical products as well as the manufacture of various kinds of science instrumentation equipment. An important point to emphasize is that India has been a very bad 'copyist' of foreign technology but an excellent learner and adapter of technology. Further, it should be emphasised that when technology is copied and not adapted to suit local conditions or circumstances it merely turns that country into a dumping ground of such technology. There is no attempt to add value to it by modifying or improving it for the production of more competitive goods and services that are able to stand their own and yield bigger returns on investment both locally and in the export market.

It is also important to take note of India's vast investment in human capital development through tertiary education. Although India has been justifiably criticised for neglecting basic education she cannot be faulted on higher education, particularly in terms of liberal university education and science and technology.[28] India produces some of the best scientists, doctors, not to mention professionals in information technology. Bill Gates' Microsoft Incorporated knows how valuable Indian expertise is, which realisation made the company to set up base in India for the production of computer software and peripherals.[29] The outsourcing by various companies in Western countries into India is based on the same recognition of India's comparative advantage in abundance of expertise, labour-intensive and cost-effective production.[30] India's taxes are also many times lower than Zambia's. This enables industry to thrive in India and cause many foreign companies to extend or even shift their production lines to India. The Indian government's tax gains are based on economies of scale rather than on high tax margins as the case is in Zambia.

Therefore, in the field of science and technology India stands out from the rest of developing countries. Her capabilities in literally all scientific and technological fields put her in front of the bandwagon of developing nations. India's commitment to research and development (R&D) testifies to the country's vision in development. Research yields desired results, which are then passed on to industry where such findings are used for goods and services production and improvement. India's successful research, for example, in low-cost HIV/AIDS antiretroviral drugs has turned her into the world's cheapest source of this life-prolonging drug. Many life-saving drugs are produced in India because of the investment that keeps being pumped into research and development (R&D). Many developing countries send their personnel to India for training in various scientific fields and for collaborative efforts with Indian scientists and expertise in other fields of science and technology. India's pioneering role in tele-medicine and cost-effective neurosurgery and other complex medical situations put India in the front row of developed/developing countries. India has since increased Zambia's access to Indian Technical and Economic Cooperation (ITEC) training slots in India from thirty to fifty per annum, while over 2000 Zambians have been trained through ITEC.[31] To re-emphasise the point, the Zambia-Indo relations is a means that should enhance cooperation in science and technology, but more so, it should be used by Zambia to build up capacity to adapt and innovate in the world of science and technology. Merely copying and using such scientific and technological products cannot be a panacea.

Zambia-Indo Relations in Agriculture and Food Security

While it is true that many African countries were self-sufficient in food and some even exported food in the 1950s and 1960s,[32] Zambia was an exception. Zambia was a perpetual importer of food, given her then abundant revenues from copper exports upto the mid-1970s. President Kaunda during the post-colonial period once complained that Zambians were born with a copper spoon in their mouths![33] There have been very few years in which Zambia was self-sufficient or exported food from the colonial days to the year 2000. Generally Zambia, unlike other African countries, has been a victim of occasional (not prolonged) drought.

Like many other countries, Zambia has her own share of the impact of unsustainable population growth rates of 2.8 - 3.4 per cent for the most part of the country's post-colonial period. These are unsustainable when related to Zambia's fluctuating economic productivity indicators of between below zero and 3 per cent up to the year 2000. The World Bank indicates that between 1975 and 1998 Zambia's population annual average growth stood at 3.4 per cent for the period 1975-84, at 3.0 per cent for 1985-89 and 2.8 per cent in 1990 working out to an average of 3.06 per cent per annum between 1975 and 1990.[34] During the same period Zambia's average annual percentage growth of agriculture value added production picture was 0.5 per cent from 1975 to 1984, 5.6 per cent for 1985-89 and -5.2 for 1990,[35] while growth domestic product (GDP) for the same period was 0.2 per cent, 2.3 per cent and 0.9 per cent respectively.[36] The *World Bank Development Report 1991* also states that:

> Among 38 mixed developed and developing countries, Zambia, Ghana and Nigeria stand out as the only countries whose per capita income declined between 1960 and 1980. Of the three Zambia's per capita income declined the most...[37]

The World Bank further records that Zambia's real growth domestic product declined by 5.1 per cent in 1994, despite an increase of 6.5 per cent the previous year, which marked a significant recovery from the 2.5 per cent decline in real growth domestic product in 1992 due partly to a severe drought in the 1991-92 farming season.[38] The point that the less dependent a country is on agriculture in terms of GDP growth the better off it is does not hold much for Zambia, just as it doe not for many other developing countries. The industrial sector, which is supposed to overtake agriculture as an engine of economic growth, is not sufficiently developed. Industrial production, especially of exportable finished products is literally non-existent in the Zambian economy. Even the once robust import substitution industrial complexes have atrophied. These industries were not given sufficient time to blossom into fully-fledged producers of goods and services. The collapse was partly due to the multilateral lenders' mistaken perception that the industries were ill-conceived and unsustainable. The stand point of their argument was based on the Berg Report's recommendations that Africa's comparative advantage lay in agriculture so long the state removed itself from it to leave it to market forces.[39]

The alternative to state participation proposed by the Breton Woods Institutions in collusion with Zambia's bilateral lenders, through the *Paris Club*, of leaving agriculture to forces of the market (liberalising agricultural commodity prices), did not deliver the expected phenomenal growth. Zambia, instead, witnessed deterioration in food security and a rapid rise in the country's poverty levels, partly due to spiralling food prices. That Zambia's poverty levels have grown fastest and highest during the time Zambia has been under the dogmatically implemented World Bank and IMF prescriptions is not an exaggeration. Sapire and Beall argue that:

> Since the 1980s much of this (Zambia's poverty) has been 'new poverty' resulting from the impact of the economic reform measures and 'conditionalities' accompanying IMF and WB structural adjustment programmes.[40]

That these conditionalities have tended to aggravate the levels of poverty, unemployment, and alienation, and has contributed to deepening class contradictions,[41] is no secret.

Zambia's agricultural lag can be traced to the colonial economic set up where commercial agricultural production was a preserve of the few white settler commercial farmers dotted along the line of rail from Livingstone in the south to the Copperbelt in the north of the country. This shackled African producers into mere subsistence production, for even when they were later allowed to grow maize commercially their sale of the grain to the Grain Marketing Board attracted a lower price than that paid to the white settler commercial farmers for the same type of grain.[42] Due to the late entry of indigenous producers into the commercial market, the lack of expertise and skilled labour resulting from the late start of independent economic development coupled with the neglect occasioned by the colonial administration,[43] Zambia's agricultural production could not hope to compete even with that in neighbouring countries like Malawi and Zimbabwe. Back in 1972 Lombard and Tweedie stated that:

> Unlike many other developing countries, Zambia has not relied on agricultural exports as the basis of her economic

development. Zambia has a large and increasing dependence on imported agricultural commodities to feed herself and provide raw materials for industry'.[44]

Whatever attempts have been made at ensuring food security in the post-colonial period have been neutralised either by drought or unsupportive policy frameworks.[45]

Given the above scenario, of failed advanced technologies copied from abroad, a huge debt burden, failed structural adjustment programs, and a slender agricultural base susceptible to drought and other natural vagaries, Zambia's agricultural industry needed a major paradigm shift. It is argued that:

> The urgency for the less developed nations (is) to not only tap into the existing pool of technology available on the world level but also of developing over time autonomous technological capacity.[46]

Like in the field of science and technology India offers great opportunities of agricultural technologies that can be adapted (not merely copied) to the Zambian situation. India's agricultural development model based on high yielding seed varieties, cost-effective irrigation formulae, improved agricultural practices and innovative extension techniques have considerable lessons for Zambia. This is buoyed on by India's successful development of small scale or cottage manufacturing industries using improved traditional techniques, which have been responsible for successfully industrialising rural India over the years and have alleviated the problem of unemployment to an extent.[47]

On a bilateral level of cooperation in agriculture Zambia has to date received increasing assistance from India. However, like help from all other donors, it has mostly behaved the way rain behaves on a roof; it falls on the roof and flows away down the roof if it is not harvested. During President Mwanawasa's maiden visit to India in April 2003 India gave Zambia an agro-equipment grant worth Rs. 25 million and promised to send Indian expertise to help Zambia learn how to utilise and manage the equipment. India also gave Zambia a grant aid of US $100 000 in form of anti-retroviral drugs, plus 10 000 tons of rice.[48] If put to use without locally based backup service, the equipment would merely go down the same drain where all others from elsewhere have gone in the past. The point being made is that no matter what donations Zambia receives, they will end in the same situation as all others have done in the past. The assistance that Zambia needs most and should get is technology adaptation in form of training slots for higher-level agricultural manpower development. Another level is that of setting up industries that manufacture such agricultural equipment in Zambia using Zambian inputs. However, for this to reach fruition Zambia needs to put her own house in order by way of establishing an iron and steel industry. There is not one technologically developed country today on the face of the earth that reached the developed status without an iron and steel industry. Without this key sector development is compromised and rendered next to impossible, for where it is possible it remains the dependent type of development. The Indian agricultural expertise, if not used to train local personnel would also only be useful while the experts are in place, once they leave the expertise leaves with them and stagnation continues.

The agreement between Zambia and India, through the Federation of Indian Chambers of Commerce and Industry (FICCI) to collaborate in the fields of agro-products and other areas is an important development. FICCI's participation in Zambia's trade and agriculture shows for the last few years has given impetus to the bilateral relations in the filed of agriculture. But still, emphasis should be placed more on technology transfer to Zambia. India allowed the Japanese company Suzuki to set up a car production base in India on the understanding that the latter would use local labour and expertise as well as local materials and, over the years, manufacture all components for the Maruti Suzuki cars in India. The end result has been genuine acquisition of technology by India rather than mere assembling of the cars. India is able to design, build and use cars that Maruti Suzuki manufactures to Indian tastes, standards and are environmentally friendly. If similar arrangements could be made between Zambia and India, with trained Zambian expertise, the agricultural industry that would be set up on such lines would be most lasting and suitable, with both skills and technology genuinely being transferred. Zambia and India have to avoid the Italian Fiat and the ITT Supersonic transistor radio fiasco of the 1970s; whereby all components and most expertise were from Italy to Zambia. In the end the two industries proved unviable and eventually outran their course of usefulness and collapsed.[49]

Conclusion

The restructured Zambia-Indo cooperation in science and agriculture is a milestone in economic development . The salient point about this renewed cooperation is that it is between two countries with similar and yet dissimilar political and economic backgrounds. The similarity in the economic background stems from the fact of both countries having attempted development acceleration on the basis of using imported technology without adapting it to their needs and desires. However, India realised quite early and saw the imported technology as unworkable, unreliable and a mere inducement to dependence, if not adapted to local needs. It would result in mere duplication of the old dependency instead of promoting collaboration. This often results in what Boratav calls relations of exploitation and dependency.[50] India would merely replace or even join the old *club* of exploitative metropolis, having graduated from dependency, if her collaboration with Zambia in science and agriculture does not involve adaptation of suitable technology. Then there would be no difference between Western domination and Indian domination. As such most emphasis should be placed on collaborative efforts, both private and public rather than the lender-borrower, giver-receiver or donor-recipient, benefactor-beneficiary mechanisms. These propel and nurture dependency and underdevelopment, and should be avoided at all cost. Zambia and the rest of the Sub-Saharan African experiences during the 1970s to the 1990s are too harsh to be repeated.[51] The hope is that collaboration between Zambia and India would help break rather than enhance Zambia's dependence on Western donations and loans.

The Zambia-Indo cooperation in science and technology and agriculture fields, it should be emphasised further, can yield positive results beyond mere trade relations, if it is ensured that the relations are translated into a bipolar channel of exchanges. Technical know-how, scientific expert training, agricultural and general scientific research should be streamlined into linkages that promote exchange of information, scientific research results and the collaborative use of such information in both countries. India's scientific, technological and agricultural comparative advantage advances can make this happen. For example in the field of food security, India's irrigation technology and capacity can be harnessed for mutual benefit by setting up irrigation projects to grow non-GM (genetically modified) food crops whose products can then be accessed by both countries. However, there should be caution to avoid the old pitfalls of the developed/developing countries quagmire of diverting most land to the growing of such *cash* crops at the expense of locally consumed crops, and turn the food growing countries into net food importers.[52]

India's position in the field of food security is very strong because at independence India inherited a food deficient economic set-up, but thereafter managed to overcome the food deficiency burden. Today India is a net exporter rather than importer of food.[53] India also donates to other less able countries like Zambia.[54] The Zambia-Indo collaborative efforts should be targeted at enhancing investment opportunities in science and technology and agriculture, because 'effective globalisation relies on efficient localisation'.[55] Therefore, only when the Zambia-Indo relations in science and agriculture, is harnessed and adapted to the two countries' local needs, would the benefits foster mutual developmental benefits. Jawaharlal Nehru's words are very befitting if applied to the Zambian situation. Nehru stated then that:

> We have been backward. We have been left behind in the race, and now we have a chance again to make good. We have to make good rapidly because of the compulsion of events. If we do not make good now we shall fade away not to rise again for a long time to come.[56]

Nehru's words were true of the Indian predicament then as they are for the Zambian situation today. India took heed then and has since emerged economically stronger than ever before, particularly in science and agriculture. Zambia needs to heed the same words in order to invigorate the economy by the use of science, technology and agriculture combined with other developmental factors to push the pedals of development forward, and get her people out of the perpetual poverty cycle that has bedevilled the Zambian socio-economic landscape for ages.

Endnotes

1 Anwar, Tilak, 2002. 'Impact of Globalization and Liberalization on Growth, Employment and Poverty: A Case Study of Pakistan', World Institute for Development Economics Research (WIDER) Discussion paper, WDP2002/17 January, p. 1.

2 A.P. Thirlwall, 2003. *Growth and Development, with Specific Reference to Developing Economies,* 7th Edition, New York: Palgrave Macmillan, p. 3.

3 Joseph, Stiglitz, 2003. *Globalization and its Discontents,* New Delhi: Penguin Books India, p. 3, notes that riots and protests in the developing world against harsh austerity measures by the Breton Woods Institutions have gone unnoticed in these institutions.

4 Jeffrey, Sachs, 2005. 'Debt of the Rich', *Times of India,* New Delhi, February 10, p. 16.

5 http:/www.ambedkar.org, *Ancient Indian Ocean Trade;* W.H. Schoff, 1974. *The Periplus of the Erythraean Sea,* New Delhi: Oriental Books Reprint Corporation, pp. 46-49. Pranab, Kumar, Mukherjee, 'Indo-Africa and South-South Cooperation', in N.N. Vorha and K. Mathews eds., 1997. *Africa, India and South-South Cooperation,* New Delhi: Har-Anand Publishers, p. 41, Mukherjee posits the view that India's contacts with Africa stretch back to 2500 BC and even earlier.

6 Benudhar, Patra, 2005. 'Maritime Contact of Ancient Orissa with the Western World', *Orissa Review,* January, pp. 1-4.

7 Prunab, Kumar Mukherjee, 1997. 'India-Africa and South-South Cooperation', in N.N. Vorha and K. Mathews eds., *Africa, India and South-South Cooperation* (New Delhi: Har-Anand Publications, p. 41.

8 http://www.ydn.org.za, says that Zambia has a small but economically important Asian population, most of whom are Indians.

9 K.K. Virmani, 1989. *Zambia: The Dawn of Freedom,* New Delhi: Kalinga Publications, p. 113.

10 Government of India, Ministry of External Affairs, 'Zambia', http:/www. Meaindia.nic.in; K.K. Virmani, 1989. *Zambia: The Dawn of Freedom,* New Delhi: Kalinga Publications, p. 110; Anthony, Martin, 1972. *Minding their Own Business: Zambia's Struggle against Western Control,* London: Hutchinson and Co. Ltd., p. 77. Simon Mwansa Kapwepwe who became Zambia's first Vice President, and Nalumino Mundia who later became a Prime Minister during Zambia's One-party State era were trained in various fields in India in preparation for independence. The author is currently studying for PhD in history at Jawaharlal Nehru University.

11 Republic of Zambia, 1965. *Transitional Development Plan, 1 January 1965-30 June 1966,* Lusaka: Office of National Development and Planning, p. 73.

12 Republic of Zambia, 1966. *First National Development Plan, 1966-70,* Lusaka: Office of National Development and Planning, p. 2.

13 *First National Development Plan, 1966-70,* p. 2; see also James, Fry, 'The Zambian Economy', in William, Tordoff. 1980. eds., *Administration in Zambia,* Manchester: Manchester University Press, p. 44.

14 National Archives of Zambia (NAZ)/MF1/2/106, Village Regrouping: Planning, Lusaka, 1966-67, Correspondence between Permanent Secretary, Office of National Development and Planning and Permanent Secretary, Ministry of Agriculture.

15 Government of India, 2005. Ministry of External Affairs, 'Indo-Zambia Bilateral Relations', New Delhi, December, http://www.meaindia.nic.in; http://itec.nic.in/about.htm.

16 Raj, Sharma, 1993. *The 'Missing Middle' in Sub-Saharan Africa: Role of South-South Cooperation,* New Delhi: Interest Publications, Foreword.

17 Sharma, *The 'Missing Middle' in Sub-Saharan Africa: Role of South-South Cooperation,* p. 3.

18 S. N. Chipungu, 1988. *The State, Technology and Peasant Differentiation in Zambia: A Case Study of the Southern Province, 1930 - 1986,* Lusaka: Historical Association of Zambia, 193-194.

19 Pranab, Kumar, Mukherjee, 'India-Africa and South-South Cooperation', in N.N. Vorha and K. Mathews eds., *Africa, India and South-South Cooperation,* p. 43.

20 Utsa, Patnaik, 'On the Inverse Relation between Primary Exports and Food Absorption in Developing Countries under Liberalized Trade Regimes', paper presented at a Conference on 'The Agrarian Constraint and Poverty Reduction: Macro-Economic Lessons for Africa', organized jointly by International Development Economics Associates (IDEAS), Ethiopian Economic Association (EEA) and Council for the Development of Social Science Research in Africa (CODESRIA) Addis Ababa, 17-18 December 2004.

21 Hans-Otto Sano, 1988. 'The International Monetary Fund (IMF) and Zambia: The Contradictions of Exchange Rate Auctioning

and De-subsidization of Agriculture', *African Affairs,* vol. 87, no. 349, October, p. 571.

22 'Employers Want Mining Tax Concessions Reviewed', *Zambia Daily Mail,* 6 April 2005. The Zambian Government gave post-1991 FDI a tax holiday of six years but none to local investors. Several FDIs fled the country upon the expiry of their respective tax holidays. In the Export Processing Zones the Zambian Government intends to give a tax holiday of fifteen years!

23 Julius, K. Nyerere's statement cited in Vorha and Mathews, 'Introduction' in Vorha and Mathews eds., *Africa, India and South-South Cooperation,* p. 29.

24 Jonathan, H. Chileshe, 1986. *Third World Countries and Development Options: Zambia, New Delhi: Vikas Publishing House,* p. 86.

25 K.S. Jomo, 'Some East Asian Lessons for African Development?', paper presented at a Conference on 'The Agrarian Constraint and Poverty Reduction: Macro-Economic Lessons for Africa', organized jointly by International Development Economics Associates (IDEAS), Ethiopian Economic Association (EEA) and Council for the Development of Social Science Research in Africa (CODESRIA) Addis Ababa, 17-18 December 2004.

26 Julius Nyerere, 'Understanding Africa', in Vorha and Mathews eds., *Africa, India and South-South Cooperation,* p. 38.

27 Rodrik, Dani and Arvind, Subramanian, 2004. 'Why India can grow at Seven per cent a Year or More: Projections and Reflections', *Economic and Political Weekly,* 17 April, pp. 1591-1596.

28 Armatya, Sen, 1990. 'How is India Doing?' in R.A. Choudhury et al. eds., *The Indian Economy and Its Performance since Independence,* New Delhi: Oxford University Press, p. 15.

29 'The World Today', BBC Radio, Monday, April 11, 2005, states that Indian exports of software total US 17.5 million dollars per annum.

30 Rodrik, Dani and Arvind, Subramanian, *op. cit.* p. 1593.

31 Government of India, Ministry of External Affairs, 'Zambia', http:/www.meaindia.nic.in; http:/www.indiainbusiness.nic.in/commercial-relation/zambia.htm.

32 Pranab, Kumar, Mukherjee, 'India-Africa and South-South Cooperation', *op. cit.* p. 44.

33 *Zambia Daily Mail,* 22 June 1983.

34 World Bank, 2000. *African Development Indicators 2000,* Washington DC: World Bank, pp. 6-7.

35 World Bank, 2000. *African Development Indicators,* p. 18.

36 World Bank, 2000. *African Development Indicators,* p. 17.

37 World Bank, 1991. *Development Report 1991,* Washington DC: Oxford University Press, p. 37.

38 World Bank, 1995. 'Zambia', *Trends in Developing Economics,* Washington DC: World Bank, p. 568.

39 K.S. Jomo, 'Some East Asian Lessons for African Development', paper presented at a Conference on 'The Agrarian Constraint and Poverty Reduction: Macro-Economic Lessons for Africa', organized jointly by International Development Economics Associates (IDEAS), Ethiopian Economic Association (EEA) and Council for the Development of Social Science Research in Africa (CODESRIA) Addis Ababa, 17-18 December 2004, p. 19.

40 Hilary, Sapire and Jo, Beall, 1995. 'Introduction: Urban Change and Urban Studies in Southern Africa', *Journal of Southern African Studies,* vol. 21, no. 1, March, p. 16.

41 George, A. Abiozor, 'Governance in Africa', in N.N. Vorha and K. Mathews eds., *Africa, India and South-South Cooperation,* p. 84.

42 S.N. Chipungu, 1988. *The State, Technology and Peasant Differentiation in Zambia: A Case Study of the Southern Province, 1930 - 1986,* Lusaka: Historical Association of Zambia, p. 106.

43 Joachim, Voss. 1973. 'Introduction' in Joachim, Voss eds., *Development Policy in Africa,* Bonn: Verlag Neue Gesellschaft, p. 16.

44 C.S. Lombard and A.H.C. Tweedie, 1972. *Agriculture in Zambia Since Independence,* Lusaka: National Educational Company of Zambia, p. 87.

45 The Minister of Agriculture in Zambia has already declared 2005 a year of maize crop (the national staple diet) deficit due to drought in the southern half of Zambia. The 1991-2001 period saw declining food crop harvests due to disincentives in the crop production and marketing arrangements, which disadvantaged peasant farmers who grow the bulk of Zambia's staple crop, maize.

46 James, M. Cypher and James, L. Dietz, 1997. *The Process of Economic Development*, London and New York: Routledge, p. 16.

47 Pranab, Kumar, Mukherjee, 'India-Africa and South-South Cooperation', *op. cit.* p. 44.

48 Government of India, Ministry of External Affairs,'Zambia', *op. cit.*

49 Both FIAT and ITT-Supersonic were Italian companies formed through collaboration between the Zambian and Italian governments and both companies were based in Livingstone.

50 Korkut, Boratav. 2004. 'Net Resource Transfers and Dependency: Some Recent Changes in the World Economy', paper presented at a Conference on 'The Agrarian Constraint and Poverty Reduction: Macro-Economic Lessons for Africa', organized jointly by International Development Economics Associates (IDEAS), Ethiopian Economic Association (EEA) and Council for the Development of Social Science Research in Africa (CODESRIA) Addis Ababa, 17-18 December, p. 1.

51 Boratav, *Ibid.*, p. 9.

52 Utsa, Patnaik, 'On the Inverse Relation between Primary Exports and Food Absorption in Developing Countries under Liberalized Trade Regimes', p. 1.

53 Pranab, Kumar, Mukherjee, 'India-Africa and South-South Cooperation', *op. cit.* p. 44.

54 In April 2003 when President Mwanawasa visited India the latter donated tons of rice for distribution to underprivileged citizens in Zambia.

55 K.S. Jomo, 'Some East Asian Lessons for African Development?' paper presented at a Conference on 'The Agrarian Constraint and Poverty Reduction: Macro-Economic Lessons for Africa', p. 21.

56 Pranab, Kumar, Mukherjee, 'India-Africa and South-South Cooperation', *op. cit.* p. 42.

Developing a Fruitful Partnership between India and D.R. Congo

Mwamba-Tshibangu

The main purpose of this paper is to bridge the gap between Indian and Congolese people by suggesting a careful framework, based on related literature, and also some important steps to be taken at the highest level of the governments of both the countries. These steps will lead to the creation of an enabling environment whereby the Congolese people will be aware of the Indian finished products and technology, which on one hand they need at the moment and on the other the Indian people will be aware of the Congolese raw material, which India needs at the moment.

Such awareness will be the blood-life of the partnership between India and D.R. Congo. As a result, people of India will have a direct access to the Congolese raw material ,which they are now getting through a third country, likewise the Congolese people will have a direct access to the India finished product, which they are also getting through a third country.

Introduction

In the new phase of globalization, there is a great need for a fruitful partnership between India and the Democratic Republic of Congo.

In partnership, both the partners have their own attributes, which can be their strengths or needs/requirements to support their weakness. If the strength of one partner is the need of another partner then there evolves a fit case for collaboration[1]. Since, the Democratic Republic of Congo possesses substantial mineral wealth and oil that Indian industries need daily for producing finished products on one hand, on the other hand, India has developed technology that the Democratic Republic of Congo needs at the moment for exploration of oil and mining of minerals, construction of roads and bridges, railways, construction materials and low cost housing complexes. Therefore, there is a fit case for collaboration. Specially now that diplomacy and economics go side by side[2], new trade policies need to be implemented on both sides. As the structure of import and export of a country depends among other things on the trade policies adopted by it. The term trade policy refers to all the policies that have either direct or indirect bearing on the trade behaviour of a country.[3] The new policies, which will bring India and the Democratic Republic of Congo closer, are policies that are based on strategic partnership in such a way that a mechanism is put in place by both parties to facilitate and promote international trade based on their needs and strengths.

However, a fruitful partnership between India and the Democratic Republic of Congo cannot be developed as long barriers, such as trade economic weaknesses, policies and medium of exchange, continue to hinder its development.

Economic Weaknesses

In order to understand implications of the import and export between India and the Democratic Republic of Congo, it is very important for us to understand the concept of balance of payments.

According to Vij[4], the fundamental determinate of a country's vulnerability is its balance of payment. The balance of payments management is a function of, among other things, internal goals, and changing external circumstances.

A very useful indicator of a country's risk analysis is the current account balance. It summarizes the country's total transactions with the rest of the world for goods and services (plus unilateral transfers) and represents the difference between national income and expenditure. It also indicates the rate at which a country is building foreign assets or accumulating foreign liabilities.

The balance of payments on current account is negatively related to the probability of default since the current account deficit broadly equals the amount of new financing required.

Countries with large current account deficit are thus less credit worthy.

Another useful indicator of the balance of payment position of a country is the reserve to imports ratio. Reserves provide a short-term safeguard against fluctuation in foreign receipts. The larger the reserves are relative to imports, the more reserves are available to service debt and the lower is the probability of default.

Developing countries, such as India and the Democratic Republic of Congo, are more vulnerable than mature economics to balance of payments difficulties because of high import properties and a heavily skewed dependence on few exports[5] .

India's Balance of Payments

The situation by the end of 1990 had become so critical that the country was almost on the brink of default. Foreign exchange reserves of the country were barely adequate to finance three weeks imports.

The Gulf crisis of 1990 led to an unprecedented crisis in the balance of payments. The immediate impact was the rise in the oil import bill. It also resulted in a decline in workers' remittances as well as additional burden on repatriating and rehabilitating non-resident Indians from the affected zones in West Asia. As a consequence of the increase in the price of oil as well as certain other oil related imports, the trade deficit for the year 1990-91 deteriorated by around US $ 2 billion. Since, there was deterioration in the invisible account also; the overall current account deficit in 1990-91 at US $ 9.7 billion was US $ 2.8 billion higher than in the previous year.

During 1993-94, a distinct improvement in the balance of payments occurred. A strong export growth of over 19 per cent in US dollar terms, fall in international prices of crude oil and the continuing slack in non-POL imports have resulted in a sharp contraction in the merchandise trade deficit. During April-November 1993, it was US $ 532 million as against US $ 3097 million in the same period of 1992.

Imbalances in the external sector reflect the fundamental fact that aggregate absorption in the economy is in excess of the domestically produced goods and services. Measures to reduce excess demand in the economy, therefore, constitute an important policy ingredient of the adjustment towards creating a sustainable balance of payments environment. Excess absorption can originate either from the private or the public sector or from both. In reality, however, it is the fiscal deficit of the public sector that is found to be associated with excess demand and the consequent deterioration of the current account balance. The link between the fiscal deficit and the current account balance can be derived from the following economy-wide financial balance identity.

An improvement in the current account balance can be achieved either by an improvement in the combined balances of the private and public sectors or by an increase in national income relative to domestic absorption.

A domestic economic policy aimed at maintaining absorption at an appropriate level has an important role to play in an effort to maintain a reasonably comfortable level of current account deficit.

Any external shock, such as a rise in oil prices, can put the economy in a serious situation[6], specially now that India's oil demand jumped by 11.3 per cent in March to a record 2.57 million barrels a day [7] .

A tight balance of payments situation is, however, endemic for developing countries. Literature on development economics used to emphasis the two gaps that countries in the process of development were likely to face, namely, the domestic savings and investment gap and the external gap between imports and exports. To be comfortable, the current account deficit must be kept at a level that can be financed by normal capital flows. When the total stock of external debt is low, it becomes possible to finance a fairly large level of current account deficit because the lenders are prone to be less[8]

Democratic Republic of Congo's Balance of Payments

The present Government of Democratic Republic of Congo, headed by His Excellency President Joseph Kabila, has inherited an economy, which was crippled by war and mismanagement of previous regimes. This is, therefore, not the right time for India to expect billions of dollars from the Democratic Republic of Congo for the purpose of importing Indian finished products.

Since both of our countries are likely to have a tight balance of payments situation, which is endemic for developing countries[9] while importing from abroad. The barter system of trade is the only option we have as medium of exchange otherwise we will wait for the next 40 years to see the fruits of our partnership while we need them now.

If the barter system of trade is properly implemented we will not face the Managing Risk in Foreign Exchange Trading. The performance of banks or other institutions trading in the foreign exchange market depends on how well they assess the nature and type of risk and accordingly measure and manages the risk. There are basically two forms of risks that are faced in foreign exchange trading and the issue of managing risk is a continuous and exacting part of trading in foreign exchange.

1. *Market Risk :* This risk refers to the risk of advance changes in a currency rate or in an interest rate. Two major forms of market risk are exchange rate risk and interest rate risk. They are inherent in foreign exchange trading. A trader - when he buys or sells foreign currency to a customer or to another bank - is creating an "open" or "uncovered" position (long or short) for his bank in that currency, unless he is covering or transferring out of some previous position. Every time a dealer takes a new foreign exchange position – in spot, outright forwards, currency options– that position is immediately exposed to the risk that the exchange rate may move against it and the dealer remains exposed until the transaction is completed. Interest rate risk arises when there is any mismatching or gap in the maturity structure. Thus, an uncovered outright forward position can change in value, not only because of a change in the spot rate (foreign exchange risk), but also because of a change in interest rates (interest rate risk), since a forward rate reflects the interest rate differential between the two currencies. In an FX swap, there is a no shift in foreign exchange exposure and the market risk is interest rate risk. In addition to FX swaps and currency swaps, outright forwards, currency futures and currency options are all subject to interest rate risk.

2. *Credit Risk :* This refers to the risk of not getting back the payment on time. Credit risk, inherent in all banking

activities, arises from the possibility that the counter party to a contract cannot or will not make the agreed payment at maturity. When an institution provides credit, whatever the form, it expects to be repaid. When a bank or other dealing institution enters a foreign exchange contract, it faces a risk that the counter party will not perform according to the provisions of the contract. Between the time of deal and the time of the settlement, be it a matter of hours, days, or months, there is an extension of credit by both parties and an acceptance of credit risk by the banks or other financial institutions involved. As in the case of market risk, credit risk is one of the fundamental risks to be monitored and controlled in foreign exchange trading.

3. *Sovereign Risk :* It is a variation of credit risk which is very important and relevant in foreign exchange trading. It refers to, the political, legal and other risks associated with a cross-border payment. In many cases, many governments have interfered with international transactions in their currencies. Although in today's liberalized markets and less regulated environment, there are fewer and fewer restrictions imposed on international payments, the possibility that a country may prohibit a transfer cannot be ignored. In order to limit their exposure to this risk, banks and other foreign exchange market participants sometimes establish ceilings for individual countries, monitor regulatory changes, watch credit ratings and, where practicable, obtain export risk guarantee[10].

Bilateral Trade between India and the Democratic Republic of Congo

India's trade with the Democratic Republic of Congo is almost one sided affair, as exports from India to the Democratic Republic of Congo is very negligible.

Like other developing African countries, Industrial countries namely Belgium, the USA, the UK, France, Japan and Netherlands have been the major trading partners of the Democratic Republic of Congo. These countries accounted for more than 60 percent of the Democratic Republic of Congo's total trade. Though India is one of the trading partners, her share in the total trade of the

Democratic Republic of Congo accounted for very small especially in case of imports from India. India's share in the total exports of the Democratic Republic of the Congo, however, show an increasing trend after 1975, which rose from 0.8 per cent in 1975 to 6.7 percent in1979[11]. The composition of India's import from the Democratic Republic of Congo included: pearls; precious and semi-precious stones and non-ferrous metals (copper, Zinc, lead etc.) accounted for about 100 per cent of India's imports from Zaire during the period from 1970-71 to 1983-84.

Composition of India's imports from the Democratic Republic of Congo

Precious and semi-precious stones and non-ferrous metals (copper, Zinc, lead etc.) accounted for about 100 per cent of India's imports from the Democratic Republic of the Congo during the period from 1970-71 to 1983-84.[12]

For the period, between 1995 and 1999, the PHD Chamber of Commerce had released the following report:

(Value in Rs. millions)

	1995-96	1996-97	1997-98	1998-99 Apr-Sept
India's exports to D.R. Congo	9.438	16.463	531.271	516.672
India's Imports from D.R. Congo	0.000	16.436	302.191	422.003

Source: DGCI&S

Exports of India to the Democratic Republic of the Congo

Drugs, pharmaceuticals and fine chemicals; transport equipment; cotton yarn, fabrics, made-ups, etc.; manufactures of metals; ready-made garments of colon including accessories; machinery and instruments; tea; rice; spirits and beverages; fresh vegetables; miscellaneous processed items; meat and preparations; processed minerals; footwear of leather; dyes/intermediates and coal tar chemicals; inorganic/organic/agro chemicals; cosmetics/toiletries, etc.; rubber manufactured products. Except footwear; paints/ enamels/varnishes, etc.; glass/glassware/ceramics/refractors/

cement; paper/wood products; plastic and linoleum products; residual chemicals and allied products; non-ferrous metals; residual engineering items; electronic goods; man-made yarn, fabrics, made-ups, etc.; ready-made garments of man-made fibres; handicrafts.

There exists immense potential for export of engineering goods from India to Congo like agricultural implements and machinery, machinery for construction of roads and bridges, irrigation equipment and water pumps, diesel sets, mining machinery, etc. Other potential items of exports from India to Congo include textiles and garments, drugs and pharmaceuticals, electronic goods, household appliances, bicycles and parts, automobiles and auto components, gems and jewels, foodstuffs, leather and leather goods, rice, machine tools, processed fruits and vegetables and their products, computer.

Potential items of imports from Congo to India include wood pulp; and wood products, crude minerals and mineral products, non-ferrous metals like copper and cobalt, rough diamonds and other precious stones, various types of agro-produce, etc.

This review reveals that the bilateral trade between India and the Democratic Republic of Congo is not what it was supposed to be, so far has been it is like a drop of water in a big ocean therefore, there is a great need for strategic partnership based on their mutual and urgent need, such as oil exploration, mining machinery and construction of roads and bridges, irrigation equipment and water pumps etc..

Many Indian companies are unable to import items such as copper and cobalt, rough diamonds, precious stones, and timber directly from the Democratic Republic of the Congo, in stead, they get them from a third country at a very high price. Likewise, many Congolese companies are still buying Indian products from a third country at a higher price. India's share in the total exports of the Democratic Republic of Congo, however, does not exceed 8 per cent. In many cases, people have complained about current medium of exchange making it difficult for them to transfer funds.

The bilateral trade between India and the Democratic Republic of Congo, so far has been like a drop of water in a big ocean. Therefore, there is a great need for strategic partnership based on their mutual and urgent need, such as oil exploration, mining machinery and construction of roads and bridges, irrigation equipment and water pumps etc.

Trade Policies

The structure of import and export of a country depends, among other things, on the trade policies adopted by it. The term trade policy refers to all the policies that have either direct or indirect bearing on the trade behaviour of a country.[13] Therefore, the barter system as a medium of exchange requires a careful intervention of the policy makers of India and Democratic Republic of Congo,, since, there is a general feeling that India is not taking Africa as a priority.[14]. But this general feeling was given a blow when His Excellency the President of India met the former South African President Nelson Mandela on 16th of September 2004 and announced $50 millions assistance to connect 53 African countries through a satellite and fibre optic network donated in honour of Indo-African partnership.[15] Specially now that diplomacy and economics go side by side, [16] help in construction, agriculture, small industries, electrification and other infrastructure work is most needed and India needs to evolve such a foreign policy with emphasis on the economic factor,[17] which is a big stepping stone towards fruitful partnership between India and the Democratic Republic of Congo that will cause them to give priority to each other as far as trade is concern.

The Barter System of Trade

The barter system of trade as a medium of exchange is the only solution at the moment for the partnership between India and the Democratic Republic of Congo to be fruitful. Since, it implies that the two parties must have a reciprocal need for merchandise, the value of which is determined by the extend of their demand. This medium of exchange can be traced back to the stone age, when the tool making industries having fairly specialized required some sort of exchange between the manufacturers and the users giving birth to the barter system to facilitate a regular trade between the consumers and the factory sites.[18]

Contrary to common misconceptions, barter is not a thing of the past. It is still quite actively used by many companies. Today, over 500,000 businesses worldwide are involved in barter and it is estimated that 65 per cent of the Fortune500 companies use barter. These interesting barter statistics demonstrate that barter is consistently growing in popularity.[19] (See Table no. 1).

From the table, it is very clear that barter system of trade as a medium of exchange has been successful in North American Trade Companies, therefore let us give it a chance in the partnership between India and the Democratic Republic of Congo.

Important Steps to be taken

The following steps need to be taken in order to enhance economic cooperation between India and Congo that will result in a fruitful partnership.

1) Since the review of literature has revealed that barter system of trade arrangement is the only option, therefore, the trade policies of both our countries need to be amended towards barter system of trade.
2) Dialogue at the highest level of our Government officials regarding new trade policies will boost the economic cooperation between India and the Democratic Republic of Congo paving a way to the creation of a joint research and development committee.
3) Research and development committee that will have to deal with the identification of each other's urgent needs and evaluate the value of the finished products as well as services from India, which are needed in the Democratic Republic of Congo on one hand and on the other to evaluate the value of the quantity of oil, and other raw materials that India needs. Laying down of the guidelines for barter system of trade is also needed.
4) The joint research and development committee will have to create data banks and institutionalized mechanisms for

exchange of commercial intelligence and information on business opportunities and available technologies to bridge the existing information gap and create awareness will be the blood-life of the partnership between India and D.R. Congo. As a result, people of India will have a direct access to the Congolese raw material, which they are now getting through a third country, likewise the Congolese people will have a direct access to the India finished products, which they are also getting through a third country.

Conclusion

From the above discussion, it can be concluded that: There is a great need for a fruitful partnership between India and the Democratic Republic of Congo.

Since both the partners have their own attributes, which can be their strengths or needs/requirements to support their weakness[20], specially now that India's oil demand jumped by 11.3 per cent in March to a record 2.57 million barrels a day,[21] a fruitful partnership between India and the Democratic Republic of Congo is likely to be a permanent solution. The removal of barriers related to the medium exchange and mainly from the trade policy will definitely create an enabling environment for a fruitful partnership to flourish between India and the Democratic Republic of Congo.

The above mentioned steps will lead to the creation of an enabling environment whereby the Congolese people will be aware of the Indian finished products and technology, which they need at the moment on one hand and on the other the Indian people will be aware of the Congolese raw materials, which India needs at the moment.

The above steps will be the blood-life of the partnership between India and D.R. Congo. The next generation of the Congolese as well as Indian people will rise up against our generation in judgment and condemn us if we do not act now, therefore let us not pass this unfruitful partnership between India and the Democratic Republic of the Congo to the next generation, instead, let them lay a strong foundation from which they can take our fruitful partnership to the next level.

Table No. 1

Dollars Bartered by North American Trade Companies

(In Millions)

Year	Corporate Trade Companies	Trade Exchanges Companies &Trade Exchanges	Total Corporate Companies	Number of Trade Clients	Number of Trade
1974	850	45	895	100	17,000
1976	980	65	1045	120	24,000
1977	1130	80	1210	150	30,000
1978	1300	110	1410	180	40,000
1979	1500	165	1665	230	60,000
1980	1720	200	1920	280	70,000
1981	1980	240	2220	340	90,000
1982	2200	270	2470	330	100,000
1983	2440	300	2740	350	110,000
1984	2680	330	3010	370	120,000
1985	2900	380	3280	390	140,000
1986	3200	440	3640	410	160,000
1987	3470	500	3970	430	180,000
1988	3750	566	4316	440	200,000
1989	4050	636	4686	450	220,000
1990	4550	707	5257	470	240,000
1991	5100	781	5881	500	260,000
1992	5570	858	6428	540	280,000
1993	6050	938	6988	570	300,000
1994	6560	1084	7644	610	340,000
1995	7216	1248	8464	650	380,000
*1996	*7749	*1356	*9105	*686	*408,000
*1997	*8205	*1464	*9699	*700	*436,000
*1998	*9265	*1572	*10,837	*708	*464,000
*1999	*9404	*1596	*11,000	*719	*470,960

*1996-99 figures are estimates for retail based upon the average increase of the prior 5 years. Corporate are based on study commissioned by the Corporate Barter Council.

Endnotes

1 Jain, Kirti & Jain, Sudhir K. 2004. *Partner Identification Strategy for International Joint Venturing in India*. Decision. Culcutta: Indian Institute of Management Studies, vol. 31, no.1, Jan-June, p. 100.

2 Jha, Uma Shankar. 2003. *Recast Foreign Policy*. Delhi: Association of Indian Africanist, p. 32.

3 Panchamukhi, V.R 1977 *Trade Policies of India. A Quantitative Analysis*. Delhi: Concept Publishing Company, p. 33.

4 Vij, Madhu. 2004. *International Financial Management*. Delhi: Excel Books, pp. 485-86.

5 *Ibid.*, p. 428.

6 Rangarajan. 2004, pp. 196-202.

7 Ye, Xie. 2004. 'Rising energy demand won't impact globally'. *China Daily*. http://www2.chinadaily.com.cn/english/doc/2004-06/22/content_341408.htm

8 Rangarajan. *op. cit.*

9 *Ibid.*

10 Vij, Madhu. 2004. *op. cit.*

11 Mathew, M.J. 1988. *International Trade: Policies and Prospective in Developing Economy*, Jaipur: Prateeksha Publications, p. 109.

12 *Ibid.*

13 Panchamukhi , V.R 1977. *op. cit.* , p. 33.

14 Jha, Uma Shankar. 2003. *op. cit.*, p. 32.

15 *The Times of India*, 2004. New Delhi 2004 Friday 17 September.

16 Jha, Uma Shankar. 2003. *op. cit.*, p. 41.

17 *Ibid.*

18 Prasad, Prakash Charan 1977. *Foreign Trade and Commerce in Ancient India*. New Delhi: Abhinav Publications, p.156.

19 Kneeland, Joseph http://www.barterexchange.info/contact.html Last updated 2004-09-27.

20 Jain, Kirti & Jain, Sudhir K. 2004. *op. cit.*, p. 100.

21 Ye, Xie. 2004. *op. cit.*

India and Horn of Africa: Towards a Meaningful Partnership

Nivedita Ray

Introduction

India's relations with the countries of Horn of Africa i.e. Ethiopia, Somalia, Eritrea, Sudan and Djibouti are marked by friendship, cordiality and understanding. Since the dawn of history, the people of the two regions came together and interacted. Their linkages can be traced back to ancient times. The Indian Ocean and the Red Sea were and continue to be the vehicle of trade, peoples and ideas. Some historical researchers established trade and cultural links between India and the Horn of Africa region and the Red Sea as early as early as 538 B.C. Though contacts were largely based on trade, it had a wider dimension and found expression in many cultural similarities between the two regions. Their relations were multifaceted covering not only trade but also art, architecture, agriculture, music and others. They share similar histories and legacies of colonialism as well as struggle for independence. India supported their fight against anti-colonialism and anti racialism after it gained independence in 1947. The post-colonial era witnessed an integrated pattern of relationship ,where the scope of economic activities were extended beyond mere trading activities to include joint -venture participation and supply of both middle and high level technical and managerial manpower to the independent countries. The establishment of Special Commonwealth Africa Assistance Programme (SCAAP), in 1963 and Indian Technical and Economic Co-operation (ITEC), in 1964 aimed at providing a firm institutional leverage to developing relationship with these concerned countries. The countries of Horn of Africa have been co-travellers with India in the NAM, Commonwealth, and South-South co-operation and other international fora, sharing similar perceptions on global issues.

Nature of Relationship

A glance at the past reflects that there is a bond, an affinity, a common vision, and a genuine sense of empathy, which have brought India and Horn of African countries together in fostering political and economic relations. The present and future partnership rests on these strong foundations of close ties they have been sharing in the past. India's approach has been to consolidate the gains of these traditional ties that it has with these countries. In recent years, their relations have been steadily forging ahead and acquiring greater significance, as they share common interests and understand each other's importance. There is, indeed, a growing desire in each side to enhance and promote partnership in various spheres, for which new areas of mutually beneficial cooperation are being identified and explored. While India with a vibrant democracy, rich culture, developmental experiences and economic prowess assumes importance for Horn of Africa, so also the region as a whole with its proximity to the sea has a geo-strategic significance as well as potential in the economic arena in terms of oil, water reserves, agricultural capacity and human resources for India. Both the sides have certain common security challenges and problems such as terrorism that has to be addressed jointly for mutual benefit. A need is also being felt to promote regional cooperation for the common benefit of India and the region. In this joint effort India can contribute in maintaining peace and stability in the region by addressing the problem of conflict and instability, which is an important factor in Horn of Africa. In the light of this backdrop we aim to understand-

- First, India's relations with the countries of Horn of Africa, taking into account each others strengths, where they can benefit from cooperation and their weaknesses, where they can complement each other. The focus will remain India's specific engagement with each of the countries in the Horn of Africa i.e. Sudan, Djibouti, Ethiopia, Eritrea and Somalia in different spheres (political, economic, educational and cultural).
- Secondly, discuss the common threats and India's endeavors towards promoting peace in the region.

India-Sudan Relations

Sudan and India are linked by strong bonds of common heritage and unique similarities. They are both countries of diversities and demographic wealth. Relations between the two countries have always been warm and cordial. These relations have long history of contacts.

Historical Perspective

In ancient times, the Nile Valley Civilization and the Indus Valley Civilization mutually interacted. The Nile and the Red Sea also provided well-known routes to Indian traders and visitors. Many aspects of culture and traditions in India and the Sudan have had a common source of origin. The large Indian community in the Sudan as well as the presence of many Sudanese of Indian origin, are clear examples of such interaction between the peoples of the two countries.

Indian and Sudanese people also came closer to each other during the British colonial era, which dominated both of them. Shortly before independence, and in preparation for that historic event, Sukumar Sen, an Indian representing the Indian Election Commission conducted the first election in the country. Prior to independence too, the very establishment of the Sudan's Forest Service in 1901 was based on a report by an Indian forester, Mr. Murell. The establishment of Sudan Railways drew also from the Indian experience. Likewise, the well-known Indian National Defence Academy in Pune was contributed by Sudan. The largest Indian School in Africa located in Omdurman, Sudan, was also a gift from Sudan to India on the occasion of the visit of the then Prime Minister Late Pandit Jawaharlal Nehru to Sudan. As founding members of the Non-Aligned Movement whose seeds were sown at Bandung Conference, leaders of the two countries have maintained regular contacts: Sudanese leader Ismail Al-Azhari visited India in 1955 followed by late President Ibrahim Abboud.

Political Relations

Political relations between India and Sudan are cordial and both sides have recently sought to widen the scope of their cooperation. Exchange of high-level delegations between the two countries have been taking place since long which includes the visit to Sudan by the late Indian President Fakhruddin Ali Ahmed in 1975, following the visit of the former President Numeri to India in 1974. The then Sudanese Foreign Minister Ali Osman Mohammad Taha visited New Delhi in 1996 followed by Dr. Mustafa Osman Ismail, the minister of external relations in 1997, as the leader of the Sudanese side to the meeting of the Indo-Sudanese Joint Ministerial Commission.

The latest of these contacts was the visit of Dr.Mustafa Osman Ismail on 6 June 2005 which was in keeping with the tradition of high level visits between both the countries including the Indian President's vist to Sudan in October 2003 and the visit by H.E.Mr. Osman Mohammed Taha, first vice president of Sudan to India in 2002. Besides, many visits to both Sudan and India are currently performed by many visitors, experts, businessmen and tourists as well as official delegations representing various fields of human endeavor, which has reinforced the friendly relations that both the countries have. The Indian and Sudanese leaders have underlined the need for urgent and meaningful reform of the UN and its organs, in particular the Security Council to reflect the needs and aspirations of the developing countries, the Sudanese leaders have expressed their consistent support for the early entry of India to permanent membership of the UNSC. India on its part respects the sovereignty, unity and territorial integrity of Sudan. It also maintains that the situation in Darfur is an internal crisis that has to be resolved by the Government of Sudan in consultation with AU in bringing the situation to normalcy.

Economic & Commercial Engagement

India is among Sudan's important trading partners. Both countries are determined to achieve, once again, the highest possible performance in their bilateral dealings. They have signed eleven agreements on trade, economic, cultural and technological fields. The signing of the North-South peace agreements in Sudan has also brightened the prospects of economic trade relations. Various Indian companies from public and private sector are trying to register their presence in Sudan.

The main items that are exported from India to Sudan are drugs and pharmaceuticals, agro-chemicals, machinery and instruments, transport equipment and vehicles, man-made yarn/ fabrics/made-ups, plastic and linoleum products, miscellaneous processed products and manufactured metals. The main items imported from Sudan are raw hides and skins, leather, ores and metal scrap.

A Joint Committee for Economic, Technical, Commercial, Information, Trade and Cultural Co-operation was set up in January, 1995 to facilitate trade and economic relations between both the countries. It was later upgraded to the Ministerial level in June, 1995. The first session of the Joint Commission was held at New Delhi from 6-9 November, 1997. The last session of the JCM was held in Khartoum from 8-9 April, 2000. There is a proposal to set up a Joint Business Council between FICCI and Sudanese Union of Chamber of Commerce (SUCC).

A Protocol for Science & Technology Co-operation was signed on 4 November, 1985 at Khartoum between the Indian Council for Scientific & Industrial Research (CSIR) and the Sudanese National Council for Research. The Sudanese Embassy has recently made a proposal to reactivate the Protocol as per the Agreed Minutes of the JCM held at New Delhi from 6-9 November 1997.

Oil Factor

One among the key resources of Sudan is hydrocarbon. India along with other countries is participating in the discoveries of oil and gas. India has got a stake in a producing oil block in Sudan, and is now looking at two other oil blocks for which the competition is bound to be tough. India has now 25 percent equity stake in the Greater Nile Oil Project in Sudan, which consists of four blocks in the Muglad Basin and a 1,500 km pipeline from the producing fields to Port Sudan on the Red Sea. It currently produces 12 mm tpy of oil (240,000 bpd). India's share from the block works out to 3 mm tpy of oil. The oil being of good quality from a reliable source, India is keen to not only bring its entire share but also persuade the other partners in the block to let it have the remaining supplies on commercial terms. OVL's other partners in the Sudan field are the Chinese National Petroleum Company (CNPC) with 40 percent stake, the Malaysian National Oil Company Petronas with 30 percent and the Sudan National Oil Company with five percent stake. 'OVL is looking at two more oil blocks in the same

Heglig field. Sudan wants India's involvement in exploration and value added sectors like petrochemicals, refining and marketing, in fact, in all aspects of the oil industry given its expertise. It is interested in encouraging Indian investment not only in the oil sector, where India could step up investment and help to enhance production, but also other areas. In fact OVL's investment in Sudan's oil sector has generated interest among Indian companies, businessmen and other experts to explore possibilities of cooperation in Sudan.

Other Areas of Partnership

A Memorandum of Understanding in the field of Health Co-operation between India and Sudan was signed in October, 1996 at New Delhi during the visit of the Sudanese Minister of Health Mrs. I. El Gabshani. Protocol for cooperation in the field of Radio and Television between Prasar Bharti and the Sudanese Radio and Television was approved by the Cabinet in 2004. Ministry of Information later signed this protocol with the Sudanese Government.

Under the ITEC Programme, Sudan is offered 35-40 scholarships annually. Sudan is one of the largest beneficiaries of our ITEC Programme. In the sphere of cultural relations a cultural agreement was signed in New Delhi in the year 1974. The last Cultural Exchange Programme under the agreement was signed in August, 1996, for the years 1996-99 in Delhi. Under this Programme, Sudan was offered 16 Scholarships.

The various areas of cooperation and collaboration between India and Sudan suggest that both the countries are striving to synergize their development goals and policies. Those create a possibility for both nations to acquire enviable capabilities in the coming years.

India-Ethiopia Cooperation

Historical Background

Ethiopia's contacts with India, and the East, though less well documented than those with the West, were important, and long-enduring. The economies of the two regions were to a significant extent complimentary, and commerce between them was facilitated by the trade winds. The sub-continent was thus a major source of cotton, silks, and spices, and various luxury items, among them pearls. Ethiopia, by way of return, supplied India with such exports as gold, ivory, and slaves. This commercial pattern, first evident in ancient times, continued substantially unchanged, into the medieval period. Contacts across the Red Sea and Indian Ocean, though largely based on trade, also had a much wider dimension, and found expression in many cultural similarities between the two countries, not merely, as often noticed, in that of food and dress. These ancient traditional ties have expanded over a period of time in various areas of cooperation. Both the sides have tried to consolidate the gains of their close relationship.

Ethiopia-Indian bilateral relations have been reinvigorated from time to time in various areas of cooperation. The main areas of partnership are related to trade, human resource development, and agriculture.

Ethiopia-India Trade Relations

The volume of trade between the two countries crossed the US $ 100 million mark in 2001-02 with exports from India standing at US$ 90.4 million and imports from Ethiopia at US$ 18.4 million in 2000-01. The main items of exports from India included iron and steel products, manufactures of metals, drugs and pharmaceuticals, machinery and instruments as well as yarns and fabrics, among others, and the export items from Ethiopia included pulses, raw hides and skins as well as raw cotton and leather.

Of late various Indian entrepreneurs have evinced interest in doing business in Ethiopia. For instance an Indian entrepreneur has signed a contract agreement with the Oromia State administration to set up a sugar processing factory at a cost of 131 million Birr. Another Indian company, E.V. Industries showed interest in establishing sewing and embroidery threads manufacturing factory in Ethiopia with a capital of US $ 550,000.

The first India-Ethiopia Joint Trade Committee that met in Addis Ababa on 25 and 26 February, 1998 to review the implementation of the provisions of the Trade Agreement has given a fillip to bilateral trade and promotion of closer relations with Ethiopia. The Indian delegation was led by Shri P.P. Prabhu, Commerce Secretary, and the Ethiopian delegation by Mr. Brook Debebe, Vice Minister of Trade and Industry of the Federal

Democratic Republic of Ethiopia. Two sides also had explored the new areas of cooperation in trade and investment and had extensive discussions on the ways and means to further enhance trade and technical cooperation between the two countries. The new areas of cooperation identified were agriculture, water resources, power, electronics and computer software, telecommunications, drugs consultancy, science and technology and small scale sector and pharmaceuticals and construction.

Human Resource Development

The government of India has a keen desire to further bolster bilateral cooperation with Ethiopia particularly in the area of human resources development. India is ready to share its successful development experiences. India is poised to further explore the potential of bilateral cooperation in the fields of agricultural research and education, irrigation development, information and technology; among others.

Several Ethiopian delegations have so far visited India to exchange views and share experiences in the fields of agricultural research and education. According to the Charge d'Affaires, Prime Minister Meles Zenawi's visit to India in 1997 has given a fresh impetus to further consolidate the bilateral relations between the two countries. He has also called upon the business communities of both countries and the pool of the ITEC scholars to explore possibilities for further expanding the bilateral trade and entering into joint venture projects.

Ethiopian Government has lauded initiatives being taken by the Indian government to share its valuable experiences and expertise knowledge to Ethiopia through the ITEC. It is desirous to share all available India's development experiences in a bid to prop up the country's human resources development endeavors.

Cooperation in the fields of Education and other capacity building activities are priority areas between India and Ethiopia. More than 3000 students are at present pursuing their education in India in various fields of study. Currently there are 40 Indian professors and instructors at the Debre Zeit Defence Engineering College, 29 at the Addis Ababa University and 63 others in the Civil Service College and some other universities in the country.

Ethiopia faces a grave problem of food scarcity. It needs to share India's experience in overcoming drought and ensuring food self sufficiency, through enhanced agricultural research, water conservation and natural resources management as well as revised land tenure and irrigation development schemes.

It is observed that while main areas of cooperation between India and Ethiopia have been trade and human resource development, yet new sectors are being identified and explored for mutually beneficial partnership.

India-Djibouti Partnership

Relations between India and Djibouti can be traced back to the ancient times. The port of Adulis was the hub of maritime trade where Indian seafarers have traded in spices and silk for gold and ivory. The people of Djibouti are born from a contact among the cultures of East Africa, the Arab peninsula and the Indian sub-continent. The relations between both the countries received a boost with the historic visit of the President of Djibouti to India in May 2003. New vistas of opportunities opened up in many areas of mutual interest with the visit. It has led to enhanced contacts and business linkages.

Establishment of Diplomatic Relations

Djibouti is concurrently accredited from Japan. India's diplomatic footprints in Djibouti dates back to 1969 when the Honorary Consul of India started functioning in Djibouti. The present Consul Mr. Nalin J. Kothari is the son of the first Honorary Consul of India Mr. S. I. Kothari who was Honorary Consul of India for 25 years. The setting up of the consul led to strengthening of ties between the two countries.

Political Relations

The relations between India and Djibouti have traditionally been warm and friendly and have been reinvigorated following the visit of the President of Djibouti to India. Indian ships make regular calls at the Port of Djibouti on transit. We share similar perception on issues of common concern and those that affect developing countries. Bilateral contacts have increased in the last one year.

Bilateral Visits

H.E. Mr. Ismail Orner Guelleh, President of the Republic of Djibouti made a historic visit to India in May 2003. He was accompanied by the Minister of Foreign Affairs and International Cooperation, the Minister of Defense, the Minister of National Education and the Minister of Public Works and Public Transport. A 30-member business delegation also accompanied the official entourage.

Apart from high level visits various treties and agreements have been signed some of them are mentioned as below:

Important Bilateral Treaties and Agreements

- Bilateral Investment Promotion and Protection Agreement (BIPPA) signed at New Delhi on 19th May 2003.
- Civil Aviation Agreement signed at New Delhi on 19th May 2003.
- Cultural Cooperation Agreement signed between India and Djibouti on 31st, January 1989 and Executive Programme of Cultural, Education and Scientific Cooperation for the year 2003-2005 signed at New Delhi on 19th May 2003.

Commercial and Economic Relations

Djibouti is keen to develop economic partnership with India and would like to learn and receive assistance from India especially in areas of education, information technology, agriculture, small scale industries, portable electricity generating units, fisheries, water resource development, etc. Our Economic and Commercial relations picked up momentum following the visit of President of Djibouti to India. It was agreed to strengthen cooperation in various spheres. In order to contribute to the economic development of Djibouti, India provided an EXIM Bank Line of Credit of US$ 10 million in 2003. India also enhanced the number of training vacancies under the ITEC programme and provided humanitarian assistance worth US$ 1 million in the form wheat, rice and medicine to meet the requirements arising from drought in 2003. The Djibouti side has requested for an additional credit of US$ 10 million. During the Djiboutian Presidential visit both sides also felt that bilateral relations had reached a stage at which an institutional mechanism such as a Joint Commission could be useful.

Among the areas of cooperation, a Cement Project is being set up in Ali Sabieh under GOI credit of US$ 10 million. Cooperation in other sectors like, to transform the Salt Lake by developing a chain of chemical industries to produce caustic soda, etc are being explored. Djibouti is also interested in training for small and medium scale enterprises to acquire skill for using the tools. Indian side has offered assistance in areas such as setting up Tool Centres in different parts of the country where small tools could be produced. Similarly, in the area of rural electrification, IRCON has conducted feasibility study for rehabilitation works of rural electrification in Djibouti. M/s Kirloskar have supplied generator sets for power production.

Trade relations have picked up considerably following the visit of the President of Djibouti to India in May 2003. India's export to Djibouti increased by 68% (US$ 72.9 million) during April 2003-March 2004 as compared to US$ 37.2 million during the corresponding period of 2002-2003. India's import from Djibouti was US$ 0.81 million and US$ 1.2 million during the period April 2002-March 2003 and April 2003-March 2004 respectively. Most of the trade between India and Djibouti is conducted primarily by the small Indian community in Djibouti numbering around 300. The major items exported by India to Djibouti are iron and steel products, paper and plastic products, machinery, metals, yarns and fabrics, food items and drugs and pharmaceuticals. Main import items are raw hides and skins, metal scraps and leather. (See Table no. 1)

Table No. 1

Indo-Djibouti Trade

Year	India's Exports to Djibouti		India's imports from Djibouti	
	Lakh Rs.	Million US$	Lakh Rs.	Million US$
April 1996 – March 1997	2919.79	8.3	262.50	0.74
April 1997 – March 1998	3278.27	8.7	56.89	0.15
April 1998 – March 1999	5587.23	13.6	78.33	0.19
April 1999 – March 2000	3992.28	9.3	86.37	0.20
April 2000 – March 2001	9559.77	21.2	207.81	0.46
April 2001 – March 2002	7736.80	16.2	352.86	0.74
April 2002 – Sept. 2002	7137.71	14.6	154.25	0.31

Source: DGCI&S

Investment/Joint Ventures

The first project of India-Djibouti Cooperation is the setting up of a Cement Plant in Ali Sabieh under GOI Credit. Cooperation in other sectors is also being explored.

Humanitarian/Emergency Assistance

In 2003, India donated wheat/rice and medicines valued at US$ one million to help in mitigating the shortages caused by drought.

ITEC Assistance and Programmes

Currently, two slots are allotted to Djibouti under the ITEC programme. Following Presidential visit in 2003, the ITEC slots have been increased to 25.

Cultural of Education Cooperation

ICCR sponsored an 8-member composite troupe of Kuchipudi dance and Hindustani violin in July 1998 which was hosted by the Indian community.

Student Exchange Programmes

These were covered under the Executive Programme of Cultural, Education and Scientific Cooperation for the year 2003-2005 signed at New Delhi on 19 May 2003. Djibouti students are also studying in India under self-financing scheme.

Indian Community

The Indian community in Djibouti at present is comprised of about 300 persons including family members. Majority of them belong to Gujarat and a few from Kerela. Late Mr. J. J. Kothari, grandfather of the present Honorary Consul of India was one of the 10 persons who initially came to Djibouti in 1910 and initiated shipping and import business. The Indian community in Djibouti is mainly involved in trading and agency business representing companies from India, China, and South Korea etc. Some of them work as corporate employees holding positions in accounts and management and as computer programmers.

Multilateral/Regional/Sub-Regional Organizations

IGAD or Intergovernmental Authority on Development is headquartered in Djibouti. It consists of seven member States, viz.,

Djibouti, Eritrea, Ethiopia, Kenya, Somalia, Sudan, Uganda. Its basic principles are economic cooperation, regional integration, enhancing and promoting peace and stability. In the joint Indo - Djibouti Statement Djibouti has expressed the belief that India's membership of the IGAD partner's Forum would add to the strength of their organization.

Both the sides have the interest and inclination to promote their relationship by strengthening cooperation in various spheres. The two sides also endeavour at establishing a joint commission to coordinate bilateral engagements in political, commercial, economic, cultural and other fields.

India-Somalia Partnership

India has maintained traditional friendly relations with Somalia. However, the unstable situation in Somalia, since 1991, has disrupted the normal conduct of bilateral relations and co-operation. The situation in Somalia continues to be unstable. India supported UN efforts to restore peace and normalcy. India has taken note of Cairo Declaration on Somalia after the meeting of the leaders of various Somali factions at Cairo from 12 November to 22 December, 1997 including their decision to convene a National Reconciliation Conference.

India has taken note of the outcome of the meeting of the leaders of four main factions in Somalia at Nairobi in April, 1998 to discuss restoration of lasting peace in Somalia. The Nairobi Conference was a follow-up to the Cairo Accord of December, 1997.

India participated in the UN operation in Somalia - UNOSOM- and contributed the second largest contingent of 5000 defense personnel. The Indian contingent also rendered much appreciated humanitarian assistance before its return to India in December, 1994.

India had donated relief supplies consisting of medicines worth Rs. 1 million in June, 1991. India again donated relief supplies of medicines and baby food worth Rs. 2 million in November, 1992 and seeds and medicines worth Rs. 0.6 million in 1994. India also contributed US$ 250,000 to UNOSOM out of Africa Fund.

India's relationship with Somalia had not developed much because of instability factor in Somalia. Its cooperation towards Somalia has only been on the areas of humanitarian assistance and promotion of peace. But the recent political developments show signs of encouragement in reinvigorating their past bilateral relationship. Somalia undoubtedly assumes importance for India in strategic terms.

Common Challenges (Combating Terrorism)

India and the region of Horn of Africa face certain common challenges like terrorism, which they resolve to fight together for their mutual benefit. India and the countries of the Horn condemn all form of terrorist attacks. It is estimated that there are more than a dozen countries in Africa, where terrorist groups (mainly as part of the AI Qaida network) have established a strong presence. Sudan and Somalia figure prominently in that list. Sudan was declared a rogue state by the US because it provided a safe haven to a number of terrorist organizations, including the Al Qaida. Osama bin Laden was quite active in Sudan from 1991-96. Nevertheless, the Sudanese and the Somalian governments joined other African countries in condemning the terrorist attacks against the US. In the war against terrorism Djibouti offered access to sea and airport facilities to the US military. The September 11 attacks and the subsequent attacks on the Indian parliament on December 13, 2001 have led to a greater understanding of the Indian position on terrorism by these countries. They supported in the past India's moves to deter terrorism, at multilateral fora. Both the sides understand the urgency to fight terrorism together for a meaningful partnership to be constructed.

Promotion of Peace

Peace is an elusive commodity in Horn of Africa, which has witnessed scores of conflicts over the years. In a number of these conflicts, the UN peace keeping forces were deployed. India has participated in a number of these peacekeeping operations. It was involved in the United Nations operations in Somalia (UNOSOM II) and in Ethiopia and Eritrea (UNAMEE). India has also encouraged the peace developments in Sudan and Somalia in the recent times. It has also shown its willingness to join the IGAD Forum, which works towards peace process in the region. India understands how essential it is to maintain peace and stability in the region for a viable partnership to sustain and nurture.

Conclusion

India has lot of goodwill in the region. They acknowledge its support in the past and are attracted towards its image as a new centre for technology and commerce in Asia. India also realizes the vast potential of the region as strategic and economic space in terms of energy, water reserves and human resource. With immense potential in both the sides they are nurturing the present relationship and building for future a more permanent and collaborative socio economic infrastructure for sustained growth and modernization. The trajectory of India's relations with the Horn of Africa reflects a change as well as continuity. While traditional ties have been consolidated a new meaning and substance has been given to their relationship. New mutual beneficial partnerships are being built on the strong foundations of the past emotional and political solidarity. Complementarities and interrelationships on the issues of security, stability and prosperity have further been forging there bonding. Both sides are emerging with well-defined joint missions, programmes and projects that have the following broad objectives:

1. To work together for creative, balanced and sustainable democratic socio-economic growth in both nations.
2. To create new programme management organizations and joint venture institutions and forge strong linkages between existing institutions for specific developmental missions.
3. To enable each other to attain and sustain self-sufficiency in energy, food, water, health care and critical new technologies (especially analysis and use of remote sensing data) and to develop surplus capacities to assist other nations.

In addition they are also trying to evolve a common stance for common threats like terrorism and jointly working towards promoting peace in the region, which is very much necessary for a meaningful partnership to endure.

Endnotes

1. *Ministry of External Affairs, Government of India.* 2005 'Joint Statement of India and Sudan at the end of Visit of H.E. Dr. Mustafa Osman Ismail, Foreign Minister of Sudan' http://

meaindia.nic.in/speech/2005/06/08js01.htm, accessed on 10 June 2005

2 *FICCI,* India and Sudan Economic Relations, http://www.ficci.com/international/countries/sudan/sudan-commercialrelations.htm,accessed on 12 June 2004

3. 'Sudan's Oil Industry', http://www.sourcewatch.org/index.php?title= Sudan's_oil_industry, accessed on 13 February 2004

4. Suniti Kumar Chatterji *.1971,India and Ethiopia from the Seventh Century, B. C.* by, *Journal of the American Oriental Society,* Vol. 91, No. 4, pp. 568-569

5. Muthanna, I.M. 1995. *Indo- Ethiopia Relations for Centuries,* Vancouver: James Waix. pp. 5-10

6 'India-Djibouti Bilateral Relations', http://www.embassyofdjibouti.org/Relation.htm, accessed on 3 February 2004

Culture, Education, Literature and Diaspora as Issues and Factors in Indo-African Relations: Focus on India-South Africa Relations

Usha Shukla

The statement 'There is always something new emerging from Africa' (*ex Africa simper aliquid novi*) is an old one, and may have various interpretations. In the sense of things that capture the romantic notions of the human spirit, it challenged adventures and discoverers. To the rapacious and acquisitive, Africa became a rich object of plunder, conquest and exploitation. In this context, it is a curious irony that the people who termed Africa the Dark Continent, coveted it so earnestly that they agreed amongst themselves to partition Africa for each one's exploitation. They did, however, bring their missionaries to enlighten the people. A remark attributed to Jomo Kenyatta, father of modern Kenya, 'when the white man came to our country, we had the land and they had the Bible, now they have the land we have the Bible' sums up the colonial past of Africa. It would seem that the exchange was not very beneficial to Africa. To conclude, the reference to the Latin statement, indeed, much that is new and momentous has been emerging out of Africa, which point in the direction of its having been the cradle of humanity. Extricating itself from its shortcomings of the past and the effects of colonial and oppressive rule, Africa is beginning to tread the path of 'African Solutions to African Problems'.

Africa has had commercial interaction with India over a long period of time. Africa's expeditions outside its continental boundaries were not for conquest or domination; even though involuntarily, her children contributed with their sweat and blood to the prosperity of countries in North and South America and the

Caribbean, in the form of slaves in the initial stages. Asian countries, too, contributed later to similar development of western powers who emerged as the determiners of the world's destiny. Africa evolved and survived by its philosophy of *ubuntu* (Humanism) and Asian countries which were influenced by Buddhist and Hindu thought, applied the maxim: the world is one family (*vasudhaiva kutumbakam*). The following remark, made in the context of India, easily characterizes the role and contributions of both India/Asia and Africa in the History of human civilization:

> India conquered and dominated China culturally for 2000 years without ever having to send a single soldier across her border[1].

If one considers carefully, Mahatma Gandhi spent more than a quarter of his life in Africa, and evolved the doctrines of Ahimsa, Satyagraha, Savinaya Avagnya (civil disobedience) and Sarvodaya on African soil. In this respect, too, many marvellous things have come out of Africa. The mutual relationship between India and Africa may be more founded in the inherent spirituality of the peoples of these land masses, and less on the fact that they were probably part of one continent - as the theory of Gondwana suggests. The considerable similarities in the religious and philosophical thinking in what is called African Traditional religion (for want of a better name) and Hinduism would support such a view[2].

In the twentieth century, India and much of Africa were under colonial or imperial domination of various European powers such as Britain, Spain, France, Portugal, Italy, Belgium and Germany. Whereas Africa at one time supplied labour to the west, in colonial times it provided resources in the form of its mineral wealth and also its labour to the colonialists. The long and painful march towards freedom and sovereignty began to fructify during the middle of the twentieth century with the withdrawal of colonial powers from India in 1947, Ghana in 1957, followed by the rest of the African countries except the then Rhodesia and South Africa.

Both Africa and India have borne the brunt of the colonial powers' negative and cynical perceptions whilst they found it acceptable to use and abuse the human and material resources of their colonies. Hence statements such as 'Naked Fakir' uttered by Winston Churchill for Mahatma Gandhi and the inscrutable expression 'noble savage' employed to denote social, political and spiritual leaders of Africa persist to the discredit of European powers. Perhaps Joseph Conrad, novelist in the English language, in a satirical novel 'Heart of Darkness', conveyed the supreme irony of the situation, when he wrote about the exploitation in the Belgian Congo. Mr Kurtz, a Belgian agent, whilst furthering the interests of his mother country, in ways not reconcilable with decent human standards, orders the following treatment to be meted out to dissidents: 'Exterminate the Brutes'. Author Joseph Conrad leaves it to the reader to determine who the brutes deserving extermination are. Africa has suffered many ignominies at the hands of civilized nations whilst its explorers and writers portrayed it as a place of exciting discovery and natural wonders and wealth. Writers such as Mungo Park (Travels in Africa), H Rider Haggard (King Soloman's Mines) and explorers like David Livingstone and Henry Morton Stanley achieved much in bringing Africa to the attention of the world. It is noteworthy that the potential of Africa was realized by Cecil John Rhodes a century ago, who wished to build a railway line from Cape Town to Cairo! However, the outrageous deeds of some peoples against the children of Africa still rankle: South Africa has been successful in recovering the Head of Hintsa, a local chief, which was taken away to Britain as a trophy. More brutally dehumanising was the treatment meted out to Sarah Bartsman, an indigenous South African woman, who was taken to Britain as a curiosity, and whose body was on exhibition in Paris when she died of neglect and disease. Her remains have been brought home and interred with the appropriate respect for the human dead.

It is not likely that the developing world would soon find itself on an economic par with Europe or America; nor will it get much material support to attain such an elusive status. Leaders of Africa, under the inspired vision of President Thabo Mbeki of South Africa, are engaging in a united effort to find the African solutions to Africa's problems. The formation of the African Union and the opening of the Pan African Parliament recently in Midrand (Johannesburg) are the engines that will drive this endeavour to lift Africa from its present human and natural calamities and economic underachievement. It is indeed heartening to see the determination of the African leaders to make an earnest beginning, in spite of the negativity of the not unexpected detractors. The initial hiccups in setting up such an important body attracted comment. The first President of the Pan African Parliament, Tanzanian Gertrude Mongella, had to slash the parliamentarian's daily allowance by one third. The task of the Pan African Parliament (facetiously referred to by the acronym PAP–the South African staple maize diet) is enormous because it will have to be a 'catalyst for greater democracy on the continent. Only fourteen of the continent's 53 countries can be considered democratic, and most of the PAP's seats will be filled by MPs from repressive nations'. The title of the article quoted, by Tom Nevin, is indicative of the cynicism towards this initiative, as well as the financial burden on South Africa, viz. 'Pan African Parliament – money pit or a beacon of hope?'[3]

Whilst the Pan African Parliament seems to be an answer to the present needs of Africa in the global world, more than the mere establishment of this body redound to the credit of the government of South Africa. Numerous bilateral commissions– with USA, India and China amongst others, have been created. Moreover, a more significant initiative is the joint commission involving Brazil, South Africa and India which ought to produce much needed results with regard to technological cooperation, environmental issues, agricultural and economic benefits and cultural collaboration.

This paper focuses on South Africa and India where there may be common concerns, areas of interest and issues of importance. The long-standing relationship between the two countries, their present state of development in relation to their geographical positions and the leaderships' determination to improve the lot of their own and each other's peoples will be the necessary lubricant in their relationship. The recent state visit of the President of India Dr A P J Abdul Kalam, the first by an Indian Head of State to South Africa, created much goodwill throughout the country. Besides the diplomatic and political significance of this visit, the simplicity, warmth and the intellectual dimensions of His Excellency made a lasting impression on South Africans from all walks of life. This ought to herald a new era of India–South Africa cooperation to help the two countries develop, and assist in the upliftment of the vast underdeveloped and developing world to meet the challenges and opportunities of globalization. The two countries are sufficiently imbued with the desire of doing so, and endowed with the cumulative vision of Albert Luthuli,

Nelson Mandela, Mohandas K Gandhi and Jawaharlal Nehru to be able to work harmoniously and successfully. A considerable extent of this success will depend on the abilities of the various teams and task groups to work together for a common goal to serve humanity.

The presence of 1.2 million South Africans of Indian origin in South Africa, and the sojourn of Mahatma Gandhi in the country for 21 years, is a factor not to be underestimated when considering the relationship between India and South Africa. Similar elements were instrumental in forging bonds with countries in East Africa for the past one century, and India's offer of human aid in the form of teachers and other professionals to West African countries since the 1960s helped their development. The South African community of Indian extraction is a settled one, in the sense that they are South Africans in the full sense of the word. Granted citizenship a hundred years after arriving here (1961), and having survived the social engineering of Apartheid and separate development, the 'Indosafricans' began to experience full citizenship and protection under the law after the advent of democracy in 1994. Questions of their being a minority, and therefore, in some way vulnerable, often arise. However, the Constitution being the supreme law of the land is cited to allay these. It may be inappropriate to consider a community as a minority under constitutional rule; and our leaders have often appealed to South Africans of Indian origin to become part of the majority who were at some time or other disadvantaged, since our laws are explicit that Africans, Coloureds and Indians fall into the category of disadvantaged. Hence, the existence of political parties that put forward the notion of 'minority' is questionable. Identity, on the basis of religion, language or culture is a separate matter. 'To assert one identity is not to deny another' states an article in Post[4]:

> The Indian identity, like the identities of all of the minority groupings, be they Portuguese, Congolese, Bohemian or Mongolian, is not just a surviving one but also an absorbing one ......the Greek, English, Zambian, Swazi, Zanzibari, Zulu, Tswana, Xhosa or Indian identities are not a unique feature of the South African rainbow, and to assert one identity is not to deny another identity.

The relationship between India and South Africa developed on the basis of mutual support in world fora. India early became conspicuous as a supporter of the oppressed peoples of South Africa. Lawyer and commentator Pat Poovalingam wrote the following in his weekly column in the 'Post[5]'

> After Srinivasa Sastri publicly condemned 'the sonorous hypocrisy of Smuts' who was then South Africa's Prime Minister, India took its firm stand. And as several African National Congress leaders have stated, from that time on, for nearly fifty years until the *uhuru* of 1994, India gave very considerable material, moral and diplomatic support to the ANC.

I shall now examine some aspects of the bilateral relations to determine the factors and issues that require attention.

The imperatives of globalization and certain changes in world power balance in the post-cold war period could lead to the marginalization of some of the world's poorest nations. It is hence incumbent on the leaders of the 'second world' foremost amongst these being South Africa and India, to adopt measures that would create solidarity with the understanding that we have a common destiny. The broad cultural aspects of the lives of different nations and communities need to be understood to deepen the feeling of a common humanity. India and South Africa have measures in place to facilitate cultural exchange through their diplomatic missions. Much good work is being done through the Indian High Commission in South Africa, as well as the Consulates-General in Johannesburg and Durban. South Africa must augment its cultural ventures in India, so that the people of India, who are always eager to know about South Africa, get a clear understanding of our history and culture. There is tremendous regard for South Africa's icon the Hon. Nelson Mandela in India, just as there is reverence for Gandhi in South Africa. The feeling of 'ownership' of these two figures on both sides of the Indian Ocean creates the environment for the meeting of hearts and minds of the peoples of the two countries. It is, therefore, necessary to extend the cordiality existing between the governments, and also business leaders, to the common people.

Language and Literature are important components of culture and the means of communicating thoughts and values to others. In the colonial period, the colonial powers imposed their languages and literature on their subjects whilst giving some support to the indigenous languages. In the present era, when many languages are under threat of becoming obsolete, India and South Africa have both given constitutional protection to the major languages of their territories. The South African constitution provides for the respect and promotion of Eastern Languages as well- Hindi, Tamil, Telugu, Gujarati, Sanskrit, Urdu and Arabic in addition to eleven official languages. There is provision for the teaching of most of the Eastern Languages in the South African school system. The cultural memories of people are sustained through their languages, hence the maxim-if language disappears, then culture also disappears. The appointment of the Commission for the Rights of Cultural, Religious and Linguistic Communities, in terms of our Constitution, will bring greater support to languages and culture.

Literature in or on Africa up to a hundred years ago was scant. During the twentieth century novelists and explorers wrote about their experiences in Africa, or on mythical topics such as the figure Prester John, a supposed potentate in the Middle East. John Buchan's novel 'Prester John' portrays the figure of the Reverend John Laputa who tried to revive the cult of Prester John and his opulent empire. Freedom from colonial rule encouraged African writers to express themselves through literature, although often in the language medium of the colonists. African countries are now taking the initiative of developing their own intellectual outlook. Writers have been engaged in the process of creating African paradigms, following the publication of Ngugi Wa Thiong'o's celebrated work "Decolonising the Mind". An 'African Intellectuals Conference' held in Dakar, Senegal, in early October 2004, included many writers amongst the 700 delegates. It is an encouraging step, and came at a time when even the British government is looking at new and appropriate ways to aid Africa's development through its Africa Commission.

Another African writer, Wole Soyinka, added a new dimension to the concept of African solidarity in an article analysing Western and African responses to acts of terrorism in their territories and elsewhere. He describes how fear muted the voices of African leaders when an airliner carrying hundreds of passengers was shot down in Niger's airspace in 1989. He says, 'the world jettisoned all notion of a common humanity'. He further states, 'from Lockerbie through Niger to Manhattan (World Trade Centre) the trail of fear had stretched and broadened to engulf the globe, warning its inhabitants that there was no longer any categories of the involved or the non-involved. No longer could, not just innocents, but even the community of historical victims that inhabit the African continent lay claim to a protective immunity'[6].

Soyinka tries to exhort African leaders to prepare to defend their own, because the reactions of world powers only tend to secure their own interests. India and South Africa have a vast body of 'struggle' literature which should be made available to each other. The common goal of freedom and love of country and compatriots are to be found in the literatures of both countries. India's vast literary heritage can be not only of interest, but value to other countries and cultures, and must be disseminated.

The speed of globalization and the Information Technology revolution have perhaps begun to outstrip the educational systems of developing countries. For economic and industrial progress, technology and innovation have become indispensable. Moreover, the needs of people with regard to food, clean water, sanitation and health care are major challenges to be met by the science and technology institutions of the world. Educational systems are being reformed in order to achieve the developmental goals, even while there are millions of children in India and South Africa not attending school, or attending 'open air' schools. Earnest efforts have to be made to build schools, and get the proper equipment and teachers, and more importantly, the pupils to learn to become competitive in the market of life. Adult literacy must also be tackled with greater vigour to empower the disadvantaged. Concepts of 'each one teach one' and the 'Ekal Vidyalaya' system being tried out by some movements in India must be examined for ideas on tackling ignorance. The availability of IT and the modern 'open' universities will be fruitless if the infrastructure does not provide for exploiting the scientific development.

Indian sage and reformer, Swami Vivekananda, had said that education is the manifestation of the divinity already in man. Holistic education must aim for the material as well as the moral/spiritual development of people. Whilst the governments of India and South Africa are both secular in nature, there is a difference in their approach to religion in the educational system. Whereas there is no religious education in the Indian state schools, South Africa has embarked on a new educational policy whereby religious education will be provided to learners up to the twelfth grade in order to equip all the learners with knowledge of the world's major religions. This is in keeping with our constitutional goals of respect for the people of different religions / cultures, respect for diversity and other human rights goals. In a world torn by intolerance and alienation, this aspect of the curriculum would bring about a change in peoples' mindsets towards the faiths of others.

Education at higher levels is well catered for in both countries, and there is already much cooperation and exchange in the fields of science, medicine and technology. There is need for concerted and combined action to find ways to beat the AIDS scourge, India and South Africa being the leaders in the numbers of victims of the epidemic. Use of modern science and traditional, indigenous healing systems will have to be explored and developed to fight this disease, as well as other life threatening diseases that afflict the developing and underdeveloped world. Both countries have the scientists and the researchers, as well as indigenous materials: they must be given the facilities to expedite progress.

An important outcome for the citizens of India and South Africa is opportunities for them in the educational-cultural field. Many hundreds of Indian citizens are employed at South African tertiary educational institutions. Our government had earlier this year announced its intention of recruiting large numbers of civil service staff from the Indian sub-continent to boost service delivery. South Africans too will increasingly enjoy opportunities in India, once joint ventures in mining, manufacturing etc. are finalized. The need to know the culture of both countries, as well as their official languages, becomes apparent. South Africa welcomes the opportunity given to Ms Ilene Hamann of Jeffreys Bay, a South African, to act in the Hindi film *Rog,* directed by Pooja Bhatt, actress and producer daughter of the renowned Mahesh Bhatt. Whilst Mahesh Bhatt, commenting on the charm and suitability of Ilene, said 'she is a dewdrop from heaven', unfortunately Ilene had no knowledge of India, its culture or the Hindi language. Only loving care from Ms Bhatt prepared Ilene for her role[7]. How much easier would things have been, had there been a facility for the preparation of South Africans and Indians for movement from one country to the other, especially in terms of language and culture.

An encouraging development at the University of KwaZulu Natal in Durban is underway. In new moves to bring Africa and Asia closer to work on common goals, the governments of India, South Africa and Indonesia took the decision to revive the spirit and goals of the Bandung (Afro-Asian) Conference (1955). At the Association of South East Asian Nations (ASEAN) Conference in Phnom Penh, Cambodia, November 2002, President Thabo Mbeki, as chairman of the African Union briefed the leaders on the origins and aims of NEPAD (New partnership for Africa's development). As a result, an Asian African Sub-regional Conference (AASROC) was held in Bandung, Indonesia in July 2003. This conference discussed ways and means by which the people of Africa and Asia could achieve full economic, social, political and cultural cooperation.

In pursuance of the above, steps were taken at the University of KwaZulu Natal to establish the Centre for Africa-Asia Studies whose main objectives are:

- To strengthen Africa–Asia relations and cooperation by providing a platform for dialogue and the exchange of data, information and knowledge;
- To increase opportunities for international student / faculty exchange, with a particular emphasis on expanding post-graduate activities;
- To explore and record historical links and shared experiences between the two continents;
- To facilitate innovation and aid in bilateral skills transfer;
- To foster mutual understanding of the various languages, traditions and belief systems of the two continents;
- To promote interaction and collaboration in the visual and performing arts and other modes of cultural representation and expression.

An immediate result of this initiative was the activation of the Gandhi-Luthuli Peace Institute (GLPI), which was in planning for over five years. This Institute, which will offer courses and promote research in Peace Studies, will be headed by a Professor appointed and paid by the Government of India for an initial period of three years. Another positive outcome of the launch of the Centre for

Africa-Asia Studies was the decision to reinstate the offering of Eastern Languages, viz. Hindi, Sanskrit, Urdu, Tamil, Telugu, Arabic and Gujarati; which were discontinued six years ago.

It is with the provision of educational facilities that countries can equip their people to achieve development goals and interact with other peoples in this era of globalization. Isolation, as in the case of South Africa during the apartheid era, can only be detrimental to development of knowledge, peoples and countries, and the solution of critical problems. In this context, it would be imperative that India also offers Studies in African Languages and cultures at its major educational institutions.

South Africa has had an 'Indian' presence for one hundred and forty five years, beginning with the arrival of Indentured Labourers from the ports of Madras and Calcutta in November 1860. Hence, in spite of the isolation during colonial rule and the apartheid era, South Africa also forms part of the Indian Diaspora. The South African people of Indian origin are fully integrated into the national life of the country. However, they cherish the religio-cultural links with the land of their forefathers. Unlike in the original meaning of Diaspora (nurturing the feeling/expectation of returning permanently to the land of origin) the South African Indians do not harbour such intentions. Professor R Sitaram encapsulated the stance of the majority of South African Indians thus[8]:

> The South African Indians are committed to doing their duty towards their country. Their expectations of India are that they continue to get support and cooperation in the fields of business, culture and education; nothing else is sought.

Africa and India both have a common interest in the Diaspora—particularly in the Caribbean and America, where people of African and Indian origin settled; the African people as slaves long before Indentured Indians whose exodus from India started after the abolition of slavery in 1834-Mauritius—1834, Guyana 1838, Trinidad 1845, South Africa 1860, Suriname 1871 and Fiji 1879.

The situation of Mauritius is unique amongst these: it is geo-politically part of Africa and a major constituent of the Indian Diaspora, although it also refers to itself as 'Little India'. Its proximity to both mainland Africa and India has favoured it with regard to cultural and educational support. In Mauritius one can see the mother-country strongly embracing its separated offspring and making a variety of opportunities available to them. Being in the majority, Indo-Mauritians probably feel comfortable with their expression of affinity to India. As an Indian Ocean Rim state Mauritius has an important role to play in Asian-African relationships. The sizeable Creole population of Mauritius emphasizes its African links. The socio-economic upliftment of the Creoles is a significant challenge for Mauritius as a role player in the African Union.

India as the Mother country of the Indian diaspora containing PIOs (People of Indian Origin—who left India in the 19th century) and NRIs settled in USA, Britain, etc. during the latter part of the 20th century has been playing its supportive role wherever physically and diplomatically possible. Since the turn of the 20th century, Indian missionaries and teachers have been travelling the "indentured" diaspora imparting religious knowledge and encouraging the retention and study of the Indian Languages. South African Indians benefited from the work of Prof. Bhai Paramanand, Swami Shankeranandaji amongst a number of others. In recent decades, journalists and scholars have also taken greater interest in the Indians overseas. The Antar Rashtriya Sahayog Parishad under the leadership of Sri Baleshwar Agrawal has been publishing "Mother India, Children Abroad" with special issues focussing on different countries, such as Trinidad, South Africa, Suriname etc. "Pravasi Sansar" is a new addition to this, being published by Sri Rakesh Pandey of New Delhi. The Government of India helps to organize the World Hindi Conferences in these countries, and copious amounts of literature are made available on these occasions when the members of the diaspora find the opportunity to meet one another. The holding of Pravasi Bharatiya Divas, marking the date when Mahatma Gandhi returned to India from South Africa (1915), provides an opportunity to recognize and meet the offspring of the Pravasis — the emigrant Indians. There is even a Ministry for Overseas Indians established in Delhi. This Pravasi Bharatiya Divas is seen as a gathering of PIOs, and also some Non-Resident Indians. Although there are some differences between the PIOs and NRIs, and they may have not been able to embrace each other as long lost cousins, an attempt should be made to efface the differences, which will persist if the distinction as PIO and NRI remain.

The African Diaspora is located in the Caribbean Area and the United States of America. Although most of the people of African origin who are in the diaspora were from the West African region, South Africa does not make any distinction, but embraces them in the spirit of African solidarity amongst the children of Mother Africa. Hence when African leaders and intellectuals talk of Africanism, they include all the offspring of Africa, wherever they may be and whatever language or religion they profess. A noteworthy event occurred earlier this year when President Jean-Bertrand Aristide was ousted from Haiti. He first took refuge in North Africa, but returned to Haiti. The South African Government offered him sanctuary with his family in South Africa until the situation in Haiti normalizes. Whilst this prospect does not seem to materialize soon, our government has considered it appropriate and necessary to assist our fellow African who was removed illegally from office after having been elected duly to that office. Interpretations and comments on this move by our government varied from cynicism to support. The following note in the journal "African Business" reflects the negativity surrounding our government's action. Captioned "Aristides R1million Joyride" the article reads[9]:

> South African taxpayers forked out nearly a Million Rand to send Thabo Mbeki's presidential jet to Haiti to fetch former President Jean-Bertrand Aristide, his family and entourage and take them to Pretoria..........

The next line reveals the shallowness of the criticism and lack of understanding of the situation as well as the factors motivating President Mbeki to send his jet:

> The 26000 kilometre round trip was two and a half times more expensive than if the exiled group had travelled business class on a commercial airline.

President Mbeki's and the Government's refusal to engage in polemics over this indicates the new thinking on international and African issues.

Fiji, part of the diaspora, also had an incident of this type some years ago, when Prime Minister Mahendra Chaudhary's government was held hostage in the Parliament buildings. This type of occurrences can be avoided by creating an environment wherein democratic processes are followed and respected.

There is a very delicate population balance in some of the diaspora countries, e.g. Trinidad, between people of Indian origin and those of African origin. Various accommodations between the political parties representing these people succeed in maintaining socio-political stability. Just as India and Africa are moving closer to each other through common ideals and interests, this relationship should be reflected in the diaspora, where people of Indian and African origin begin to appreciate each other's humanity and needs. Perhaps the Pan African Parliament and the African Union can devise means of attaining this goal.

In the context of diaspora issues, a few matters require decisive action. Access to the countries of the diapora in the Caribbean is made difficult because of absence of consular or diplomatic missions within South Africa, and other countries of Africa, for the issuance of travel documents. South Africa is a popular destination for people seeking a better life; and a new phenomenon has emerged, which creates problems, particularly for the women of our country. Marriages of convenience, with the knowledge of the South African citizen (and generally for a financial consideration) enable males from African countries and the Indo-Pak Subcontinent to gain entry into South Africa. The problem aspect arises when, through illegal means, access is obtained to the citizenship details of the women and they are 'married' to people without even knowing about it.

The foregoing problems, compounded by influx of refugees, 'illegal' immigrants and the need for repatriation, created enormous human suffering and inconvenience. Governments involved in these matters need to harmonize their rules and regulations with regard to immigration, travel, residence etc. in order to create a better environment for international relations.

Endnotes

1 'Hu Shih-Chinese Ambassador to USA 1938-1942' in Deshmukh, V.V. 2000. *Khoj: Sachche Bharat ki*. Pune: Deshmukh Lokahita Pratisthan.

2 Literature on Research carried out at Centre for Afro-Hindu Studies and International Centre for Cultural Studies, Nagpur.

3 *African Business*, 2004. August/September, p. 39.

4 Nanackchand, Ami. 2004. 'Fourth Column'. *Post,* Durban, 6-10 October.

5 Poovalingam, Pat. 2004. 'Straight Talk'. *Post,* Durban, 6-10 October, p. 16

6 Soyinka, Wole. 2004. 'Living in the Shadow of Fear'. *Sunday Times.* Johannesburg. 25 March, p. 21

7 *Daily News.* 2004. Durban. 8 October, p. 3.

8 Sitaram, R. 2004. 'Pravasi Bharatiya: Sanskritik, Rajnaitik evam Arthik Ayam tatha Apeksae' in *Pravasi Sansar.* Delhi. January / March p. 6.

9 *African Business.* 2004. August-September. p. 8.

African Indians: Settled Stereotypes and Limits of Socio-Cultural Adaptation

Vyacheslav Usov

Introduction

Although Indian-African contacts were known from the times immemorial, there was not a considerable Indian immigration to Africa until the 19th century when the British brought a number of indentured laborers in their colonies in Southern, Eastern and Central parts of the 'Dark' Continent. Later, these indentured labourers were followed by so-called free passenger Indians. Notwithstanding usually bad treatment, harsh climate and unfriendly social environment, the Indians had met in their land of adoption, they managed to uplift the social ladder. By the end of 19th century Indian settlers occupied the important positions in colonial business and trade.

Today around one million people Indian origin live in South Africa and about 130 thousands of them in Eastern Africa. Many African Indians in African countries are businessmen and usually far well-off than the indigenous Blacks. They run an enormous bulk of national trade and industries, however, their political and social status is not equivalent to the high economic status. The political and economic status is rather low Moreover, well-being and thriving of the Indians have paved the way for Black majority's resentment and hostilities towards the 'Asians' (nickname for immigrants from Indian subcontinent).

In spite of living for so long in Africa, Indians are often considered by indigenous population as aliens from racial, political and economical point of view. They have often been targeted by populist Black politicians for their alleged disloyalty to the countries of their adoption and fall victims to ethnic-motivated crimes and harassment. However, the degree of animosity is mutual. This mutual perception of Africans and Indians is to a great extent tangled with prejudices and distrust. This paper is aimed to clarify the main characteristic features of African perception of the Indians and otherwise Indian perception of the Blacks.

Colonial Legacy and Post-colonial Development

Certainly there is a plain difference between the Indian communities in East Africa and South Africa respectively. From the very beginning the Indians arriving in the then East African colonies were seen by the British colonial administration as the 'second tier' in three-tier structure of the colonial society with Whites in the upper position, Indians in the middle and Blacks at the bottom. Some political activities of the Indians there, including a famous demand pursued by some of the prominent Indian political leaders to turn former German East Africa (Tanganyika) into a colony of India after Germany's defeat in the World War One and further Indian hartal strikes or closure of shops movement in 1920, generated deep African resentments against 'Asians'. The hardest hit of this movement were African consumers who saw prices of food stuff rise from 100 to 300 percent as a result of the strike, which apparently seriously increased racial tensions between Indians and Africans.

A growing alienation between two racial groups resulted finally in Africanisation policy pursued by the new native rulers of East African countries after they got their independence. Indians were subjected to different forms of discrimination with Idi Amin decision to expel all the Indians from Uganda in 1972 as the most dramatic moment.

From the late 1980s, the governments of East African countries abandoned their early policy of clamping down of 'Asian' business. A new, more liberal and encouraging economic policy impacted a lot on a relatively successful economic development of Uganda and Tanzania in 1990s. The end of Ujamaa and self-reliance policy in Tanzania in late 1980s and early 1990s marked a moment of celebration to the 'Asian' business. The 'Asians' turned out to be financially better-equipped to apply for trade licences than the Blacks. As one 'Asian' said: 'We bring containers full of televisions or refrigerators, we sell them. There is quick turnover and then we import again. We have no industries, no investments. All we have are containers.'[1]

The arrival of 'containers economy' in spite of its plain speculative nature to great extent revitalized Tanzanian depressed economy. By the middle of the 1990s, the number of Asians in East Africa rose from 100 thousands to 130 thousands[2] but the process of 'Asian' rehabilitation was not easy.[3] Public opinion of the country was not as welcomed towards foreign investors as Tanzanian ruling classes. There was a rise of anti-Asian moods before coming October 1995 elections that made some Indians close their enterprises and left the country for a while.[4] In January 1999, the late president of Tanzania, J. Nyerere, criticized the privatization programme, which meant in his words that national property would be handed over to foreigners. Later that year some Tanzanian officials declared that there was a necessity for indigenisation of national economy.[5] Additional interracial conflicts were generated in Tanzania when the Indians were allowed to acquire farmlands, which for a long time before had been used by local people to graze cattle.

One of the most difficult and potentially provoked problem, facing the Indian communities in Africa and liberal-minded African governments too, is return of former properties of Indians who had to fled the East African countries in 60-70s to its former owners. It has not special importance for Kenya where in spite of some ethnical limitations the percentage of firms owned by Indians from the colonial period through the 1980s varied from 71 to 85 percent. In Uganda such a policy is an integral part of wide economic reforms promoted by the President Y. Museweni who repeatedly called all of expatriates to come back and some really did.

Aside from their compatriots in East Africa, where colonial administration de-facto was successful in using the Indians as a buffer between white rulers and black subjects, the Indians in South Africa were treated as 'blacks'. After apartheid was established in South Africa in 1948, a large number of Indians fought with Africans against the suppressing regime. While the relations between Black and Indian leaders were often friendly, the bursts of hatred happened and mutual animosity was preserved for a long time. The position of the Indians was further deteriorated in the eyes of Blacks during the latest years of apartheid rule when three-chamber legislative body, which included Whites, Coloureds and Indian representatives, was established and a number of

Indians were given ministerial posts with fat salaries. Notwithstanding their inferior position to the Whites during the days of apartheid, a lot of Indians supported the National Party of F. De Clerk in the first non-racial elections in 1994.

Actually, the first truly democratic election in South Africa had substantial implications for the South African Indian community. The high profile of the Indians in the ANC hierarchy was very beneficial. When Nelson Mandela became the President of South Africa he included six Indians in his cabinet of sixteen members. The Indians, making up three percent of the population, were over-represented at executive level. They also had a proportionally larger number of members of Parliament. With Mandela and Buthelezi being the only traditional 'chiefs' in the cabinet many Africans were reported to grumble that 'there were too many Indians and not enough chiefs'.[7]

By every indicator of economical and social well-being and development, the Indian South Africans were until recently the most successful minority both economically and politically and come next to Whites. 92 per cent of the community lives in a house or a brick structure; 99 per cent use electricity; 96 per cent use piped water; 77 per cent have telephones and so on. The average national profile of South Africa presents a rather different picture with Blacks as the most disadvantaged category.[8] However, the recent outburst of hostility against the ethnic Indians caused by Mbongeni Ngema song has become a sign, which shows how fragile and unstable the well-being of Indians is even in the country where they were at least from 1994 regarded as respected and deserved minority.

Mbongeni Ngema Song and Major Challenges Facing Indians in South Africa

The song 'Amandiya' (Indians in Zulu), written by a noted antiapartheid song and playwriter Mbongeni Ngema, who for long was a champion of a multiracial society, stirred up racial and ethnic tension in KwaZulu-Natal province of South Africa in 2002. The lyrics of the song are: 'Oh brothers, Oh my fellow brothers. We need strong and brave men to confront Indians. This situation is very difficult, Indians do not want to change, whites were far better than Indians. Even Mandela has failed to convince them to change.' They [Indians] also 'keep coming from India' to South Africa. [9]

Ngema declared that the views of black people who gathered at taxi ranks and bus stops, at shebeens, soccer matches and 'many other places' were expressed in his song. 'I believe it is my role as an artist... to mirror the society and highlight the plight of the people on the ground. The leadership relies on us artists to voice out issues where there is perceived oversight.'[10]

The song has been widely condemned as racist and provocative by almost every significant person in South Africa from Nelson Mandela to the leaders of the New National Party, the remnant of the party that built apartheid. The South Africa Human Rights Commission received several objections against the song and lodged an official complaint with the Broadcasting Complaints Commission.[11] South Africa's Broadcasting Complaints Commission (SABC) banned the song from the radio on the grounds that it constituted hate speech. Despite the official condemnations, Ngema consistently refused to apologies to Indian community. He told the SABC that the song tried to address the fundamental problems between blacks and Indians, rather than creating confrontation. 'The song is intended to begin a public debate on the issue (as the opening line of the song says) and not to cause racial hatred,' he said.[12]

The song has struck a chord among many South African blacks, particularly in Durban, where Ngema lives and Indians make up 27 percent of the urban population. Ngema's album was selling rapidly since its release in March 2002, and bootleg copies made the rounds in local townships. A number of violent acts and atrocities against the Indians were reported to take place in Durban after the song had been written and the members of Indian community believe that the wave of crime had been caused by the song. On June 25, 2002, probably under the growing pressure, Ngema announced that he has started to work with local Durban churches and community leaders to schedule several events to encourage community dialogue between Blacks and Indians.[13]

Some commentators made a suggestion that ultimately the song may serve to mend fences. And indeed, a number of Indian and African businessmen frightened by a potential danger to their business and stability planned a summit of Indian and African businessmen to address escalating concerns and defuse 'potentially explosive situation'. Vivian Reddy, an Indian and a self-made businessman with links to the African political and business community, proclaimed: 'While there are legitimate concerns that need to be addressed in creating a combined ethos of business, public perception has been steered totally by a one-sided perspective and therefore an urgent debate of the issues needs to be engaged in as a matter of national importance.'[14] He also had discussions with Deputy President Jacob Zuma, who allegedly supported the forum.

Zuma, however, was once accused by then National Director of Public Prosecution of South Africa, Bulelani Ngcuka of being 'corrupt and in trouble because he had surrounded himself with the Indians'.[15] This incident greatly troubled Indian community. The president of the Indian Academy of South Africa, Dr T. P. Naidoo said 'any person reading this [the news report] will have the distinct impression that most, if not all, Indians are either corrupt or conduct business unlawfully'. 'Once perceptions have been established, they are difficult to wipe out', he noted.[16]

This note obviously takes à point. Two years after Mbongeni Ngema had released his song, it is still stirring up the tensions. A burst of hatred against the Indians has recently taken place in Ntha, small settlement near Bethlehem in South Africa. A store of Abdul Khan, the Indian, a formerly thriving business, was stoned and looted by angry African mob after a Black employee of the Khan's had a fight with another Black youth and stabbed him to death. As the police inspector, investigating this matter, explained: '...people in the community somehow got the impression the Khans were responsible' and '...were making all sorts of allegations against the Khans'.[17] He added the safety of the family had only been secured at midnight, after the arrival of police reinforcements.

One of the men at Ntha bottlestore explained the situation from his point of view: 'Life in these rural areas is very different from urban living...' 'We adhere to old values and beliefs and respect one another. But these Indians... You've heard Mbongeni Ngema's song, Amandiya. It's all true. You can't run away from that...' It was not only unbridled racism that the men voiced, but also hate speech, and threats. 'What's happened will spread. Coolies have got it coming for them, also in KwaZulu-Natal.'[18]

While Indian community of South Africa was greatly resented at Ngema and Ngcuka, some of its prominent members have to admit real problems in relations between Indians and Blacks. 'You've got the Indian trader, the Indian shopkeeper who is constantly in the eyes of the African because he trades with them,' says Dr. Fatima Meer, head of the Institute for Black Research at the University of Natal. 'The African looks at him and thinks, "even he has more than I do."'[19] 'They [Indians] treat you like an animal,' says Sfiso Ngcobo, an off-duty policeman outside the Marketplace mall, to the reporter of Daily Mail & Guardian. He said that the song of Ngema reflects the way most Africans views about the Indian community. 'Sometimes you try to help an Indian person and they just think you're going to do something to them.'[20]

Certainly not every crime committed in South Africa against the Indians is caused by the racist prejudices and ethnically motivated hatred. The escalation in crime in South Africa has often been attributed to the youth, many of whom have fought the good fight but are otherwise ill-prepared to deal with the realities of post-apartheid South Africa. The crime has also been attributed to the influx of Africans from neighboring countries. These migrants have entered the borders of the country and set up squatter camps in Indian neighborhoods. Non-militant and usually peaceful Indians are often considered by the criminals as easy targets.

However, more fundamental reasons for South African Indian community to worry exist. When the ANC Government was formed it systematically began to abolish apartheid discriminatory legislation. All the previously disadvantaged groups benefited and the Indians prospered the most because of the advantages of superior education and greater wealth. The ANC Government introduced legislation to empower all previously disadvantaged communities. But eventually because of many companies had previously discriminated against local Blacks their affirmative action polices tended to favour the Blacks. They also interpreted Blacks as meaning people of African origin. The Indian community objected strongly and on several occasions Nelson Mandela and his senior officials assured the Indian community that all previously disadvantaged communities (African, Coloureds and Indians) should be treated equally in affirmative action programmes.

Despite of the government assurances the Indian community felt that they have been marginalized. For instance, Indians previously were the majority at the University of Durban-Westville. The University systematically increased the intake of Black students in many courses where they had previously had no access. Medicine was one course where few Blacks were able to enter at local universities. The University of Natal was the only university that enrolled Black students and even there more Indians were accepted than Blacks. The decision, by the University of Natal, to let student registration be dictated by population demographics resulted in an outcry from the Indian community and had some political implications. Prof. Narendra Bhana, University of Durban-Westville said that the Minority Front Party, by the maverick politician Amichand Rajbansi, attracted many followers as he had pledged to fight for a better dispensation for the Indian community.[21]

Since South Africa's transition from apartheid to democracy, Nelson Mandela has endeavoured to make the country's minority communities feel more secure. He has held many meetings with White, Coloured and Indian opinion-makers to address their insecurities. In May 2000, Mandela held a meeting with about 30 young Indian graduates and professionals. He wanted to discuss pertinent issues related to the Indian community. Mandela opened the meeting by asking Indian intellectuals for their assessment of the ANC Government's performance since 1994 and to raise issues of concern to the Indian community. The President was surprised at the level of insecurity expressed by the Indian youth. There was a litany of complaints about the Indian not having a place in the 'rainbow nation', resentment about the progress of unqualified and inefficient Blacks, the hackneyed line about Indians not being Black enough, insecurities about affirmative action and fears about Blacks 'taking over our schools, suburbs and jobs.'[22]

The real problem of post-apartheid South Africa is that the long awaited peace dividend has only partly materialized. The poor economic prospects and the high level of unemployment has resulted in minority groups such as the Whites, Coloureds and Indians being fearful and suspicious of the Blacks who have been the main beneficiaries of the policy of affirmative action. Indians have always expressed admiration and support for the ANC but in the general election of 1994, over fifty percent of Indians voted for the National Party. It was the Indian support that enabled the Inkatha Freedom Party to become the ruling party in KwaZulu-Natal province by a small majority. Why were the Indians acting this way? According to Bhana, there is a general suspicion among the Indian community that while the ANC has appointed many Indians in key government positions, it has, in its actions, tended to marginalize the Indian community as a whole from mainstream economic activities.[23]

A major challenge facing the Indian community today is their perceived disloyalty to South Africa. This is based more on the experience in the rest of Africa rather than the reality of the South African situation. For the vast majority of Indians, South Africa is their natural home. Indians have very little contact with their kith and kin in India. After 129 years in the country the Indian community here has the largest population outside India. Compared to Whites very few Indians have emigrated. Contrary to the Indians in Eastern Africa they do not have British passports. The vast majority of the South African Indians belong to the middle class and even the wealthy do not export excess capital to India or any other country. The stringent foreign exchange regulations, which until recently had existed in the country since 1960 precluded the possibility of diverting any meaningful amount of capital out of South Africa. Nevertheless, Prof. Bhana regrets, the old arguments about the Indians who prefer 'milking the cow' to 'feeding the cow' still prevail.[24]

Asians and Blacks in East Africa

While the South African political and social situation is unique one in Sub-Saharan Africa there are likely growing similarities in mutual perception of two racial groups, Blacks and Indians, in both South Africa and the rest part of the continent. Not only economic inequality and unfair business competition seem to be the important sources of interracial tensions but a deep cultural gap that divides two communities. This is less visible in South Africa where the Indians, although assimilated western culture and lifestyle, regard South Africa as their 'natural motherland'. But the same is rarely true for the Indians in East Africa.

Abdul Sheriff, Prof. of History at the University of Dar-es-Salaam and principal curator of the Zanzibar museums, expresses his regrets about his Indian compatriots on the mainland

[Tanzania and Kenya]. They regard Africa as nothing more than a 'transit lounge'. In his interview to *The Times of India* he says the Indians in Nairobi, for example, had assimilated western culture but hardly anything at all of African culture.

The prejudices against the 'Asians' have been inadvertently reinforced by the Indian community itself, with its custom of holding itself culturally and economically separately, shop separately and rarely mix or marry outside their own groups. In spite of their own differences, sometimes as deeply divisive as those dividing Indians from their African neighbours, 'Asians' are perceived by native population as a homogeneous and exclusive or, some say, even reclusive group. Intensely focused on family and community, 'the Asian is the eternal other,' wrote a world famous writer Shiva Naipaul after visiting East Africa in the 1970s. Naipaul, a native of Trinidad, where Indian immigrants had become an inalienable part of nation, was struck by how 'the Indian in East Africa brought India with him and kept it inviolate.'[25]

Mistrust and friction between Blacks Africans and Indians in East Africa has been so famous for a long time that *The Lonely Planet* travel guide for Kenya, by Hugh Finlay and Geogg Growther, gives the following description: 'They [Indians] kept very much to themselves, regarding the Africans as culturally inferior and lazy'.[26] This, in turn, provoked black Africans to regard 'Asians' as clubby and standoffish.

Agehananda Bharati, a professor of anthropology at Syracuse University examines Afro-Indian race relations in his 1972 book *The Asians in East Africa.* He asserts that many South Asian merchants held negative attitudes against Africans:

> Some of the more liberal among the Asian educated readily admit the exploitation of native customers...the discourteous treatment given to them...but the majority of the Asians do not see it his way: 'we Asians,' so several small *duka*-owners told me, 'do not care much for public relations with our customers; we do not treat them politely...whether they are Asian, African or white.'

The book of Prof. Bharati was written more than thirty years ago but the same opinion is still common among many Indian traders and entrepreneurs. An interesting discussion about promoting the indigenous participation in economy took place in Tanzanian mass media last year. The discussion began when MP and former minister for industries and trade Iddi Simba declared, 'the government should set up policies that encourage indigenous to do business' and accused government officials of facilitating the enrichment of 'Asians and Arabs' alone.[27] Idi's speech entailed a number of very negative replies from Tanzanian Indians. One of them called Ahmed Sachedina, probably an Indian, finally concluded that so-called 'sera ya wazawa' (encourage of indigenous in Swahili) policy is equivalent to eviction of Indian businessmen as it was done by Idi (another Iddi) Amin in Uganda.

In tone of his article, this author was of the opinion that Asians are hard working and highly disciplined than the 'wazawa (indigeneous)' and hence the status quo should be maintained and nothing should be done to promote economic emancipation of the 'wazawa'. Answering this article another person M.F. Selekwa, probably a Tanzanian of African origin, noted: 'Unfortunately, this attitude exists among many Indians in Tanzania; they don't want to see wazawa (indigeneous) coming out of poverty.'

He told a story about the conflict that reached a point of threatening the life of one prominent black businessman by a group of Indian businessmen in Dar-es-Salaam in 1994/95. For his opinion that was a typical result of such attitude by these fellow Tanzanians, that 'wazawa' should not run businesses. The problem for Tanzanian Indians, Selekwa concluded, is that they want to be the only ones in business. That is why they moved from all places where a few 'wazawa' took up strongly in business: you don't see many Tanzanian Indians in places like Arusha, Moshi, Iringa and Mbeya.

The same situation is true for another East African country, Kenya. In Kenya, where the Indian community accounts for much, if not most, of the merchant class, there is open resentment and anger from a black African majority mired in poverty. 'Most of them are businessmen,' said native Kenyan Festus Muasa standing just near the National Museum of Kenya, where 'The Asian African Heritage Exhibition' was representing a community that spent so many years avoiding the spotlight. 'They are traders, the ones who are owning most of the companies, the big companies we have.' 'Some of them behave like colonizers, the way they pay Africans,' explained Muasa.[28] Another Black Kenyan, fisheries official George Oduor, said about the fish processing industry, 'The whole area is dominated by them. There is not one African. There was one or two coming up. They collude and make sure you go down.'[29]

'All Indians are rich', proclaimed another Kenyan of African origin. 'Ordinary Kenyans have said enough is enough to all forms of exploitation and plunder of the national economy by the largely cunning Asian population,' 'and we all know that the people's own responses are in place already to deal with, and totally eradicate, the Asian malaise in the country.'[30]

Indians in East Africa know the anger and resentment too well. In Kenya, Indian-owned shops and homes were looted and Indian women were raped in the chaos that followed an unsuccessful coup attempt in 1982. 'I think of "Kenyan Asians" like "German Jews," says Sultan H. Somjee, the National Museums of Kenya ethnographer and a fourth-generation Kenyan who curated the exhibit. "Of course Asian Africans are always accused of being a closed society. But what did this closed-ness contain?"', asks Somjee. According to him, it is the very components of 'civil society' so crucial to the struggling democracies of the Third World. Unable to rely on either British colonialists or post-independence governments for protection, the subgroups of the Indian community – Sikh, Ismaili, Goan, Hindu – turned self-reliant, building welfare organizations that all Kenyans have come to depend on.[31]

Indeed, when a terrorist bomb exploded at the U.S. Embassy in downtown Nairobi on August 7, 1998, the Kenyan government was unable to muster a single trained disaster response crew to bring order to the chaos. But within hours, Indian businessman had cranes and loaders at the site. Thousands of victims were taken to M.P. Shah Hospital and Aga Khan Hospital for emergency care. 'Not all of them are bad,' said George Oduor, when reminded of that day.[32] Not only the social activity of the Indians but also better education of the Blacks can change attitudes. A black student at Aga Khan Academy, Elaine Adema, says, she hears derogatory references to 'Asians', 'but I ignore it because it doesn't help my life.'[33]

Some Indians see a chance for the Kenyan Indian population to simply be accepted as one more ethnic group within the Kenyan nation. Pheroze Nowrojee, chairman of the Asian African Heritage Trust and a civil rights lawyer, insisted that Kenya's Indian community is no more economically exclusionary than other ethnic elites that have thrived here: The Kalenjin of President Daniel arap Moi; the Kikuyu of founding father Jomo Kenyatta.[34] According to Dr. Somjee 'I do not see resentment against Asian Africans out of the overall national context, that is, it is not any different from resentment of one tribe against another in the context of poverty, inequalities, power games, corruption and lack of pluralism.'[35] Yet, in Kenyan media and everyday conversation, Indian businessmen or 'tycoons' are far more likely to be labeled 'Asian.'

Business Solution and Cultural Differences

To overcome anti-Indian stereotypes, it is essential that Indians increase their social contact with the Blacks. In South Africa especially a number of Indian organizations are striving to be seen involving in the development of the Black communities. In this regard, certain religious bodies such as the Ramakrishna Vedanta Society and the Divine Life Society have spearheaded the movement of building schools and clinics in Black areas. They have also made arrangements with Indian medical practitioners to provide medical services free of charge in severely poor areas in the Black townships. On the economic front, many Indian businessmen are taking on Black partners to improve their image with Black consumers and the government.

In East Africa too, the Asian community is trying to improve their image by the involvement in building school, hospitals and mosques for use by the general African population. The restructuring of Indian business into more social-oriented forms along with removing of restrictions for Indians to make their business in other markets, except trade and services, can be another important factor for overcoming of image of 'Asians' as ruthless money-launders. Returning Asians in Uganda and their disproportionate role in a successful story of the country's recent development is one more step in this direction appreciated by African media in headlines such as 'Asians Recover Ugandan Wealth.'[36]

Some of these efforts seem to have really hit a target. 'Follow example set by Indians' is a title of another article written by South African Mduduzi Xakaza who appraises those Indian qualities as a strong sense of community and togetherness that usually make Africans to be suspected of the Indians. Then the author goes further and points at the Indians as an example for Africans how to succeed economically. The success of an individual benefits the whole group, says Xakaza. 'To end up as masters of their economic destiny, they [Africans] have to be humble enough to learn from their Indian counterparts and borrow some of their economic upliftment tools - unity and solidarity.'[37]

But for how long all that activities can be a solution capable to secure an existence of the Indians in Africa? Each reader more or less interested in diasporic and migration studies knows that the virtues of togetherness and solidarity are an inalienable part of any significant 'trading minority' Diaspora, notwithstanding a region of its settlement. There are striking similarities in a destiny of the Jews in Middle Ages Europe and Middle East, the Armenians and the Greeks in Ottoman Empire, the Chinese in Southeast Asia, the Indians in Africa and so on.

The common feature of all these minorities drawing from ancient and self-confident civilization centers is their trading and entrepreneur specialization caused not the least by their religious, cultural or physical distinction from the host population, which was usually staying in a lower level of social and cultural development. No wonder this population had often been perceived by immigrant community as backward and less-civilized. Traditional or transitional nature of host society is likely to be another important factor in getting the immigrant community a status of 'trading minority', who in the eyes of natives may be useful but remains low-profile and contemptible aliens.

Meanwhile the exclusive nature of Indian community that has long preferred to remain socially isolated and aloof from the rest of society is not the sole African phenomena. A Report by the International Commission of Jurists in Guyana (1965) pointed out:

'the tendency of the Indians was to stay aloof from the society about them; they remained agricultural and uneducated, alien and socially disinterested. (p. 25)'[38]

The Indian communities in two Caribbean countries, Guyana and Trinidad, are about a half or slightly less of total population. They largely involve in agricultural sector and can't be treated as 'trading minority' or suspicious aliens. Their compatriots, that is, the other half of population are the Blacks of African origin and a mixed group. In spite of the fact that no group has a privilege position and all of them are descendants of immigrants, slaves or indentured workers, mistrust and animosity between the communities still flourish. One elderly African in Guyana is quoted as follows:

'we very fearful of the coolieman taking over the whole country. Dey band themselves together to get all we own. Dey so wicked I want to cry. I cry for my children. I see the terror–the spirit of their activities. Dey loan black people money and take all dey own. Dey smart people, you know. Cunning. Dey work cheap, eat cheap and save and save. If we punish ourselves as coolieman we slave again.'[39]

Similar perceptions also prevail in Trinidad. Indians are said to be more kin-oriented, uncultured, prone to promote their kind and overly thrifty; Africans are said to be lazy, spendthrift and prone to dependence on the state.[40]

Probably there is no other category to indicate the gap in mutual perception and misunderstanding between Indians and Africans more visible than Indian matrimonial traditions. According to Prof. Bharati, there were about 5000 people of mixed African-Asian origin in East Africa before 1972, most of them along the coast and in Zanzibar. Those people, who called *jotawa,* a slighty derogatory term in Gujarati, or a pejorative word *chottara,* were mainly children of informal liaisons.[41] Although rarely some Gujarati Muslims did marry native women the Indians, both Hindus and Muslims have not accepted progeny.

The Afro-Asian intermingling trend has always been an unequal one, typically involving an Asian male and an African female, and almost never the converse. The Africans have obviously seen it as a sign of Indian superiority position toward them and resented. Bharati quotes one of his interviewees, an East African girl, as saying, 'Asians...slept with our women for decades, and thought it perfectly in order to make passes at them. Then why should our men not make passes at Asian women?'[42]

Probable answer to that question and much more behind it is a cultural and religious tradition of the Indians and, first of all, caste structure. Rehana Eb.-Valley examines the problem of caste preservation and evolution among the South Africa Indians in her book 'Kala Pani: Caste and Colour in South Africa', 2001. According to the author having arrived in South Africa as mainly indentured workers 'Indians started the reconstruction of their relational networks from value internalised in India.'[43] The author proceeds to divide the Indians into two main groups, namely Hindus and Muslims. For the Hindus, regardless of their regional or linguistic heritage, she concludes, 'the predominance of religion as an identity marker notwithstanding, there are vestiges of the caste system still operating among the Hindus community.'[44]

As for the Muslims, caste does not exist but caste-like structures do. The author plausibly suggests that Muslim converts retained a 'Hindu collective memory' and points to a whole range of cultural and religious practices among Hindus and Muslims that are similar. While many Hindus and Muslims identify themselves as 'South Africans' and say that religion is not a significant factor in how they see themselves there are layers of identity that suggest that ethnicity remains a significant factor.

Having been throughout all its history a core of Hinduism and Indian civilisation itself, a caste to a great extent defines the main features of Indian communities both in India and abroad. Ideas of exclusiveness, ritual clearness/unclearness, hierarchy and social inequality of the different groups of people, the pillars of caste structure, are deeply engraved in Indian mentality. These moral and social principles have greatly impacted on lifestyle and social behaviour of diasporic Indians, even in the postindustrial Western societies where Indian immigrants met the most comfortable economical and political conditions. Therefore, it is hardly surprising that Indian communities living in developing, especially African, countries in harsh and often unfriendly environment have always been striving to preserve their traditional socio-cultural code. For Indians, especially Hindus, to abandon these principles is as the same as to reject that Indianness itself.

Obviously the solution of the problem is laid not only in the Indian communities but also in host societies itself. And perhaps there is a chance for it. Muthoni Wanyeki, the Executive Director of the African Women's Development and Communication Network, Kenya, after visiting India, wrote an article in Kenyan newspaper. She concluded: 'Not for us the necessary but tortured attempts to build American-style melting pots, Canadian-style cultural mosaics or even South African-style rainbow nations. We simply are a racially mixed country. And an awareness of our diverse traditions has seeped into our consciousness in spite of us and our many prejudices.'[45]

Conclusion

In spite of the fact that Indian communities have been living in Africa for more than a century, they are still conspicuous and alien to the African majority and known as 'Asians' or 'Coolies.' Having started as humble indentured workers on sugar cane plantations or as petty traders and low-level colonial officials, a name of 'Indian' by now has almost meant 'businessman' and 'trader'. While the situation in South Africa is rather different from the rest of Africa, the growing tensions between Indians and Blacks after the apartheid system was deconstructed, make the Indian community feel increasingly insecure. Indian communities' involvement in improving life conditions and helping the Blacks emerge out of misery can be fruitful to calm down the resentment of native majority against the 'Indian traders'. However, unless the social, economical and political situation in African countries change the core features of Indian cultural and religious tradition will probably prevent the Indians from assimilation.

Endnotes

1 Singh D. 2001. *The Asian Diaspora in Tanzania*. Paper presented at the International conference 'Indian Ocean Island States and Littoral: Conflict and Cooperation'. Mumbai, 19-21 April, p. 15.

2 Pavlova V.V. 2001. *Africa in the Labyrinths of Modernization* (*In Russian: Africa v labirintah modernizacii).* Moscow, p. 84.

3 ITAR-TASS. 10.09.1999 Cit. on: Associated Press. Dar-s-Salaam, 10.09.1999 or ITAR-TASS 27.08.2001.

4 Pavlova V.V. *op. cit.* p. 88.

5 *Ibid.* p. 113.

6 Himbara D. 1994. 'Kenyan Capitalists, the State, and Development', in *Ethnicity and Investment Promotion: A*

Thorny Path for Policy Makers.www.eagerproject.com / brief49.html. p. 3.

7 Bhana, Narendra. 2000. 'South African Indians: the past, the present and the future'. University of Durban-Westville, Durban, vol. I, p. 5.

8 South African Indian Glossary. 1999. 'How We Live: Indian Households of South Africa'. Indigo Publications. April.

9 Black Racial Slur against Indians. From the News Archives of: www.AfricanCrisis.org. 2002/05/31 or http:// allAfrica.com/ stories/20020703117.html.

10 Mbongeni Ngema poet, 2002. artist, racist. Daily Mail & Guardian online. Johannesburg. 1 January.

11 *Ibid.*

12 *Ibid.*

13 Itano, Nicole. 2002. 'Blacks and Indians clash over divisive Zulu song'. 2002. *The Christian Science Monitor.* 16 July.

14 Hassen, Fakir. 2002. 'Business solution to South Africa's anti-Indian song tension'. *Indo-Asian News Service.* 14 June.

15 Taschika, Pillay. 2003. 'Ngcuka reported for 'Indian Slur"'. www.sundattimes.co.za/Durban news. 05 October.

16 *Ibid.*

17 Kockott, Fred. 2004. 'Racism still stalks Free State Indians'. *Sunday Tribune.* 25 April, p. 7

18 *Ibid.*

19 Ngema refuse to apologise for song. http:// www.sabcnews.com/entertainment/music.html or Itano, Nicole. *op. cit.*

20 *Ibid.*

21 Bhana, Narendra. *op. cit.* p. 5.

22 *Ibid.*

23 *Ibid.*

24 *Ibid.*

25 Vick, Karl. 2000. 'A New View of Kenya's 'Asians'. *Washington Post.* 15 March.

26 African Dispatches. 1998. Allen Varney's letters from Africa (2 to 5). 13 August. www.allenvarney.com/TANZAN.html.

27 Pkema, Michael. 2003. 'Patriotism: Flight Capital Has No Colour'. *The East African (Nairobi).* 19 February.

28 Vick, Karl. *op. cit.*

29 *Ibid.*

30 Mampilly, Zachariah. New Exhibit Highlights Kenyan Asians. http://www.africana.com/articles/daily/index_20000730.asp

31 Vick, Karl. *op. cit.*

32 *Ibid.*

33 *Ibid.*

34 *Ibid.*

35 Mampilly, Zachariah. *op. cit.*

36 *New Vision.* 2004. 15 April, Kampala, Uganda.

37 Xakaza, Mduduzi. 2002. Follow example set by Indians. Echo. 23 May. www.witness.co.za/content/2002_05/6952.htm.

38 Cit. on: Bessesser, A. 2003. 'Gender and Ethnic Imbalance in the Politics of a Plural Society: The Case Trinidad and Tobago' in *Indians Abroad.* ed. S.M. Singh, M. Singh. Kolkata :Maulana Abul Kalam Azad Institute of Asian Studies, p. 89.

39 La Gueree, John Gaffar. 2003. 'Convergence and Divergence in the Organization and Politics of Two Plural Societies: Guyana and Trinidad and Tobago'. in *Indians Abroad. op, cit.* p. 103.

40 *Ibid.* p. 104.

41 Jotawa: Afro-Asians in East Africa. http://www.colorq.org/MeltingPot/Africa/Indians.htm.

42 Cit. on: Jotawa: *op. cit.*

43 Rehana Ebr.-Valley. 2001. *Kala Pani: Caste and Colour in South Africa. Social Identities South Africa Series.* Cape Town: Kwela Books, p. 140.

44 *Ibid.* p. 150.

45 Wanyeki, Muthoni. 2002. 'India or Nairobi, the Devil's in the Detail'. *The Nation.* Nairobi. 9 February.

'Hindu' Dance Groups and Indophily in Senegal: Cultural Translation and the Imagination of the Exotic Other

Gwenda Van Der Steene

'L' Afrique indou' ('Hindu Africa')

At the beginning of my fieldwork period on dance in Senegal I was not very skilled in the typically Senegalese *sabar* dances. However, I was always very proud to tell I was a dancer as well. I didn't usually mention I practice *Bharata Natyam,* a South Indian dance style, as I thought people had probably never heard of such a thing as 'Indian dance'. I was surprised when people reacted enthusiastically, saying they loved 'Indian dance'[1], and was even more astonished when they told me they practised 'Hindu' dance (*dance indou-indo-hindou*)[2] as well in some of the numerous Hindu dance groups indu dance" troupsin Senegal. Not long after I started my quest for Hindu dance in Dakar, I learned there was a real federation (UNAIS, *Union Nationale des Indouphiles au Senegal*),[3] grouping over twenty associations of India-lovers throughout Senegal, with activities, *soirées indous* ('Hindu evenings') and rehearsals.

When you turn on your radio, you are likely to come across one of the many Hindu programs broadcasted almost every day on different radio stations. The presentators often have their own association in the form of a fan club.

It only took me a couple of weeks to become aware of the fact that Indophily (the love for 'Indian' music, dance and films) is more than merely superficial in Senegal. Surprisingly enough, there is no Indian expatriate community in Senegal, which can account for this, as is the case in e.g. eastern Africa or the Caribbean[4]. Moreover, being a francophone country, one would presume Senegal lies out of the English influence sphere, which is much stronger in Anglophone Africa. The little research devoted to Indophily in Africa has all concentrated on Anglophone Africa.[5] In this article I want to fill this gap by looking at a francophone country without an Indian expatriate community.

Analysing this Senegalese Indophily, we found that it has its origin in the massive import and immense success of Bollywood films. Looking at Africa in general and Senegal in particular, it is interesting to investigate why this import has been so successful and how this gave rise to lots of Indophile associations imitating Bollywood song and dance. Who are these Indophiles, and how do they interpret/imagine/exoticise or even 'Senegalise' this 'other' culture which is, at first sight, so different from their own. I will deal with all these questions with special reference to dance. I also want to look at the relation between this Indophily and the collaborative research project on comparative linguistics between the University of Cheikh Anta Diop in Dakar and the University of Annamalai, India.

BOLLYWOOD FILMS AND AFRICAN AUDIENCES

Africa

Research on Indophily and the popularity of Bollywood films in Africa (outside Indian expatriate communities) is a rich but mostly virgin territory. Although the import of Bollywood started already in the '50s, only during the last decade it has caught the attention of several researchers. In his article, *Itineraries of Indian cinema*, Brian Larkin tries to answer the question why Indian films travel. He explains the popularity of this genre throughout the world (in 'Third World' countries, with or without an Indian expatriate community, as well as in lots of socialist countries such as Eastern Europe) because it offers a way of being modern that does not necessarily mean being western [6]. In northern Nigeria, where his own research is focussed, it is also a way of distinguishing themselves from the south which is much more oriented towards the West. Thus these transnational cultural flows become 'a foil against which postcolonial identity can be fashioned, critiqued, an debated. They allow an alterity to Hollywood domination'[7]. This is not to say the story of Africans turning towards Bollywood films is a discourse of 'local' resistance to 'dominant' Western culture.

Arabic and Bollywood films were first imported by Lebanese cinema owners in the '50s, who thought Arabic films would become very popular in African Islamic countries[8]. Bollywood, however, turned out to have a much bigger success. The explanation for this phenomenon is still to be found. Is it because Arabic film is too 'familiar' or has less song-and-dance sequences so typical of Bollywood? Larkin also suggested Arabic language is associated with religion, making it difficult to be associated with profane domains such as films.

Lots of Hausa state 'Indian culture' (at least how it is presented in the films) is 'just like' Hausa culture [9]. In Senegal, I heard exactly the same explanation over and over again. According to Larkin, the popularity of Indian films among Hausa rests, in part, on this dialectic between sameness ('just like') and difference. [10] Characters in Indian films struggle over whether they should speak Hindi or borrow from English; whether they should marry the person they love or wed the person their parents choose, elements, which are very relevant for Hausa viewers[11].

Senegal

A lot of elements pointed out for Nigeria by Larkin also hold true for Senegal. According to my informants, the first Bollywood films appeared in Senegalese cinemas around the '50s and were an immense success. They soon became much more popular than Arabic films and were turned daily in most of the urban cinemas. But why does Indian cinema appeal to a Senegalese audience? Most Bollywood films are in Hindi, sometimes English, meaning not understandable for the Senegalese. So why would people watch films in a language they can't understand, about a culture so different from their own[12]?

From numerous talks with Indophiles, I tried to draw a model. When being asked what they like about Indian film, most informants answer surprised 'because it is good, beautiful, romantic...'.They probably find it a rather weird question, something they had actually never thought of. The more I was surprised at Senegalese going crazy about Indian film, the more they seemed to find it absolutely normal, an integral part of Senegalese everyday life. Indophily has now attended the third generation. Even more strange that it has only recently attracted scholarly attention.

Indophiles say they love 'Indian culture' because it makes them think of their own, how paradoxical that may sound to us. They point out all kinds of comparisons, some of which seem somehow far-fetched to me. Of course it is not about actual similarities but about perception of similarities (whether real or not). Though in my eyes Islam and Hinduism are quite different, someone told me that there are a lot of similarities between Islam and Hinduism: 'in Islam there is only one god and in Hinduism this is Brahma. Even the three main gods Brahma-Vishnu-Shiva are in fact a trinity, three-in-one'[13].

The perceptions of similarities between Senegal and India can be brought together into different groups.

'Façon de vivre' (way of life)

First of all there is what some informants call 'façon de vivre' (way of life). For this they often refer to the most popular Bollywood film ever: *Mère indienne* (*Mother India*, 1957).[14] The images of village life, horses and carts, women fetching water at the well or carrying fire wood on their heads 'really make you think you are in Senegal'. Several Indophiles especially stressed similarities with the Fouta, a very rural area in northern Senegal, inhabited mostly by Fulani,[15] or with the Sereer, an ethnic group occupying mostly the coastal areas south of the Cape Vert Peninsula (on which Dakar is situated). According to several informants, the Fulani and the Sereer are strongly related groups with a common origin and a lot of linguistic and cultural similarities. They said there was much less comparisons with Wolof village life. Maybe this is due to the fact that most Wolof have a more urbanised culture, or because some informants mentioned that especially among the Sereer 'animistic beliefs' are still very lively (even though they are all Christian or Muslim). Though Hinduism of course cannot be characterised as 'animistic', according to my informants some 'animistic beliefs' have been incorporated, such as the veneration of snakes or cows, which may, according to them, account for the fact that there are more similarities with the 'more animistic oriented Sereer' or with 'the importance of cows in the religious and cultural practices of the Fulani'.

When talking about *façon de vivre,* Indophiles stress the image of women engaging in village activities as an important aspect of comparison, something I will come back to further on in this article. Some mentioned, the way women are regarded or the respect that has been attached to them is very similar in Senegal and India.

Language

Larkin mentioned the argument that Hausa language and Hindi are similar is often used by people to stress the similarities between both cultures. In Senegal this was no different. Whether one was talking about Wolof, Sereer or Fulani, all said their language is 'very similar' to Hindi. Some Indophiles, especially radio presentators presenting Indophile programs, even state they speak Hindi fluently. Most of them are self-taught, by writing down dialogues phonetically when watching Bollywood movies, though in the 80s a few took courses from an Indian adventurer who travelled the world by bike and stayed in Senegal. Indophile informants always mention the same words when asked for examples of similarities: *caabi* (key - Wolof) and *caabu* (Hindi), *asamaan* (heaven – Wolof and Hindi), *kaay* (come here – Wolof) and *aw* (Hindi), *jogal* (get up – Wolof) and *uto* (Hindi). As in the case with other mentioned similarities, these similarities are sometimes far-fetched and are nothing else but a perceived (imaginary) similarity (who would otherwise say *jogal* sounds like *uto*?). Several linguists reinforced my inkling idea that most of these words are of Arabic origin (e.g. *asamaan*)[16]. Why otherwise would Hausa *and* Wolof *and* Fulani *and* Sereer be similar to a language like Hindi? Wolof as well as Fulani and Sereer are very mixed languages, with a strong Arabic influence of which people are often unaware (Prof. Souleymane Faye, interview 10-05-04). Apart from Arabic words, people often rely on homophones to conclude that there are linguistic similarities, sometimes without knowing the exact significance of the words. Resemblance is therefore sometimes invented but people strongly believe in it [17](Prof. Souleymane Faye, interview 10-05-04).

Values

Bollywood films reinforce values which are highly regarded in Indian society, such as the importance of family relations, devotion, respect for elders, love between a man and a woman resulting in a socially acceptable marriage. Senegalese Indophiles often mention that Indians are very dignified, they respect tradition, are very religious. This appreciation of 'traditional' values also relates to a preference for older films. More recent films are often criticised (especially by the older Indophiles) for imitating Hollywood and for their 'deteriorating' values. The fact that Senegalese appreciate this aspect of Bollywood, shows how they actually would like to see themselves: it is the Senegalese ideal projected in Bollywood film.

Dance and music

Senegal is a country where people love expressing themselves through dance and music. The saying goes 'if you are born a Senegalese, you can dance'. It is therefore not surprising when people say they love Bollywood because it's full of songs and dance sequences. Even though also in Arabic film dance and music plays an important role, it is more typical for the Bollywood style. Moreover, here again people probably recognise their own culture in Bollywood dance and music. Bollywood music and dance is, like all Hindusthani music, strongly influenced by Arabic music. It must therefore not sound that unfamiliar to the African ear.

Emotion

People love Bollywood films because they are 'very emotional', 'romantic'. When a Senegalese is behaving too emotionally or if he's in love, people often say 'you behave like an Indian'.

Larkin's research among Hausa showed more or less the same perceptions of (imaginary or not) similarities: visual (dress) and linguistic similarities, way of living (marriage celebrations, village life...) and the importance of values such as family and kinship[18] . He also stresses the preference for older films: people say Indian films 'have culture' in a way American films seem to lack. Thus, the West is being defined as 'other' against which Indian culture is perceived as similar - similar because American films are different.

HISTORY OF INDOPHILY IN SENEGAL

Indophily

The first Bollywood film, *Mangala(an),* came to Senegal in '53, and, according to the first Indophile generation, created a furore.

Before that one could only watch French, American or Arabic films. Bollywood films became more and more popular, and were imported massively in the '70s. They soon outnumbered and surpassed Arabic films. All urban cinemas showed at least one Bollywood film each day. People always told as a child they watched lots of Bollywood, whether they came to the cinema for the Bollywood film or for the western or Chinese film shown afterwards. Due to the arrival of TV and home videos, lots of cinemas have been closed now, though in those still existing Bollywood is still shown.

For many Indophiles the passion for Indian dance and music came via the films. From the sixties onwards, Indophiles started organising themselves. The first association (*Les amis de l'Inde-Friends of India*) was established around '66-68. Most of the associations concentrate on Bollywood dance and music. The most popular Indian singer in Senegal is Mohammed Rafi, as is evident in associations bearing his name (*Rafi ke log - Rafi ke chandan - Rafi club*) as well as in the fact that the two largest Indophile parties (*soirées indous*) are organised on Rafi's birthday, December, 24th.[19] Apart from Rafi, other Bollywood singers such as Lata Mangeshkar are also very popular.

As more and more associations were created, the need emerged to have an Indian Cultural Centre. The Centre would be a back-up structure to spread Indian culture more systematically. Dance classes could be organised, people could get grants to go to India, Indian costumes and make-up could be made. Throughout fruitful contacts with the Indian embassy and the Ministry of Culture, there soon was a need for a federal organisation covering all the different Indophile groups in Senegal. This is how the UNAIS emerged in 2003, as a first step towards a (future) Cultural Centre. A president has been elected democratically, though again, this caused a wave of jealousy. The federation also wants to work more internationally, having contacts with other African Indophile groups outside Senegal.

Leopold Sedar Senghor and the UCAD project[20]

From independence onwards, Léopold Sédar Senghor, the first president, launched his theory of *négritude*:[21] from now on everyone could be proud to be African and should be proud of his 'own' culture. The cultural politics of Senghor were therefore marked by a 'back to our roots' movement and an intense promotion of 'traditional culture'. While this was the official road, the sixties were also the period during which the Senegalese urban population was exposed to salsa, rock, pop, jazz and Indian music. Especially salsa became extremely popular[22]. Note that jazz, blues, salsa and Indian music did not sound that unfamiliar to the African ear. They carried the original African (or Arabic in the case of Bollywood) sound and rhythms with them and now 'returned' in different variations. It seemed that Senegal searched for its 'roots' through this diverse cultural landscape.

Senghor was also a popular intellectual and poet, who liked to theorise about the universality of humankind and the mixing and origin of cultures. His visit to Chennai made him develop ideas about possible relations between (South) Indians (of Dravidian origin) and Africans. He was struck by the 'physical resemblance' between the two groups and called the Dravidians 'black Indians'. He also noted linguistic resemblances and started developing the idea of a common origin. On his return, he contacted the University Cheikh Anta Diop (UCAD) in Dakar and charged his ministry of culture to find him researchers who would work on the cultural and linguistic affiliations between India and Senegal. Three researchers set off for India, all carrying out comparative linguistic research between different local languages (Wolof, Fulani and Sereer) and Tamil[23]. Apart from them, Senghor also accorded a grant to singer Amadou Badiane, still the most popular Indophile in Senegal, to study Indian singing.

The scholars found indeed lots of affinities regarding vocabulary and grammar. They reinforced the theory developed by intellectual Cheikh Anta Diop on the Egyptian origin of most West Africans. At that time Indian researchers had developed a similar idea of an Egyptian origin of Dravidians. The resemblances can, however, not account for a genetic affiliation. For this more research is needed from other disciplines (history, anthropology etc.). Though it was Senghor's idea to develop this, and even to establish an Indo-African research institute at the UCAD, all this did not happen due to his departure in 1980, the year the research projects ended. Of course Senghor's ideas about *négritude* and theorisation on the origin of Africans have to be placed within its historical context. Until now there has been no continuation of Senghor's projects.

Links between Senghor and Indophily

Important to mention is that there is no link at all between the Bollywood originated Indophily and Senghor's project. First of all, Senghor's project encompassed Dravidian languages, not Hindi. As Bollywood films are in Hindi, there is a difference between the linguistic resemblances mentioned by people watching these movies and the resemblances pointed out in the research project. Hindi and Tamil are completely different languages, belonging to different (respectively Indo-European and Dravidian) language groups.

Furthermore, Senghor's project has never been popularised. The change of government definitely played a role in this. The only popularising attempt was the invitation of Prof. Ndiaye on a Fulani radio program. For one month, he talked about his experiences in India and about the resemblances between Fulani and Tamil. Indophily, however, has not been influenced by this whole project. The scholars were surprised to find Indophiles when they came back - people who were very eager to meet them and who always asked them loads of questions on Bollywood actors they had never heard of.

PORTRAIT OF THE SENEGALESE INDOPHILE

Gender

The first thing one notice when going to *soirées indous* is that almost all dancers are women.[24] Furthermore, most of the audience consists of women. People often say that Bollywood films have a mostly female audience because the themes (love and marriage) especially appeal to them. At the time when cinemas were still blooming, the afternoon Bollywood films were massively attended by women, who could go home around 5pm to cook dinner, before their husband comes home.

According to some Indophiles, there are also lots of male Indophiles but they keep their passion more hidden. This probably relates to the image of Bollywood films as being 'very emotional' (cf. supra), a quality Senegalese men want to distance themselves from because it does not fit the Senegalese gender norms (a man should not be emotional and weak). In Nigeria, the situation is somewhat different. As they were living indoors, women were absent in the cinemas in the '70s, but gained access to Indian films through the rise of home videos. According to Larkin, Indian films have since then become identified as 'women's films' because of their huge popularity among women[25].

Ethnic descent

Another striking thing about *soirées indous* is that most women present are very pale. This is partly due to the high amount of bleaching products they are using, but also because about 80% of those present are of Fulani origin. The reason why remains partly unclear. It is a fact that due to their paler skin colour there is closer physical resemblance with Indians. Several informants also mentioned the cultural resemblances between Indians and Fulani. As stated already, cattle are the most precious possession for a Fulani. A Fulani will never slaughter his cows, and a Fulani is said to commit suicide if he looses his whole livestock. Cows are almost holy to them, and a lot of people link this with Indian cow veneration.

The research of Prof. M. Ndiaye concerned the linguistic relations between Fulani and Tamil (1980). According to him, Negro-Africans, especially Fulani, and Dravidians are fractions from one original Indo-African culture.

Urban or Suburban Context?

In the '50s and '60s efforts have been made to modernise the popular quarters in central Dakar. Therefore, the government stimulated those people to move to newly created suburbs, and a lot of cinemas from central Dakar moved with them[26]. This might explain the popularity of Indophily in suburbs such as Pikine. Pikine is considered the centre of Indophily, a place where many Indophiles, dance troupes and *soirées indous* are based. Why this is the case, is an only partly answered question. The moving of people who used to live in the popular quarters in central Dakar definitely plays a role: only a certain kind of people (class, if you like) came to live in Pikine. There is indeed a difference between middle and lower class people living in the suburbs and the (intellectual) bourgeoisie in the residential areas of central Dakar[27].

And different people mean different kinds of film: while in big cinema's in the heart of Dakar people watch French and American films (as people want to mirror a Western oriented lifestyle), in the suburbs people go for Bollywood. Bollywood is thus a popular genre. This is not to say it only appeals to poorer people. I met several rich Indophiles, mostly well established businesswomen engaging in trade.

Age

The older (1st or 2nd) generation of Indophiles prefers older films such as *Devdas* (1955) and *Mother India*. Among the younger generation, more recent films also seem to be popular. An often heard critique by older people is that recent films are too modern, too 'Hollywood'-like, with a deteriorating quality of classical song and dance, a trend indicated by several older Indophiles as *le modernisme* (modernity).

Cultural Translation: Hindu Dance Troups

The National Palace Museum in Taipei, Taiwan, displays a ceramic vase from the Ming dynasty (15th century). The belly of the vase shows a beautiful Arabic inscription. When trying to decipher the calligraphy, however, scholars noticed that the inscription made no sense at all. Even though it seemed perfectly Arabic for an outsider, it does not mean anything, just aesthetically imitating Arabic calligraphy. This vase immediately made me think about Hindu dance troups in Senegal: people imitate Bollywood song and dancing styles for the pure aesthetic pleasure of it, but without a profound knowledge of Indian aesthetics or dance. It has, however, never been the aim of my research to make any ('colonial') judgements about who is dancing right or wrong, or who has a better knowledge of 'how it really should be'. This is irrelevant to Hindu dances. I only used my knowledge of Indian dance to see what is different and how the dances are recreated into another vital form, how these dances are translated, reinterpreted, Senegalised. Of course this cultural translation is much more than merely copying. It is a whole new interpretation and translation of Indian dance and culture. The dancers make up new choreographies in what could be called a 'Senegalised Bollywood style', emphasising e.g. big movements and waist rotations.

The dancers in a *soirée indou* wear according to me very Senegalese looking costumes, with the typically Senegalese overloaded headdress and make-up. It all fits more in Senegalese aesthetic norms and forms (e.g. sexy tops with bare shoulders, something very un-Indian). However, to the Senegalese the dancers are looking very 'Indian'. A picture of a woman with a Senegalese make-up such as those done by beauty parlours, wearing a long dress made from a typical Senegalese cloth, *kokettes* (stylish pointed Senegalese women's shoes), and the indispensable little fancy bag evoked reactions such as 'you see, she's dressed up like a Hindu (*indou*)'. Sometimes you could discern some influence from Bollywood costumes, resulting in an interesting mix.

Hindu Dance

It was a hot day in April when I set off for my first Hindu dance rehearsal. After sitting for a while watching children playing in a rather disorganised courtyard, someone put a cassette from *Kuch Kuch Hota Hai* [28]in the cassette player, and some girls started dancing on it. Bollywood dance (especially from the recent films) is closer to folk dance styles than it is to Indian classical dance (which is more prevalent in older films). Some people had told me before Indian dance is 'just like' Arabic dance. As soon as I observed the dancing, I understood why. It became obvious the Senegalese got all the bigger movements right, such as the hip movements and the turnings (which are also found in Arabic dance). Eye or hand gestures, on the other hand, were almost absent. Some advanced dancers used neck movements to add to the Indian flavour of their dance. However, they imitated Bollywood very well. They must have watched the films over and over again to achieve this Bollywood style, with an aesthetic totally different from Senegales *sabar* or *djembé* dance.

After the first group choreography by the younger girls, the director of the group put *Devdas* in the cassette player. It was time for some solo's and duo's. *Devdas* is an old film where dance is still mostly inspired by Indian classical dance forms[29] – this was definitely a job for the more advanced dancers who had already acquired more technical skills.

The other rehearsals I attended were very similar to this one. Hindu dance is not about imitating good or bad, it is about what the dancers actually do with the dances, making another vital hybrid with the material at your disposal. Whenever I performed, people said my strength was that I was a Belgian doing Indian dance. The more surprised as I was to see Senegalese dancing on Bollywood tunes, the more they were surprised about a Belgian dancing Indian dance. Lots of people said that was real cultural mixing, which shows again the importance attached to hybridity and cultural *métissage*.

Soirées Indous

Soirées indous are often organised by radio presentators of Indophile programs. *Soirées indous* usually start very late, and always have a similar course: a few group choreographies alternated with solos and duos of old and modern Bollywood films. People sit around in a circle or square around the dance space. *Soirées indous* are always occasions where lots of money is flowing. First of all, there is a guest of honour who is supposed to give - to the organiser and to the dancers. Apart from that, people stand up to throw money at the dancers during the performances. Outer appeal (women with fancy dresses, expensive make-up and lots of bank notes) seems to be important, as well as augmenting your status within the group by showing off with the money you have. On one evening the guest of honour was a super rich Indophile, a trade woman, dressed in a *boubou cocaïne*, so called because of the extremely expensive cloth it is made from. She was accompanied by her female *gewel* [30](*griotte*), who sang her praises as she showed the crowd note per note that her patron gave 500 000 cfa (the equivalent of 945 US dollars) to the organiser.

Stress on Aesthetic Aspects

The Ming vase is a good example of cultural translation on a purely aesthetic level. Imitation for the sheer aesthetic pleasure seems to be an important aspect of Hindu dance and *soirées indous*. First of all, lots of time and effort is spent on splendid costumes and make-up, not only by the dancers (who change costumes all the time) but also by the audience. Women will never go to a *soirée indou* without first spending a few hours in the beauty parlour. Furthermore, lots of the women present have burns from overbleaching their skin or from using bad bleaching products[31]. The body of the dancer also plays a role: preferably they should be young, pale and with a perfect body. Another evidence of the emphasis on aesthetics are the *miss indou* elections organised every year in July, a huge event with lots of popular (Senegalese) artists performing. After the beauty parade a girl is chosen to be *miss indou* for one year. Again, the candidates don't have a very Indian look; they get on the catwalk with fancy mini skirts and shiny tops. The only criterion for participating is being an Indophile.

Gender

It has already been mentioned that the dancers in *soirées indous* are mostly women. The few male dancers usually participate in duos – mostly some pathetic playback sequences. This can be related to the fact that dance in Senegal (especially the *sabar* dance) is mainly done by women (cf. infra).

Gender in Bollywood films has been the focus of several studies[32]. Bollywood uses images of 'female-dancer-in-traditional-dress' where women are portrayed as bearers of the collective (national) identity and caretakers of 'tradition'. Where men walk around in suits and tie, women wear *sarees*. They are usually, as devoted wives or mothers, taking care of and associated with 'traditional' values. Men stand for a 'modern' way of life, women assure tradition and stability. Therefore, they are related to national identity, as 'tradition' has become an important marker of cultural (or local) difference on a global scale.

The relation between gender and national identity has been the topic of several studies.[33] This certainly holds true for the *sabar* dances as well, something, which will be discussed in more detail below. In this light, Senegalese Hindu dances definitely play with this women-tradition-nation image. Not only are they based on this imagery as Bollywood is their source of inspiration, the same image is used in the *sabar* dances. However, a more complex process is at work here as the Hindu dancers are of course veiling themselves with another – exotic – identity which is partly similar (they wear Senegalese looking clothes and Senegalise the dances) and partly different (they dance on Bollywood music and imitate the Bollywood dances). Therefore, they cannot stand for their 'national' identity, but for a construction of national identity which is similar to their own pattern found in *sabar* dance. I will come back to this idea of difference and sameness more detailed in the next section.

This image of 'female-dancer-in-traditional-dress' has also been explored in studies on Indian dance where one can notice an evolution towards a marginalisation of male dancers[34]. Dancing in India is seen more and more as women's business, a phenomenon, which is also related to economic change and class.[35] Nowadays Indian dancers starting a dance career are mainly urban, English speaking women. There is thus a relation between economic evolution and globalisation on the one hand and the fact that female dancers are becoming more prevalent on the other[36]. We might again explain this relation between women and traditional (dance) as a pursuit of creating a 'local difference marker', which can also be exported as such.

DIFFERENT POSTCOLONIAL ANSWERS FOR A COUNTRY SEARCHING ITS CULTURAL IDENTITY

Parallel Modernities

One video of a *soirée indou* showed a young man accompanying a dancer with a self-made cardboard *sitar.* He wore a dark green open jacket without sleeves and a small red scarf attached to his head, knotted to the side, which made him look a bit like Rambo. Funnily enough he held the *sitar* as if he was holding an electric guitar, banging his head and playing it full of passion and devotion as if he was a *grunge* band member.

This scene made me think about Larkin's reflections on *parallel modernities.*[37]

> I use the term 'parallel modernities' to refer to the coexistence in space and time of multiple economic, religious and cultural flows that are often subsumed within the term 'modernity[38].

He makes a distinction with the concept of *alternative modernities* applied by Appadurai[39], who links it with increased deterritorialisation of the world and the movement of people. According to Larkin, the concept of *parallel modernities* is not necessarily linked with nostalgic needs of expat communities for establishing contact with their homelands. It is not concerning imagining a partly invented native land but about imagining other cultures (as part of daily life). His point is that for the Hausa (especially the younger people) watching Bollywood is a way of being modern without being Western, without being criticised for being 'Western decadent'[40]. Although this is very applicable for the Hausa situation, the context in Senegal might be a little different. First of all, the films are not only popular among the younger people. Secondly, Indophily in Senegal (as in Hausa culture) is not a recent phenomenon. Thirdly, older films are very popular, and seem until now even more popular than the newer ones, among all generations.

Hausa culture might be stronger oriented towards the Middle East and more resistant to the West than Senegal. Senegal is not 100% Islamic[41] and is probably more anti-American than anti-Western, at least in present times of Iraq war.[42] For lots of Senegalese 'the West (Europe) is the best'[43], France being the dream destination for many of them. Though Bollywood offers an alternative way of being modern, I would not dare to say that it is the main reason of its success, as anti-Western feelings are not that prevalent in Senegalese society as they might be in Hausa culture (as described by Larkin).

An idea, which is definitely applicable to the Senegalese case, is that Bollywood films offer Hausa viewers a third space, mediating between Hausa Islamic tradition and Western modernity, disrupting the dichotomies between West and non-West [44]. Indian films are situated in a cultural space that stands outside binary distinctions between tradition and modernity, Africa and West, resistance and domination[45] . Furthermore, the Hausa engage with forms of tradition different from their own while at the same time conceiving of a modernity that comes without political and ideological significance of the West[46].

> Indian films work for Hausa because they rest on a dialectic of presence and absence culturally similar to Hausa society but at the same time reassuringly distant[47]

This politics of absence and presence, desire and imagination, proximity and distance, difference and sameness has been referred to earlier. According to me it is also one of the constituting aspects of Senegalese Indophily. Bollywood is 'just like', but at the same time different, exotic. Maybe that is also why Arabic films have never been successful. They are not exotic enough. Moreover, this can also account for the reason why Bollywood might be conceived as 'just like', explaining the perceived similarities (cf. supra): Indian culture is similar because Western is different.

Orientalism and (self-)exoticisation

One ballet and contemporary dancer who also did some Hindu dance, used to dance with real snakes around his neck, as was obvious from a picture shown to me by his uncle. An Indophile mentioned another 'very good dancer' who used snakes in her performances. Dancing with real snakes is not found in India[48]. Dancing with snakes around your neck must therefore be a Senegalese invention. It might have been inspired by statues or imagery of Siva, the Lord of the dance, who wears snakes around his neck. However, it also made me think about Mami Wata imagery. Though Mami Wata is not venerated in Senegal, her images might have circulated, or images of a nineteenth-century German snake charmer on which most of the Mami Wata imagery would be inspired[49]. But we can say for sure that the dancing with snakes is an exoticisation of Indian dance – the dancer being presented as an exotic 'other'.

The imagination of an exotic other brings us to the concept of orientalism. Orientalism in dance has been studied mainly in Western belly dance[50]. Western belly dance reinforces several ideas typical about the male, orientalist gaze, such as sensuality, the harem as place of liberal sexuality, mystery, femininity. The image of the orient as sensual and mysterious and innately feminine exotic other is perpetuated within transnational media[51]. The image of the feminine exotic is also found in Bollywood films: not men but women are wearing traditional dress (cf. section on gender earlier), and are perceived on a transnational level as being associated not only with 'Indianness', but also with exotic otherness.

Hindu dance is all about orientalising oneself in the guise of an imagined, mysterious other. Dancers disguise or exoticise themselves in a costume which is different from those found in their own culture (or at least perceived as different), dancing on 'other' music from 'other' films. Exoticism implies 'creating power over the unknown in an act of indiscriminately combining fragments, crumbs of knowledge and fantasy'[52]. This definitely holds true for Hindu dance, as apart from a few very rich Indophiles, none of the dancers has been to India. They combine their knowledge about India, or rather about the India as shown in Bollywood, with fantasy and imagination. According to Barbara

Sellers-Young, Western belly dance also imagined the other through film: the costumes used by Western belly dancers (two piece costume, heels and veil), as well as their dance styles, are more defined by Hollywood adaptations and images of Middle Eastern dancers[53]. In these examples, imagination has become a social practice, which Arjun Appadurai relates to recent globalisation:

> The world we live in today is characterized by a new role for the imagination in social life. The image, the imagined, the imaginary these are all terms that direct us to something critical and new in global processes: the imagination as a social practice[54].
>
> Savigliano refers to the impact of orientalist imagery on dancers as a form of auto or self-exoticism [55]. The self-exoticisation of the Western belly dancer seems at first to disguise her Western identity in order to represent the East of the orientalist fantasy[56].

An important item for 'disguising' oneself is the veil. Apart from being intensively used in Western belly dance, it is also used in Hindu dance. The veil is used as a mask, enabling oneself to disguise as cultural other. In her guise as the other the dancer must remain inaccessible in order to sustain the fantasy's exoticism[57]. The guise also gives the dancer a kind of legitimacy. Apart from the practice of veiling, the dancer often unveils herself throughout the dance. According to Dox, unveiling in Western belly dance relates to flirtation and sexual pleasure: 'Western belly dancers' self-presentation as a forbidden cultural 'other' offers a protective shield unavailable to strippers, exotic dancers, or belly dancers in Middle Eastern countries' [58]. According to her, unveiling (or at least the way it is done in Western belly dance) is only thinkable in the West where overtly displaying (the beauty of) one's body is accepted. Among Middle Eastern dancers, unveiling is not a common practice, and the way it is done shows it is definitely not associated with open display of the sensual body[59]. Western belly dance plays with veil and display. In Hindu dance the veil is used in a very similar way. Unveiling also stands for an open display of one's sensual and attractive body. Earlier has been mentioned how the aesthetic (and the aesthetic of one's body) is a constitute aspect of Hindu dance.

Though orientalism and exoticism has been studied mostly within the context of belly dance, other dance practices incorporate (sometimes different forms of) orientalism. Another form of self-orientalism is the Taiwanese modern dance's *Eastern Body Aesthetics* [60] which has now deteriorated due to an orientalist demand of international curators[61] Orientalism in Taiwanese dance also recurred in the so-called *Minzu Wudao* of the Kuomintang government, which tried to capture an imagined Chinese identity 'swept out' on the mainland by the communists through dance[62].

It has become clear that Hindu dance can definitely be placed in this context of orientalism and self-exoticisation. However, just as in the Taiwanese case, it places orientalism in a wholly different light, as it is not about a colonising West imagining a subaltern colonised other. It does not hold a negative judgement about the West 'getting it all wrong', such as Western belly dancers trying to be Middle Eastern but actually being more Hollywood. As stated by Appadurai, imagination has become a social practice throughout the world due to new globalising processes. It has become clear in the previous paragraph that the veiling and unveiling as openly displaying one's sensuality is therefore not only 'Western'. Trying to trace dichotomies between West and Other has become old-fashioned. Other processes are going on, such as Africans imagining exotic others in India or Taiwanese exoticising oneself in order to meet the demands posed to them by international dance curators. This coincides with the creation of a 'third space' mentioned by Larkin.

Conclusion

In this article, I have tried to disentagle the reasons why Indophily is more than a merely superficial phenomenon in Senegal. Perceived similarities seem to be a key element in the popularity of Bollywood films and Indophily: 'Indian' culture is 'just like' Senegalese. The remarks by Larkin on Hausa Indophily as related to a discourse on absence and presence, similarity and difference, exoticness and sameness have shown to be very useful.

Hindu dance is a Senegalised Bollywood dance, performed by mostly female dancers who have learned it from watching lots of Bollywood films. As their knowledge of Indian culture and dance is very restricted (because it has been filtered through the films, the only source of information they have), people use their imagination to fills the gaps in their knowledge. The result is a very Senegalese phenomenon, Senegalese in dancing or dress styles, with lots of examples of self-exoticisation such as dancing with snakes or using veils. It can therefore be placed in an orientalist discourse, broadening the definition of orientalism towards a non-culture specific concept (more than 'the colonising West [wrongly] imagining the colonised East').

From the gender point of view, most Indophiles and Hindu dancers are women, as is the case in *sabar* dance as well. Furthermore, aesthetics and ideals about beauty and the female body are prevalent in Hindu dances. The image of female-dancer-in-traditional-dress refers to its Bollywood context, as well as to the *sabar* dances. In the latter two cases it can also be related to national identity.

More research should be dedicated to these transnational cultural flows standing outside the dichotomies of West and Other. The phenomena of cultural mixing, exoticism and orientalism as described in this article could shed a new light on global processes and on transnational and national identities.

Endnotes

1 I put this term between brackets as there is of course no such thing as 'Indian dance' (there are many different styles and techniques), though the Senegalese use this generalising term, just as 'Indian film' is a generalisation for the Hindi Bollywood films.

2 The term 'Hindu' is a literal translation from the French term used in Senegal: *indou/hindou/indo*. It always struck me why people talked about *films hindou* (thus referring to Hinduism, the religion) instead of *films indiens* (Indian films– a term used in Anglophone Africa). I suppose this is due to a confusion between Hindu (the religion) and Hindi (the language), as several people stated to me they could speak *indou* (referring to the language but by mistake using the wrong term). In Europe it is also common for non-insiders to mix up both terms.

3 National Union of Senegalese Indophiles.

4 It might also be that Bollywood is popular *because* there is no Indian expatriate community in Senegal, contrary to eastern Africa where Indian expatriates form a separate social group and are sometimes not very loved by the 'indigenous' groups. This process would be similar to Mauritius where English as national language is popular *because* no one speaks it (it is

not Creole e.g.). I am grateful to Burkhard Schnepel to point these things out to me.

5 Brian Larkin has worked on the popularity and influence of Bollywood films on Hausa culture (1997, 1998, 2003), Awam Amkpa (2004) and Albert Wuaku on Bollywood in Ghana and Deborah Rush (1999) on the incorporation of imported Hindu chromolithographic imagery in Benin voodoo. Suzanne Scheld has also come across Bollywood in her research on clothing and consumption in Dakar (2003)

6 Larkin, B.2003. 'Itineraries of Indian Cinema: African Videos, Bollywood and Global Media' in Shohat E. & R. Stam. eds. *Multiculturalism, Postcoloniality, and Transnational Media*, New Brunswick, New Jersey & London: Rutgers University Press, p. 172. ________ . 1997. 'Indian Films and Nigerian Lovers: Media and the Creation of Parallel Modernities'. *Africa,* vol. 67, no. 3. p. 407.

7 Larkin, B.2003. *op. cit.,* p. 178.

8 *Ibid.* p. 181

Larkin, B.1997. *op. cit.,* p. 411.

9 Larkin, B.2003, *op. cit.,* p. 183.

Larkin, B.1997, *op. cit.,* pp. 411, 433.

10 Larkin, B.2003, *op. cit.,* p. 183.

Larkin, B.1997, *op. cit.,* p. 414.

11 Bollywood has also had a huge impact on local video and literature production in Nigeria. See Larkin (1997, 1998, 2003) for an elaborate discussion of this.

Larkin, B.1997, *op. cit.,* p. 410.

12 It must however be said that in most Bollywood films, the narrative structure follows a prefixed pattern and the story is usually not that difficult to follow even if you don't understand the dialogues. According to Larkin, the same reason accounts for the success of action films.

Larkin, B.1997, *op. cit.,* p. 435.

13 Though some believe that Hinduism has monotheistic aspects, most scholars agree on its polytheism.

14 Larkin also mentioned this film being the most popular one in Hausa land in Larkin, B.1997, *op. cit.,* p. 433 . It is a film about a poor village woman who fights against a rich land owner who exploits the poor farmers.

15 Fulani (Peul) are nomadic groups spread over different West African countries (Guinee, Mali, Burkina Faso...).

16 Larkin made the same remark in Larkin, B.1997, *op. cit.,* p. 435.

17 Prof. Souleymane Faye, interview 10-05-04.

18 Larkin, B.2003, *op. cit.,* p. 183.

Larkin, B.1997, *op. cit.,* pp. 412-13.

19 Some people even adopted the name of Rafi.

20 Most of the information mentioned in this paragraph comes from personal interviews with two of the researchers who have collaborated in this project, Prof. M. Ndiaye (25-04-04) and Prof. S. Faye (10-05-04).

21 Though the concept of *négritude* has not been invented by Senghor, he applied it to Senegalese politics.

22 See Shain, R.M.2002. 'Roots in Reverse: Cubanismo in Twentieth-Century Senegalese Music.' *International Journal of African Historical Studies,* vol. 35, no. 1, pp. 83-101

23 Tamil is a Dravidian language spoken in southern India.

24 This is also related to the fact that dance in Senegal, especially the Wolof *sabar* dance, is mainly done by women.

25 Larkin, B.1997, *op. cit,* p. 424.

26 Prof. Benga, personal interview, 21-04-04.

27 *Ibid.*

28 *Something, Something is Happening to my Heart*—a Popular Bollywood film from 1998.

29 The first time I mentioned during a dance rehearsal I practised classical Indian dance, the director immediately said she knew what I was talking about and went into the house to get a cassette for me to dance. She came back with *Devdas.* I told her this was actually not Bharata Natyam music, but she said 'o, I know what you mean' and got an instrumental Bollywood tune. To Senegalese, classical Indian dance means 'not disco', and they use the term to refer to the dances of older films.

30 *Griots* are singers, musicians who sing praises of the noble they accompany. You are born a *griot.*

31 Pale skin is a beauty ideal in Senegal, as it is in many other African countries. The use of products for bleaching the skin is however not always without risk

32 Chakravarty, S.S. 1989. 'National identity and the realist aesthetic: Indian cinema of the fifties' in *Quarterly Review of Film and Video*, vol. 11, no. 3, October, pp. 31-48.

_______.1993. *National Identity in Indian Popular Cinema, 1947-1987.* Austin, Tex: University of Texas Press.

33 Yuval-Davis, 1997. for several essays on the relation between gender and nation, as well as Longman, 2004 and e.g. Sarkar, 2001 or Chaudhury, 2000 for its application to India.

34 Arshiya Sethi and Ananja Chatterjea, 2004 personal communication, August.

35 The same decline of male dancers is found in Egypt throughout the 20th century: female dancers were becoming much more popular, whereas male dancers faded into the background (Sellers-Young, 2004: 3).

36 Arshiya Sethi and Ananja Chatterjea, 2004 personal communication, August.

37 Larkin, B.1997, *op. cit.,* pp. 407-10, 434.,

38 *Ibid.,* p. 407.

39 Appadurai, A. 1991. 'Global ethnoscapes: notes and queries for a transnational anthropology' in R. Fox. ed. *Recapturing anthropology: working in the present.* Santa Fe, California: SAR Press, p. 191-210.

40 Larkin, B.2003, *op. cit.,* p. 172.

Larkin, B.1997, *op. cit.,* pp. 433.

41 There is a growing Christian population. Senegalese Islam is furthermore different from the Islam found in the Middle East or North Africa, consisting of different brotherhoods found only in Senegal.

42 A visit of Bush to Senegal in July 2003 made many enemies. First of all, many people were not very fond of his visit because of his anti-Islamic attitude and sayings, but his behaviour in Senegal made people really angry: bringing his own guards, police, cars, and even food, his attitude was considered very 'racist'.

43 Friedman, K. E.& J. Friedman. 1995. 'Global complexity and the simplicity of everyday life' in D. Miller. ed. *Worlds apart-Modernity Through the Prism of the Local. The Use of Knowledge: Global and Local Relations.* ASA decennial conference series. London and NY: Routledge, p. 136.

44 Larkin, B.2003, *op. cit.,* p. 172.

Larkin, B.1997, *op. cit.,* p. 414.

45 Larkin, B.1997, *op. cit.,* p. 433.

46 Larkin, B.2003, *op. cit.,* pp. 176, 183.

47 *Ibid,* p. 188.

48 There exists, however, a 'snake dance' in Bharata Natyam and folk dance (e.g. Rajasthani gipsy dance) where the dancer imitates the movement of the snake. This 'snake dance' has been adopted in movies. Now the 'snake dance' is slowly disappearing. (Rajesh Karma, Bharata Natyam teacher at Kalaksetra Institute, Chennai, personal communication September 2004)

49 Mami Wata imagery might also have been inspired directly by Indian prints circulating via Indian merchants in West-Africa. For more information about Mami Wata imagery, see Drewal, H. J. ed. 2002. *Mami Water.* Fowler Museum of Cultural History.

Rush, D. 1999. 'Eternal Potential. Chromolithographs in *Vodunland.' African Arts,* vol. 32, no. 4, pp. 61-75.

50 Dox, D.2004 . *Dancing their Way our of Orientalism.* Paper presented at the CORD/WDA/ICKL International Dance Conference, 1-4 August, Taipei, Taiwan

Sellers-Young, B.2004 . *Whose Body is This? Orientalism, Dance, and Women in Popular Culture.* Paper presented at the CORD/WDA/ICKL International Dance Conference, 1-4 August, Taipei, Taiwan.

51 Bhabha, H. K.1994. *Location of Culture.* London: Routledge, Savigliano, M. 1995. *Tango and the Political Economy of Passion.* Bolder: Westview Press. Sellers-Young, B. *op. cit.,* p. 2.

52 Savigliano. *op. cit.,* p. 169.

53 Sellers-Young, B. *op. cit.,* pp. 3-4, 6.

54 Appadorai, *op. cit.,* p. 31.

55 Sellers-Young, B. *op. cit.,* p. 2.

56 Dox, *op. cit.,* p. 10.

57 *Ibid,* p. 4.

58 *Ibid.*

59 *Ibid.,* p. 5. Dox mentions that higher-class performers in Egypt would not unveil unless the performance was intended as parody.

60 In this movement, choreographers wanted to get away from a strictly Western dominated ballet and contemporary dance vocabulary by incorporating e.g. *tai chi* (Chen 2004).

61 A space on the international stage means the need to self-orientalise. One can talk about a neo-colonial phenomenon in the world's art market where 'Third World' arts are consumed by primarily 'First World' audience Chen, Y..2004. *The making of Taiwanese/Chinese/Eastern identity on Taiwan's dance stage.* Paper presented at the CORD/WDA/ICKL International Dance Conference, 1-4 August, Taipei, Taiwan, p. 5.

62 *Ibid,* p. 3.

The New Partnership for Africa's Development: Making the African Peer Review Mechanism Work

Zein Kebonang

Introduction

Although Africa's lack of development can largely be attributed to structural factors, there could also be no doubt that the continent's lack of development stems from a general failure of Africa's political leadership. Whilst promoting good leadership at national level may be a task fraught with difficulties, it is argued that at a continental level, good leadership can be enhanced with the successful implementation of African Peer Review Mechanism (APRM) by NEPAD. This paper, first provides an explanation of the concept of Peer Review, then describes the origins of the African Peer Review Mechanism (APRM); its hierarchical structure, the types of reviews envisaged under the APRM; and provides justification for its existence; highlights the contending views on it; and argues for a hybrid model to accommodate all the contending views.

The Concept of Peer Review

Despite the importance of peer reviews, there is surprisingly scant literature on the subject. That notwithstanding, the concept of peer review has its origin in professional bodies and involves two broad areas: the evaluation of proposals and projects by experts and monitoring of state compliance with a provision of a treaty[1]. It involves a systematic examination and assessment of either the performance or practices of a state by other states (peers) or designated institutions[2]. The goal of such reviews is to assist countries being reviewed to improve their policy-making capacities, adopt best practices and comply with established standards and norms. In many ways, a peer review is a discussion among equals and 'not a hearing by a superior body that will hand down a binding judgement or punishment'[3]. Thus by their nature, peer reviews are conducted on a non-adversarial basis and rely heavily on mutual trust among the states involved, as well as their shared confidence in the process[4]. The existence of these factors ensures that peer review creates, through this reciprocal evaluation process a system of mutual accountability.

The success or effectiveness of the peer review depends in large measure, on the level of influence or persuasion that other peers may exert on the country being reviewed. This form of influence or persuasion, known otherwise as 'peer pressure'[5] may be executed through a set of recommendations; informal dialogue; public scrutiny; ranking among countries as to their levels of compliance and through domestic public opinion or pressure[6].

The Origins of the African Peer Review Mechanism

The origins of the African Peer Review Mechanism can be traced to the inaugural Summit of the African Union held in July 2002 in Durban, South Africa. At this Summit, the African Heads of State and Government not only adopted the Declaration on Democracy, Political, Economic and Corporate Government[7], whose primary concern was to foster Africa's socio-economic development through the adoption of better democratic, political and corporate governance practices. They also committed themselves to the implementation of the APRM[8]. It is through the APRM that the commitments contained in the Declaration on Democracy, Political, Economic and Corporate Government are to be promoted[9].

The African Peer Review Mechanism

The APRM is an instrument voluntarily acceded to by Member States of the AU as an African self-monitoring mechanism[10]. Participation in the APRM is open to all Member States of the AU. In this respect, it is all embracing and does not distinguish between 'good' or 'bad' States. However, countries wishing to accede to the APRM must first notify the Chairman of the NEPAD Heads of State and Government Implementation Committee[11] and deposit a signed Memorandum of Agreement (MOU) at the NEPAD Secretariat in South Africa[12]. Once a country has acceded to the APRM, it is, unless it terminates its participation in the APRM, bound to submit itself to review. The APRM has been tasked with the responsibility of ensuring that the policies and practices of participating states conform to the agreed political, economic and corporate governance values, codes and standards contained in the Declaration of Democracy, Political, Economic and Corporate Governance[13]. Its primary purpose is to foster the adoption of policies, standards and practices that lead to political stability, high economic growth, sustainable development and accelerated sub-regional and continental economic integration through sharing of experiences and reinforcement of successful and best practice, including identifying deficiencies and assessing the needs for capacity building[14]. Because its membership is voluntary, there are currently only 22 African countries that have joined the APRM out of a possible 53 countries.

The Hierarchical Structure of the APRM

Under the APRM, there are four distinct organisational components. These include;

(a) the Committee of Participating Heads of State and Government (The APR Heads of State Forum (APR Forum). This is the highest decision making authority in the APRM;

(b) the Panel of Eminent Persons (APR Panel), which oversees the review process to ensure the integrity of the process and considers review reports and makes recommendations to the APR Forum. The Panel is to be constituted by between 5 to 7 Eminent Persons[15];

(c) the APRM Secretariat, which provides the secretarial, technical, coordination and administrative support services for the APRM and

(d) the Country Review Team (APR Team), appointed only for the period of the country's review visit, it carries out the review process and examines progress made by the reviewed country on its program of action[16].

Types of Reviews under the APRM

There are basically four types of reviews envisaged under the APRM. These are:s

a) The base review—this is the first country review that is carried out within eighteen months of a country becoming a member of the APRM process.

b) The periodic review – this takes place every two to four years after the first review.

c) A member country can, for its own reasons, ask for a review that is not part of the periodically mandated review; and

d) Early signs of impending political or economic crisis in a member country would also be sufficient cause for instituting a review. Participating Heads of State and Government can call for such a review in a spirit of helpfulness to the country concerned[17].

The Stages of Reviews under the APRM

The APRM process entails periodic reviews of the policies and practices of participating states to ascertain progress made in achieving mutually agreed goals and compliance with agreed political, economic and corporate governance values, codes and standrdards enshrined in the Declaration on Democracy, Political, Economic and Corporate Governance[18]. By this process, it is hoped that countries will consider the impact of their domestic policies not only on their internal political stability and economic growth, but also the effect of such policiess on their neighbours[19]. Generally, peer review is based on a five-staged process:

a) The first stage occurs after a country has acceded to the APRM and has signed a Memorandum of Understanding (MOU) on Technical Assessment and Country Review Visit[20]. This stage involves the reviewed country making available all the information pertinent to the review process. This stage is basically a familiarization stage, which involves a study of the political, economic, and corporate governance development environment of the country to be reviewed. Such a study is based on information prepared by the APRM Secretariat and or provided by national, sub-regional, regional and international institutions. This first stage ends when the country to be reviewed has provided sufficient information on the country, including the draft Country Program of

Action, to the Secretariat and the Secretariat has prepared a background document and issued a paper on the country including the proposal on the APR Team to the APR Panel[21].

b) The second stage constitutes a Country Review Visit by the APR Team. This stage is meant to facilitate consultation between the APR Team, government officials, parliamentarians, political parties, business and civil societies (including the media, academia, trade unions, non-governmental organizations (NGOs), community-base organizations (CBOs), rural communities and representatives of international organizations[22]. It is at this stage that the draft Program of Action of the reviewed country is assessed and discussed with key stakeholders in order to address identified weaknesses and shortcomings in the various areas of governance and development. Challenges facing the reviewed country and the steps needed to address them are also discussed with the relevant stakeholders. A final draft Country Program of Action of the country being reviewed is thereafter drawn containing recommendations on required improvements identified by the APR Team[23].

c) The third stage involves the preparation of the APR Team's report, which is based in part on the findings of the Country Review Visit as well as on the findings of the research studies of the APR Secretariat prior to the visit[24]. The recommendations made are to focus on how the Program of Action of the country under review can be improved to accelerate the achievement of best practice and standards, and address more effectively the weaknesses identified[25]. It is at this phase, that the APR Team's report is discussed with the government of the country being reviewed. This is intended to ensure the accuracy of the information and to provide the government with an opportunity both to react to the accuracy of the information and to put forward their own views on how to address the identified shortcomings, including modifying the draft Program of Action[26].

d) The fourth stage involves the submission of the APR Team's country review report to the APR Panel by the Secretariat. The APR Panel meets to review the report in accordance with its mandate and submits its recommendations on the report to the APR Forum. Once the latter has received the report, it meets to consider the report and recommendations of the APR Panel and decides on what action to take[27]. This stage ends with the Chairperson of the APR Forum communicating the decisions of the Forum to the Head of State or Government of the country being reviewed[28].

e) The fifth stage is the last stage and completes the first cycle of the APR process for any particular country. This phase involves making public the APRM report and action on the country review. The final APRM Report is tabled formally and publicly in key regional and sub-regional structures such as the Summit of the African Union, the Pan-African Parliament, the African Commission of Human and Peoples' Rights, the Peace and Security Council and the Economic, Social and Cultural Council (ECOSOC) of the African Union, as well as the Regional Economic Community of the region of which the country reviewed is a member[29].

Where a country shows a willingness, based on the findings of these reviews, to rectify the identified shortcomings, then participating countries, donor governments and agencies are expected to come to its assistance[30]. Where a state wilfully fails to take appropriate measures to implement the recommendations of the review, such a deviant or recalcitrant state may be subjected to collective adverse action. Whatever, this 'collective adverse action' is, it is to be resorted to only after all attempt at constructive dialogue have failed and again only as a measure of last resort[31].

Justification for the APRM

Given that African countries are already subject to other peer reviews such as the IMF Article IV Consultations, the WTO 'TPRM', the ILO Enforcement Mechanism and the FAFT reviews, the question that immediately comes to the fore is whether there is or was any need for another review mechanism. In other words, what is the justification for the APRM, what value does it add and in what way is it different from the other review mechanisms. Unfortunately, there are no easy answers to these questions and neither NEPAD nor the APRM provide answers to these vexing questions. One is therefore left to speculate on the reasons for the APRM. Be that as it may, NEPAD as a developmental program of the African Union commits in exchange for more aid, debt cancellation and foreign investment, African states to upholding principles of democracy, rule of law, respect for human rights, good governance and political stability[32]. Giving meaning to these undertakings required that NEPAD should be seen to be more than just a pledge. It required having in place a mechanism through which NEPAD could ensure compliance with these principles lest its undertakings were to be merely rhetorical. In essence therefore, the need to give credibility to its undertakings proves a possible explanation for the birth of the APRM. Accordingly, notwithstanding the existence of other peer review mechanisms, the APRM can be viewed as a means through which Africa seeks to demonstrate its genuine commitment to change. It symbolizes and conveys to the international community Africa's seriousness about its reform agenda.

Additionally, the existence of the APRM may possibly be justified on the basis that unlike other reviews carried out by institutions such as the OECD, World Bank/IMF or WTO, it is likely to have a better informational basis than those other reviews. Country visits by the latter organizations are often brief, hardly extending beyond a period of 2 weeks! The APRM which will be carried out by people not only knowledgeable about local conditions but also having strong affiliations to the continent will be better positioned to give an 'insider view' or perspective on the real problems facing the continent without being overly doctrinal or ideological in its approach.

The Contending Views on the APRM

Notwithstanding the above concerns, the APRM has been hailed as the most innovative aspect of the NEPAD. It is seen as the most ambitious attempt by African countries to lever themselves out of the cycle of poverty, underdevelopment and instability to which the continent has been condemned, by taking responsibility for the maintenance of appropriate standards[33]. Simply, it is seen as a means through which Africans will be able to promote good leadership, good governance, and socio-economic and political development in Africa[34]. For some, the APRM is seen as the key to the successful implementation of NEPAD's lofty objectives. It represents an opportunity for countries to respond to deficiencies identified in the peer review process and to take appropriate measure to address them. Whilst for others, the APRM should 'help break a destructive solidarity between African rulers, who for too long have supported each other in holding power by rigging elections, banning opposition parties, and intimidating the press'[35]. This has been the euphoria around the APRM. However, along with the euphoria have also come doubts about whether it will succeed in its intended goals.

According to Herbst and Mills[36], while the APRM may be clear enough on paper, it still remains reliant on considerable institutional capacity and the kind of political will that has not always been there among African governments. Apart from the potential lack of political will, scepticism has also been expressed about the 'moral standing' of some of the would-be-peer reviewers. Herbst and Mills[37] rhetorically ask, 'how can Nigeria, for instance, act as a peer reviewer of its neighbour's governance policies when its own have been dysfunctional for so long?' The view that Nigeria and some other countries are 'delinquent' peers, if widely held may render the application of peer pressure by these countries ineffective.

Meanwhile, others contend that the challenge for the APRM is in its implementation, particularly the question whether African leaders would have the courage to criticise each other. The collegiality of African leaders and their propensity to rally around each other creates some doubts whether the APRM will be effective[38]. Those who subscribe to this line of thought contend that African leaders seem to share a 'membership in a cryptic club in which there is little inclination to castigate but greater tendency to empathize with members'[39]. Consequently, they argue that if the peer review mechanism is to address the very political, social, and economic malpractices of some of the African states and their political elites, some straight talk will be required. Referring to the failure of NEPAD to act in Zimbabwe, Herbert[40] tersely comments:

> While Robert Mugabe violently dismantles a state that was, until recently, functional, his peers applaud. So which vision

of peer review is it to be? Vigorous and constructive criticism or more coddling of autocrats? Africa's credibility and probably its future, hinges on the answer.

The scepticism about the APRM, that is, its ability to hold African leaders accountable, is not without substance. African group solidarity has played itself out in a number of international fora including in the Commonwealth. At the Commonwealth Meeting in 2002, the Commonwealth had to decide whether to suspend Zimbabwe's Membership, given its disputed election results, which had been marred by large-scale violence and intimidation of opposition parties, the judiciary and the illegal occupation of white farms. Although, Zimbabwe was eventually suspended from the Commonwealth, its suspension divided the association into two opposing camps, one led by Australia and the United Kingdom, which supported the suspension, and the other led by South Africa and Nigeria, which bitterly opposed the suspension[41]. Ironically, both South Africa and Nigeria are the principal architects and sponsors of NEPAD.

Other concerns that were raised during my fieldwork about the APRM included the absence of punitive sanctions and the exclusion of international partners (such as the World Bank and IMF) in the APRM process.

The Absence of Sanctions

As indicated in the preceding sections, the APRM is a voluntary monitoring mechanism, which relies on dialogue, peer pressure and monitoring of peers by other peers for its success. It is only when dialogue and peer pressure have failed that participating Heads of State and Government can notify the offending government of their collective intention to take *appropriate measures* against it by a given date[42]. It is not however clear what would constitute *appropriate measures.* The provision is vague as to whether or not the APRM can impose sanctions on it members. This vagueness, whether deliberate or not, has left room for differing and potentially conflicting interpretations on the question of sanctions. For instance, *appropriate measure* could mean anything from a fine, economic and political sanctions, suspension or expulsion. It could also mean in the extreme, armed intervention.

Some commentators such as Akokpari[43] contend that verbal condemnations in the absence of sanctions will have little impact in getting defiant states to undertake reforms without some forms of sanctions. They further argue that even in instances where sanctions create minimal economic hardship, they might still generate political change or desirable political responses[44]. Whilst this may be true, it must be borne in mind however, that NEPAD is a developmental program rather than an institution. It does not have coercive powers or the capacity to enforce anything, be it agreed declarations or reforms. Likewise, the APRM is a voluntary mechanism. States may choose to accede to it or withdraw from it without losing their membership of the AU[45]. Like NEPAD, the APRM does not have coercive powers. This lack of coercive powers reflects the nature of the APRM, that it is more of a 'soft enforcement' mechanism than a treaty. In other words, it is non-binding in the strictly legal sense and states are not bound to take on board its recommendations. However, whilst sanctions are not explicitly provided for, one may argue that the imposition of sanctions may be read into the provision, which permits for the taking of 'appropriate measure' against erring states, although the nature of such 'sanctions' has not been spelled out or elaborated.

Whilst there might be a lack of clarity and vagueness by NEPAD and the APRM about the issue of sanctions, the Constitutive Act of the AU on the other hand, provides instances where sanctions may be imposed against a state. Article 23 (1) provides for the imposition of sanctions against Members that fail or default in making their contributions to the Union. Article 23(2) expands the circumstances under which sanctions may be imposed. These would be where a Member State fails to comply with the decisions and policies of the Union. In such an event, the Union may impose a variety of sanctions, be they of a political or economic nature. Such sanctions may include for instance, denial of transport and communication links with other Member States and other measures of a political and economic nature as determined by the AU Assembly (Article 23 (2) AU Constitutive Act). Thus, it seems the imposition of sanctions, whether political or economic, may only be properly justified under the AU Constitutive Act rather than the APRM unless one takes a broader view that the AU provisions can be extended to the APRM. Such a course of action would have to be justified and premised on the basis that NEPAD and the APRM are AU initiatives or programs.

Although sanctions may have to be expressly articulated, admittedly, it may also be desirable not to have them embodied in the APRM. This is because if the peer review is understood to be a device that is meant to help rather than coerce African States to improve their socio-economic and political environments by adopting best practices, then any scheme that seeks to achieve that through sanctions will attract fewer participants. Publication of the review reports could be a sufficient incentive for countries to comply with the review recommendations. Such publication could amount to naming and shaming; a strategy that Braithwaite and Drahos[46] have found can be effective in inducing compliance and reform. Admittedly, the extent to which this strategy may work with respect to states may be limited as it depends on the value that states place on their reputation.

In an attempt to explain why states comply with international agreements, Guzman[47] posits in his 'reputational theory of compliance' that states honour their commitments because of both their reputational concerns and direct sanctions that may be triggered by non-compliance. Focusing on reputation, he argues that states' reputation has value. This value lies in the fact that by complying with its international obligations, a state signals to others that it is cooperative. This allows the state to enjoy long-term relationships with other cooperative states, provides a greater ability to make binding promises and reduces the need for monitoring or verification by other states[48]. On the other hand, the failure by the state to live up to its commitments harms its reputation and makes its future commitments less credible[49].

Whilst naming and shaming may trigger reputational concerns for some states and therefore induce them to comply with their obligations, other states may not be overly concerned with the kind of reputation they have or project. This is because a state may have a number of reputations with respect to a number of its obligations. It may be highly cooperative with respect to certain obligations and highly uncooperative with respect to others. In evaluating the importance of reputation Downs and Jones[50], argue that whilst reputation matters, states have different levels of reliability in connection with different agreements and that considerable evidence supports the view that states possess multiple or segmented reputations[51]. In this context, a failure to comply with one set of obligations will not necessarily harm a state's reputation.

Ironically, although naming and shaming could be an effective strategy in getting countries to comply with their international obligations, the mere publication of reports by the APRM without an accompanying set of punitive measures, may fail to induce states' compliance. Whilst a country may no doubt suffer a loss of reputation as a result of its failure to comply with its obligation, such a state may in fact be notorious for non-compliance or the loss it suffers may not be sufficiently high as to alter its behaviour. Furthermore, the reputational consequence of a violation will be affected by the severity of such a violation. A minor violation which causes no harm on other states will have a small impact compared to a major violation[52]. Simply stated, although reputation matters, it is not decisive in matters of states relations. Downs and Jones[53] for instance, argue that whilst the US may have on one hand an unflattering reputation for its failure to make good its financial commitments to the UN, and a complimentary one on the other, with respect to its financial commitment to NATO, its reliability as a partner has not been characterised by these organizations.

In the light of the above, one may concede that mere publication without more will not be sufficient. In this respect, the question of sanctions assumes once again centre stage. Although the imposition of sanctions is possible under the AU and possibly under the APRM if one took a broader view of what constituted 'appropriate measures' under the APRM, it is not clear whether their imposition would be effective in getting countries to comply with the APRM recommendation. There is generally a lack of consensus in the economic and political literature about the effectiveness of sanctions as a means of inducing a state being sanctioned (the target state) to undertake certain reforms or to desist from engaging in a particular conduct or course of action[54].

Although there may be instances where sanctions are able to induce certain desired outcomes, their imposition particularly when they relate to the limitations on imports and export, may affect ordinary citizens far more than the entrenched elites or leaders who actually make policy decisions[55]. Whilst, recent sanctions on Zimbabwe by the EU and USA may have adversely affected ordinary Zimbabwean citizens, they probably have had little personal effect on the country's ruling leadership and elite. As indicated in the preceding chapter, the country is experiencing a severe shortage of basic necessities (such as food, petrol and medicine), and unemployment levels have risen to over 80 percent of the population.

Additionally, if sanctions were to be imposed by the AU or APRM, the support of the international community, institutions and developed states would be crucial. Many African countries rely on aid provided by international institutions. A significant amount of their trade is also with the developed states rather than amongst themselves. For instance, the EU is Sub-Saharan Africa's largest single trading partner, providing a market for 31 percent of Africa's exports and accounting for 40 percent of Africa's imports[56]. Thus, for sanctions to work, sanctioning states must have the ability to alter the target country's terms of trade regardless of the targeted regime's efforts to substitute[57]. Except, perhaps for South Africa (in its relationship with Lesotho, a country that is within South Africa's territorial boundaries and thus exclusively dependent on it for both its exports and imports many African countries do not generally have the ability to influence the terms of trade of other members.

Furthermore, where sanctions are collectively imposed, as opposed to being unilaterally imposed by a single state, their success will depend on the existence of an effective monitoring mechanism to eliminate the problem of rent seeking by states. The problem of rent seeking arises because sanctions represent a cost both to the country or countries imposing them and the target state[58]. Because sanctions may disrupt the economic activities of those imposing them as well, there is an inherent danger that some States will backslide[59]. Additionally, the effectiveness of sanctions will depend on the countermeasures that a target state undertakes or develops. Thus, countermeasures may be fatal to sanctions as they can minimize the effects of such sanctions[60]. The challenge for the AU and APRM would be to ensure not only that none of its Members backslid but also that the target State did not find alternatives. Without the participation of the international community, this would be a task that will be fraught with difficulties.

The Role of International Institutions and Developed States

The APRM is an African self-monitoring mechanism. It is an initiative through which Africans themselves are seeking to take a proactive stance on matters that affect them. Under the APRM, all reviews are to be African led. Peer pressure is expected to come from African leaders themselves. The wisdom of excluding representatives of institutions like the World Bank/IMF, the EU and developed countries in the APRM has both its merits and demerits. Exclusion could be important in enhancing a sense that the APRM is truly an African ownership initiative. This would address concerns and criticisms that have always been levelled against the World Bank/IMF Structural Adjustment Programs that they were an imposition on African countries that discounted African input and participation and ownership. It is these factors that are often given as reasons for the failure of African reform programs initiated by the World Bank/IMF. Second, the value that could be added in having an exclusively African peer review, is that such a review will presumably be made by people knowledgeable about the local conditions, whereas World Bank/ IMF reviews may not generate the right information and pay insufficient attention to local economic institutions. Thus, the outcomes of such reviews are bound to accurately reflect African realities without being overly burdened by the World Bank/IMF ideological drives.

On the other hand, whilst the exclusion of the World Bank/ IMF and other institutions may resonate well and strongly with Africa's sense of ownership of the APRM, without some form of real pressure, the APRM may fail to influence States to comply with its recommendations. This is precisely because under the APRM, it would appear that failure to undertake the necessary reforms would not automatically attract sanctions or punitive measures. In fact, the question of sanctions is so vaguely articulated that it is difficult to say whether or not they exist! What is clear however is that, 'if the necessary political will is not forthcoming from the government, participating states should do everything practicable to engage it in constructive dialogue, offering in the process technical and other appropriate assistance'[61]. It is only when all avenues of dialogue have been exhausted, that Member States may 'put the government on notice of their collective intention to proceed with appropriate measures by a given date'[62]. Thus, these measures do not penalise a country for a failure to implement the review recommendations nor do they provide an incentive to undertake the recommendations or take steps to avoid an unfavourable review. In my view, therefore, the involvement of international institutions will provide the

APRM with some 'teeth'. Institutions such as the World Bank/IMF may be able to play a powerful role in assisting in the implementation of locally decided reforms by helping states overcome local structural problems, rather them imposing structuring adjustments.

Apart from the issue of sanctions and participation of key players in the APRM, other potential challenges facing the APRM include lack of funding, the establishment of a competent Secretariat, and a credibility and independent APRM process.

Funding the APRM

The APR Secretariat does not currently have its own funding nor has NEPAD/AU made any budget for it. States participating in the APRM are however, expected to bear the cost of such reviews[63]. As noted in the preceding chapters, Africa has not only suffered from economic stagnation but has also experienced a debilitating debt burden or a debt-overhang. Many African countries have had difficulties in paying their membership fees in the AU and its predecessor. In 1999, the Libyan government had to pay in excess of US$ 4.5 million on behalf of some of the defaulting countries in addition to its US$ 1 million grant to the process leading to the establishment of the AU[64]. Recently, the AU reported arrears of nearly US$ 39.9 million out of a budget of US$ 43 million. In the face of this reality, it is unclear how states will meet or honour their obligations to the APRM. As Bekoe[65] states, 'it is questionable if countries that have not regularly paid their dues for membership in the new African Union and other regional initiatives over the years will now pay for the operation of the APRM'. Without adequate funding, the APRM runs the danger of collapsing. In this regard, opposition to the involvement of institutions such as the World Bank and IMF must be premised on the reality of the African situation than on ideological considerations.

The Competence of the Secretariat

Until the APR Secretariat is fully operational, it is difficult to give an objective assessment of its competence. However, once operational the competence of the Secretariat will be influenced not only by available funding but also by the quality of staff employed by the Secretariat and its ability to carry out its functions. Thus, the technical competence of the Secretariat will determine whether the Secretariat is able to discharge its mandate efficiently and competently. While the APRM emphasizes the deployment of African expertise in the peer review process[66], it also acknowledges that there may be instances, where the services of non-African experts, individuals or institutions will have to be used[67].

The Independence and Credibility of the APRM

The independence of the APR Panel will be another important factor that will determine the credibility of the review process. The APR Panel's credibility will depend on whether they are able to provide accurate and independent assessments of the conditions in countries being reviewed. Thus, any signs of bias or cover-ups, will compromise the entire APRM. As Bekoe[68] states, "the members of the APRM panel should be above reproach and independent of Africa's patron-client network."

The seven members of the 'eminent persons' group that has been approved for the peer review panel include; Graca Machel (internationally known for her work with UNICEF and the effect of armed conflict on children); Adebayo Adedeji (a former Executive Secretary of the UN Economic Commission for Africa from 1975-1991. He has been critical and sceptical about NEPAD); Marie-Angelique Savane (the former Director of the UN Population Fund (Senegal); Bethuel Kiplagat (former Kenyan Ambassador to France and the United Kingdom and now a leader of the African Peace Forum); Dorothy Njeuma (former vice Minister of Education in Cameroon); Mourad Medelci (served as Minister of Trade, Budget and Finance) and Chris Stals (former governor of the South African Reserve Bank from 1991-1998).

Looking at the current panel of 'eminent persons', it is made up of highly prominent people who are unlikely to compromise their integrity by endorsing less than accurate reviews. Thus, one could argue that the composition of the current panel satisfies an important aspect of a reliable peer review commission, that is, its independence.

Publication of Review Reports

As noted earlier, the APRM provides for the publication and dissemination of its review reports in key regional places and institutions[69]. Prompt publication of these reviews would be crucial so that momentum is not lost in helping and holding states accountable. Publication will also need to be widespread so that information is not only available to government officials, other states, and the donor community but a large segment of the population such as civil societies, academic institutions and ordinary citizens. To be more effective, the APRM published reports, can draw a list of compliant and non-compliant states. This list could contain all member countries and rank them according to whether they have implemented or failed to implement the recommendations of the APRM. The list could indicate the level of compliance and suggest ways forward. In this way, non-cooperating states can be identified, assisted and if need be pressurized, even isolated unless they improve.

Making the APRM Work: The Way Forward

Although the APRM faces a number of limitations and challenges, it would appear that essentially, the critical concern is whether the APRM should embody a set of sanctions or not. As noted earlier, arguments for and against sanctions are compelling. Consequently, I propose a compromise position, which will be a hybrid of these two competing and yet compelling views. This hybrid position advocates for a mixed balance between the use of peer pressure and sanctions in the APRM. It also calls for the inclusion of all the key players such as international institutions, in the APRM process if the latter is to work. One way of thinking of this hybrid model is to think of it in terms of a regulatory pyramid as depicted by Figure 1. This regulatory pyramid is similar to the one proposed by Ayres and Braithwaite (1992) in their seminal work on responsive regulation.

To conceptualise how this compromise hybrid position would work, the regulatory pyramid as first proposed by Ayres and Braithwaite (1992) and subsequently developed by Braithwaite (2002) in his book: 'Restorative Justice and Responsive Regulation provides some useful insights. Although the focus by Braithwaite's (2002) pyramid model is more on restorative justice, its attraction is that it can be applied in any regulatory setting. This pyramid model is as Braithwaite[70] puts it, 'an attempt to solve the puzzle of when to punish and when to persuade.'

Figure 1

(An example of a Regulatory Pyramid, adapted with modifications from Braithwaite 2002).

In terms of the Braithwaite's regulatory pyramid, to secure compliance where there has been for instance, wrongdoing, breach of the peace or of agreed standards, principles or reforms, the starting point should be dialogue rather than punishment[71]. To have any meaningful outcome, such dialogue must not only be all-inclusive (involve all stakeholders) but must also be held in a non-adversarial manner. Only when dialogue has failed can punitive measures be taken by moving up the pyramid. Even so, such punitive measures must be taken only as a last resort[72]. The usefulness of the pyramid is that it does not pre-empt which matter would be resolved by dialogue and which one would attract a punitive sanction. In a sense, it is a dynamic model which according to Braithwaite[73], is not intended to specify in advance which types of matters will be dealt with at the bases of the pyramid, which ones are the more serious ones that should be in the middle and which are the most serious ones for the peak of the pyramid.

Under the regulatory pyramid model, compliance may be achieved at the initial stage of dialogue with threats of sanctions being in the background rather than in the foreground. Nonetheless, where compliance is achieved after having escalated up the pyramid, that is, through the use of punitive measures, the reforming state is still rewarded for its compliance by putting the pyramid into reverse and de-escalating down the pyramid Braithwaite[74]. Deescalation is indicative of the success rather than the failure of the punitive measure. As Braithwaite[75] succinctly state: 'The pyramid is firm yet forgiving in its demands for compliance. Reform

[is] rewarded, just as recalcitrant refusal to reform following wrongdoing... result in punishment'.

The hybrid model advocated for in the paper, just like Braithwaite's regulatory pyramid, will have dialogue at its base, as shown in Figure 1, and punitive measures up the ladder for countries that deliberately violate their obligations to the detriment of the common good. It will also be inclusive. The novelty of such an approach is that it will satisfy both the need for dialogue and the need for sanctions without the latter being in the foreground. By being inclusive, it will not only appeal to the international community but will also make the threats of sanctions more credible.

Conclusion

One of the weaknesses about the APRM is that in its present form, it is structured in such a way that its reviews are to be all encompassing. The reviews are to cover areas on democracy, economic, political and corporate governance. In a lot of ways, many of the areas that the APRM focuses on are fairly well covered by for instance the WTO and the World Bank/IMF. The value that is likely to be added by the APRM may remain suspect unless it curves-out areas of emphasis that are not already covered by the well-established review mechanisms. Until it does this, it will be handicapped in its delivery as its review process will simply be duplicitous of other reviews without much value being added. Lastly, the extent to which the APRM can promote good leadership in Africa will depend on the political willingness of Africa leaders to implement it findings and to hold each other accountable. It would also depend on whether the APRM can 'bite'. Without a clear set of sanctions and the involvement of other international players such as the World Bank/IMF, the ability of the APRM to make credible threats against delinquent states is doubtful. Yet, the provision of sanctions in the APRM is likely to encounter opposition and even render the APRM unattractive to African countries. Given this paradox, the hybrid position advocated for in this paper accommodates both arguments in favour of and against sanctions.

Endnotes

1 Ngamau, R. 2004. 'The Role of NEPAD in African Economic Regulation and Integration', *Law and Business Review Americas,* vol. 10, p. 515-544

2 OECD 2003. Peer Review: A Tool for Co-operation and Change, Paris, France.

Pagani, F. 2002. 'Peer Review: A Tool for Cooperation and Change. An Analysis of an OECD Working Method', OECD Working Paper SG/LEG (2002)1, Paris, France, and Kanbur R. 2004. 'The African Peer Review Mechanism (APRM): An Assessment of Concept and Design', available at www.people.cornell.edu/pages/sk145.

3 OECD 2003. Peer Review: A Tool for Co-operation and Change, Paris, France.

4 OECD 2003. Peer Review: A Tool for Co-operation and Change, Paris, France, Pagani, F. 2002. 'Peer Review: A Tool for Cooperation and Change. An Analysis of an OECD Working Method', OECD Working Paper SG/LEG(2002)1, Paris, France.

5 Pagani, F. 2002. 'Peer Review: A Tool for Cooperation and Change. An Analysis of an OECD Working Method', OECD Working Paper SG/LEG (2002)1, Paris, France, and Kanbur R. 2004. 'The African Peer Review Mechanism (APRM): An Assessment of Concept and Design', available at www.people.cornell.edu/pages/sk145.

6 Pagani, F. 2002. 'Peer Review: A Tool for Cooperation and Change. An Analysis of an OECD Working Method', OECD Working Paper SG/LEG (2002)1, Paris, France.

7 Paragraph 28 of the NEPAD Declaration on Democracy, Political, Economic and Corporate Governance (AHG/235 (XXXV111) Annex 1. See also paragraph 17 of the Memorandum of Understanding on the African Peer Review Mechanism (NEPAD/HSGIC/03-2003/APRM/MOU).

8 Paragraph 28 the NEPAD Declaration on Democracy, Political, Economic and Corporate Governance (AHG/235 (XXXV111) (*Ibid*). See also paragraph 18 of the Memorandum of Understanding on the African Peer Review Mechanism (NEPAD/HSGIC/03-2003/APRM/MOU) (*ibid*).

9 Paragraph 28 the NEPAD Declaration on Democracy, Political, Economic and Corporate Governance (AHG/235 (XXXV111) Annex 1 (*ibid*).

10 The African Peer Review Mechanism (APRM); Base Document (NEPAD/HSGIC/03-2003/APRM/MOU/ANNEX II), paragraph 1.

11 *Ibid*, paragraph 5.

12 Paragraph 30 of the Memorandum of Understanding on the African Peer Review Mechanism (NEPAD/HSGIC/03-2003/APRM/MOU) (supra).

13 The African Peer Review Mechanism (APRM); Base Document (NEPAD/HSGIC/03-2003/APRM/MOU/ANNEX II), paragraph 2.

14 *Ibid,* paragraph 3.

15 In terms of paragraph 3.6 of the APRM Organization and Processes, the Eminent Persons must be Africans who have distinguished themselves in careers that are relevant to the work of the APRM. They must be persons of high moral stature and demonstrated commitment to the ideals of Pan Africanism. The composition of the Panel is also to reflect broad regional balance, gender equity and cultural diversity.

16 The African Peer Review Mechanism Organisation and Processes (NEPAD/HSGIC/03-2003/APRM/GUIDELINES/O&P), paragraph, 1.1, a, b, c and d.

17 The African Peer Review Mechanism (APRM); Base Document (NEPAD/HSGIC/03-2003/APRM/MOU/ANNEX II), paragraph 14.

18 *Ibid,* paragrapgh, 15.

19 *Ibid,* paragrapgh, 16.

20 The African Peer Review Mechanism Organisation and Processes (NEPAD/HSGIC/03-2003/APRM/GUIDELINES/O&P), paragraph 7.1-7.2.

21 *Ibid,* paragraph 7.3-7.6.

22 *Ibid,* paragraph, 7.8.

23 *Ibid,* paragrapgh, 7.9-7.11.

24 *Ibid,* paragraph, 7.12.

25 *Ibid,* paragraph, 7.13.

26 *Ibid,* paragraph, 7.14.

27 *Ibid,* paragraph, 7.15.

28 *Ibid,* paragraph, 7.16.

29 *Ibid,* paragraph, 7.17- 7.18.

30 The African Peer Review Mechanism (APRM); Base Document (NEPAD/HSGIC/03-2003/APRM/MOU/ANNEX II), paragraph 24.

31 *Ibid,* paragraph, 24.3.

32 The New Partnership for Africa's Development Base Document 2001, paragraph 71, 146 and 150.

33 Cillier, J. 2002. 'NEPAD's Peer Review Mechanism', Institute of Security Studies, Occasional Paper No.64 available at http://www.iss.co.za/Pubs/Papers/64/Paper64.html

34 Akokpari, J (2004). 'Policing and Preventing Human Right Abuses in Africa: The OAU, The AU and The NEPAD Peer Review', International Journal of Legal Information, vol. 32, 461-472 and Juma, M.K 2004. 'Africa's Governance Audit: The African Peer Review Mechanism', New Economy, 178-180.

35 The Economist 2002. 'Leaders: An African Cure for Africa's ills; Africa's Economies', June 22, vol. 363, Issue 8278, p. 15.

36 Herbst, J and Mills, G. 2003. 'NEPAD and the AU: Towards a New Order?' The Adelphi Papers, vol. 361, no.1, 49-64

37 *Ibid,* p. 52.

38 *Ibid,* p. 55.

39 Akopkpari, 2004, *op. cit,* p. 469.

40 Herbert, R. 2003. 'Peer Review: Who Owns the Process?' Africa, vol.1.

41 Kebonang, Z. 2003. 'Africa and the Commonwealth: Moving from a Symbolic to a More Meaningful Relationship', Indian Journal of African Affairs, vol. 43, no. 2, 36-48.

42 The African Peer Review Mechanism (APRM); Base Document (NEPAD/HSGIC/03-2003/APRM/MOU/ANNEX II), paragraph 24.

43 Akopkpari, 2004, *op. cit* p. 468

44 Kaempfer, W.H and Lowenberg, A.D 1988. 'The Theory of International Economic Sanctions, p. 786

45 Akopkpari, 2004, *op. cit* p. 468

46 Drahos, P. 2004. 'Intellectual Property and Pharmaceutical Markets: A Nodal Governance Approach', Temple Law Review, vol. 77, 270.

47 Guzman, A.T 2002. 'A Compliance-Based Theory of International Law', California Law Review, vol. 90, 1823 -1827

48 Guzman, A.T 2002. 'A Compliance-Based Theory of International Law', California Law Review, vol. 90, 1823 -1827

and Swaine, E.T 2003. 'Unsigning', Stanford Law Review, vol. 55, 2061-2089.

49 Guzman, A.T 2002. 'A Compliance-Based Theory of International Law', California Law Review, vol. 90, 1850.

50 Downs, G.W and Jones, M.A 2002. 'Reputation, Compliance, and International Law', Journal of Legal Studies, vol. XXXI, 95-114.

51 Crossen, T. 2004. 'Multilateral Environment Agreements and the Compliance Continuum', Georgetown International Environment Law Review, vol. 16, 473-500.

52 Guzman, *op. cit,* p. 1862

53 Downs, G.W and Jones, M.A 2002, *op. cit,* p. 109.

54 Cho, S. 2004. 'The Nature of Remedies in International Trade Law', University of Pittsburgh Law Review, vol.65, 763-809, McGillivray, F and Stam, A.C 2004. 'Political Institutions, Coercive Diplomacy, and the Duration of Economic Sanctions', Journal of Conflict Resolution, vol. 48, no. 2, 154-172.

Drezner, D.W 2000. 'Bargaining Enforcement and Multilateral Sanctions: When is Cooperation Counterproductive?' International Organization, vol. 54, no.1, 73-102, Bolks, S.M 2000. 'How Long Do Economic Sanctions Last? Examining the Sanctioning Process Through Duration', Political Research Quarterly, vol. 53 no.2, 241-265, Dashti-Gibson, J; Davis, P and Radcliff, B. 1997. 'On the Determinants of the Success of Economic Stations: An Empirical Analysis', American Journal of Political Science, vol. 41, no. 2, 608-618 and

55 Dashti-Gibson, J; Davis, P and Radcliff, B. 1997. 'On the Determinants of the Success of Economic Stations: An Empirical Analysis', American Journal of Political Science, vol. 41, no. 2, 608-618.

56 Hinkle, L.E and Schiff, M. 2004. 'Economic Partnership Agreements Between Sub-Saharan Africa and the EU: A Development Perspective', World Economy, vol. 27, no. 9, 1321-1332.

57 Drezner, D.W 2000. 'Bargaining Enforcement and Multilateral Sanctions: When is Cooperation Counterproductive?' International Organization, vol. 54, no.1, 73-102.

58 Cho, S. 2004. 'The Nature of Remedies in International Trade Law', university of Pittsburgh Law Review, vol. 65, 763-809, Ehrmann, M. 2002. "Procedures of Compliance Control in International Environmental Treaties", Colorado Journal of

International Environmental Law and Policy, vol. 13, 377-442, Bolks, S.M 2000. 'How Long Do Economic Sanctions Last? Examining the Sanctioning Process Through Duration', Political Research Quarterly, vol. 53, no. 2, 241-265.

59 Drezner, D.W 2000. 'Bargaining Enforcement and Multilateral Sanctions: When is Cooperation Counterproductive?' International Organization, vol. 54, no.1, 73-102

60 Bolks, S.M 2000. 'How Long Do Economic Sanctions Last? Examining the Sanctioning Process Through Duration', Political Research Quarterly, vol. 53 no. 2, 241-265.

61 The African Peer Review Mechanism (APRM); Base Document (NEPAD/HSGIC/03-2003/APRM/MOU/ANNEX II). Paragraph, 24

62 *Ibid*, paragraph 24.

63 *Ibid*, paragraph, 27.

64 Udombana, N, J. 2002. 'A Harmony or a Cacophony? The Music of Integration in the African Union Treaty and the New Partnership for Africa's Development', Indiana International and Comparative Law Review, vol. 13, 185-236.

65 Bekoe, D.A 2003. 'Creating A Reliable African Peer Review Mechanism', USA Africa Institute, vol.1 no. 4, 2-9.

66 The African Peer Review Mechanism (APRM); Base Document (NEPAD/HSGIC/03-2003/APRM/MOU/ANNEX II). paragrapgh, 11.

67 The African Peer Review Mechanism Organisation and Processes (NEPAD/HSGIC/03-2003/APRM/GUIDELINES/O&P), paragraph 3.8.

68 Bekoe, D.A 2003. 'Creating A Reliable African Peer Review Mechanism', USA Africa Institute, vol.1 no. 4, 2-9.

69 The African Peer Review Mechanism (APRM), *op. cit*, paragraph 25.

70 Braithwaite, J. 2002. Restorative Justice and Responsive Regulation, Oxford University Press, New York, USA.

71 *Ibid*, p. 30.

72 *Ibid*, p. 30.

73 *Ibid*, p. 30.

74 *Ibid*, p. 31.

75 *Ibid*, p. 31.

Index

Notes on Contributors

Parvathi Vasudevan
Centre for African Studies, University of Mumbai

B.P. Dhaka
PHD Chamber of Commerce and Industry, New Delhi

Prof. R.L. Chawla
School of International Studies, Jawaharlal Nehru University

Dr. Vidhan Pathak
Department of Political Science, Dire Dawa University, Ethiopia

Prof. Aparajita Biswas
Centre for African Studies, University of Mumbai

Prof. Ajay Dubey
Chairman, Centre for West Asian and African Studies, Jawaharlal Nehru University

Dr. J.P. Sharma
Department of African Studies, Delhi University

Dr. Jaffar Mirghani
Director, Sudan Civilization Institute, University of Khartoum

Prof. K. Mathews
Department of Political Science & International Relations, Addis Ababa University

Dr. Euston K. Chiputa
Faculty, Department of History, University of Zambia

Mwamba-Tshibangu
Research Scholar, D. R. Congo

Dr. Nivedita Ray
Researcher, IDSA, New Delhi

Prof. Usha Shukla
University of Kwa-Zulu Natal, South Africa

Dr. Vyacheslav Usov
Institute for African Studies, Russian Academy of Sciences, Moscow

Dr. Gwenda Van der Steene
Faculty, Ghent University, Belgium

Dr. Zein Kebonang
Faculty,Department of Law, University of Botswana